CL PROGRAMMING
FOR THE AS/400

Second Edition

CL PROGRAMMING
FOR THE AS/400

Second Edition

Greg Veal, CSP, PMP

Second Edition
Second Printing—July 2000

© 1999 Midrange Computing
ISBN: 1-58347-004-2

Midrange Computing
5650 El Camino Real, Suite 225
Carlsbad, CA 92008
www.midrangecomputing.com

V4R4

To my family, without whose patience this book would never have been completed, and to the many friends, without whose support, it would never have been started.

ACKNOWLEDGMENTS

I am indebted to the following people,
and would like to acknowledge their invaluable assistance on this book:

Robert Cozzi, Jr.

Linda Collins

Jing-Hwa Wang

CONTENTS

INTRODUCTION

The role that Control Language (CL) plays on the AS/400 goes beyond that of other programming languages. No matter what other high-level languages are used, CL programs are a crucial component of every application. It is true that IBM Rochester has delivered increasing numbers of APIs as the mechanism for providing controlled, open access to OS/400. And, many APIs provide the same functions as CL commands and often work more quickly and use less system overhead than the CL commands. Yet, CL remains as the primary means of communicating with the operating system. Therefore, the first chapter of this book focuses not only on the syntax and structure of CL, but has a discussion of CL commands in general and the role they play on the IBM AS/400 computer as well. In successive chapters, readers will increase their vocabularies in CL by examining increasingly advanced examples of code.

PREREQUISITES

A basic knowledge of OS/400, the operating system of the IBM AS/400, and some prior exposure to SEU is essential to learning CL. Some exposure to DDS and any high-level language (HLL), such as RPG or COBOL, would be helpful but isn't required.

DISCLAIMERS

I leave choice of language to the programmer. I make no attempt to justify the use of CL where an API or other HLL might be available as an alternative option. I only intend to demonstrate how CL can be used to meet systems requirements.

Neither do I attempt to justify the application design criteria that might be implied by any of the examples. AS/400 application design is a topic that is well beyond the scope of this text. I do attempt to include examples that are representative of code that is likely to be found in a typical production environment, but without making judgments regarding the overall design of the application. It is impossible to evaluate design without being aware of all the design criteria.

COMPATIBILITY

This text is consistent with Version 4, Release 4.0 of OS/400.

IBM Terminology

Over the years, the terminology used by IBM in the AS/400 technical manuals and even on various screens has evolved. The terminology used by AS/400 customers, however, has, for the most part, not kept pace with that evolution. For example, most AS/400 programmers still refer to the "call stack" as the "program invocation stack." I have attempted to consistently use the current IBM terminology in this edition of the text. In order to help bridge the gap for readers, at each point in the text that an evolved term is introduced, I make a reference to the older terminology.

Integrated Language Environment

The programming model, or environment that was part of OS/400 when the AS/400 was introduced, is now referred to as the original program model (OPM). The Integrated Language Environment (ILE) is an additional, optional programming environment. Many, if not most of the changes in terminology are related to the significant operating system changes required to support ILE. Recent versions of the AS/400e series CL Programming manual are very oriented, both in terminology and function, toward ILE. I have observed, however, that the vast majority of new CL programs are still developed in the OPM. Consequently, I discuss most topics primarily from an OPM viewpoint. Specifically, I generally refer to CL programs, even though most discussions are equally applicable to ILE procedures. Where there are special considerations for ILE, I point those out. And chapter 13 is dedicated to the use of CL in the Integrated Language Environment.

CONVENTIONS

The following conventions are used in this text:

- The symbol ƀ denotes a blank character.
- The notation used to describe the size of a decimal variable is as follows:
  xx,yy

The value *xx* is the total number of digits allocated to the variable, and *yy* represents the number of decimals positions. For example, the notation 15,5 describes a variable with 15 digits, 5 of which are to the right of the decimal point.

■ Character literal values, or constants, are enclosed in apostrophes. For example: 'CL Programming'

■ Hexadecimal literal values are prefixed with the letter X and can include any valid hexadecimal digit, including 0 to 9 and A to F. For example:

```
X'12345F'
```

A hexadecimal literal must contain an even number of characters within the apostrophes. Each pair of characters represents the zone and digit portion of a single byte. For example, X'F1' represents the character "1" in EBCDIC.

RECOMMENDATIONS

The value of this text will be greatly enhanced if the reader has convenient access to an AS/400 workstation and Program Development Manager (PDM). I strongly recommend keying and compiling all CL program examples. Augmenting the reading with hands-on experience is sure to enhance the learning process.

1

INTRODUCTION TO
AS/400 CONTROL LANGUAGE

The AS/400 CL (Control Language) is a set of commands used to request system functions. CL is comparable to Operator Control Language (OCL) on System/3x computers and Job Control Language (JCL) on mainframe computers. Although it shares functions with OCL and JCL, CL is far more comprehensive than either OCL or JCL. There are well over 1,700 CL commands, and that number increases with each new release of the operating system.

CL isn't particularly complex. Despite its sheer immensity, CL is straightforward and logical, and it is a relatively easy language to comprehend. Because of its consistent naming convention, with a little experience, you can intuitively guess at CL command names with a remarkably high degree of accuracy. CL command names are composed of a verb and a noun, or a verb, adjective, and noun. For example, the command to submit a batch job is SBMJOB (Submit Job). In this case, "SBM" is the verb and "JOB" is the noun. The command SBMDKTJOB (Submit Diskette Job) includes the adjective "DKT."

The abbreviations used in command names are usually made up of one to three of the most significant consonants in the word or four letters of a word that is only four letters. This is not a hard-and-fast rule, but rather a rule of thumb that can help when you are trying to guess the name of a command. Common examples of command abbreviations are listed in Table 1.1. When vowels are found in command names, they are either the first letter in the word or the only vowel in a three- or four-letter word. Examples include CALL, CHGFORM, ENDJOB, ADDPFM, and MOVOBJ.

These abbreviations are for the most part used consistently throughout the CL language. For example, all commands that operate on a subsystem use the abbreviation SBS. All commands that start, begin, or initiate anything begin with the verb "STR" for start. Therefore, the command to start a subsystem is STRSBS. A notable exception to this rule is the CALL (call a program) command. If the term *call* weren't so thoroughly ingrained in programming, the command to invoke a program might well be STRPGM (Start Program).

Table 1.1:
Standard Command
Abbreviations.

Abbreviation	Meaning
A	Attribute
CHG	Change
CPY	Copy
CRT	Create
D	Description
DLT	Delete
F	File
L	List
LF	Logical File
M	Member
MBR	Member
MOV	Move
OBJ	Object
PF	Physical File
SBS	Subsystem
SRC	Source
STR	Start

To say the least, the thought of learning nearly 2,000 commands is intimidating, The task begins to seem manageable, however, when viewed as learning about 40 major verbs and roughly 100 adjectives and nouns (objects) in various combinations. For the more obscure commands and those that don't follow the rules, OS/400 includes layered menus that provide assistance in finding any command name.

COMMAND SYNTAX

CL syntax is not particularly difficult. Aside from a few interesting subtleties that are often misunderstood, the basic rules are relatively simple. Commands are made up of three parts: a label, the command name, and the command parameters. A *label* can be simply a descriptor for a command or the target of a GOTO command in a CL program; the *command name* identifies the command to be run; and the *parameters* identify the objects and values to be used by the command.

Command Labels

The label is optional. When used, it is the first part of a command, appearing before the command name. A label must end with a colon. In a CL program, the label can be used as the target of a GOTO command. Additionally, when using the interactive debug facility, command labels can be used as breakpoints.

A label is also commonly used as a descriptor or identifier for a command or a section of code. Used in this way, labels can enhance the readability of a CL program. An underscore (_) can be used in a label to improve readability. The GOTO command, however, cannot reference labels containing periods.

A label can be used on any command, in any environment: CL program, batch, interactive, etc. It can be convenient to use labels on the interactive Command Entry display (a display designed specifically for entering and processing commands). If you expect to retrieve and rerun one or two commands frequently from Command Entry, then adding a distinctive label can make them easy to identify. See the first and second commands in Figure 1.1.

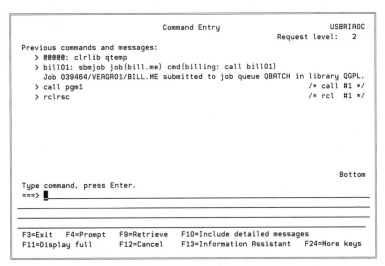

```
                              Command Entry                        USBRIAOC
                                                      Request level:    2
  Previous commands and messages:
    > @@@@@: clrlib qtemp
    > bill01: sbmjob job(bill.me) cmd(billing: call bill01)
      Job 039464/VEAGRO1/BILL.ME submitted to job queue QBATCH in library QGPL.
    > call pgm1                                              /* call #1 */
    > rclrsc                                                 /* rcl  #1 */




                                                                  Bottom
  Type command, press Enter.
  ===> ▮

  _____

  _____

   F3=Exit   F4=Prompt    F9=Retrieve   F10=Include detailed messages
   F11=Display full       F12=Cancel    F13=Information Assistant   F24=More keys
```

Figure 1.1: Command Entry display: commands with labels and comments.

Command Names

The second part of a command, the command name, identifies the command to be run; it must be specified before any parameters. A command name must follow the rules for a simple OS/400 name: it can begin with the characters A–Z, $, #, or @, and can be followed by up to nine characters or the numbers 0 to 9.

Command Parameters

The parameters identify the data that will be passed to the command-processing program (the program that actually processes data from a command.) Each parameter is made up of two parts. The first is a keyword that identifies the parameter name, and the second is the value to be used for the parameter. When the keyword and value are both used, they appear in the form KEYWORD(*value*). In this case, the parentheses around the value are required, and the left parenthesis must immediately follow the keyword.

Command Delimiters

The command name, along with any parameters (including keywords), must be separated by one or more blanks. While the command name and the optional command label are not required to be separated by a blank, commands are more readable when the label and command name are separated by one or more blanks. It is considered good practice to keep labels on separate lines.

CL Comments

CL comments are delimited by a leading /* to begin a comment and a trailing */ to close the comment. This syntax is consistent with many high-level languages. This is a significant departure from the way comments are implemented in OCL.

CL syntax offers increased flexibility over OCL because in CL a comment is not a type of line. Comments may be coded at the beginning or end of any command or interspersed between the parts of a command. They may be used anywhere blanks are allowed except within parameter values. A good illustration of this flexibility is the use of a comment at the end of a DCL (Declare) command to provide descriptive text for a CL program variable, as in the following example:

```
DCL      VAR(&X) TYPE(*DEC) LEN(7 0)  /* Counter */
```

On the command entry display, comments provide another technique for quickly locating prior commands to be retrieved. When you have a sequence of two or three commands to be rerun, it can be useful to follow each command with a comment that is right justified on the line, as in the third and fourth commands in Figure 1.1. Of course, comments may be coded as the only thing on a line. All comments are ignored by the CL compiler.

Continuation Characters

Commands in a CL program source are often too long to fit on one source line and, consequently, must be continued onto additional lines. The "+" and "–" continuation characters indicate to the OS/400 command analyzer that a command is continued on the next line. The continuation character must be the last character on the line being continued. If a "–" is coded, the command is continued beginning with column one of the next line, even if that position contains a blank. If a "+" is coded, the command is continued beginning with the first non-blank character on the next line. For example, the following CRTLIB (Create Library) commands in a source file have different results:

```
CRTLIB    LIB(SOURCE) TEXT('AS/400 source -
          code')
CRTLIB    LIB(SOURCE) TEXT('AS/400 source +
          code')
```

The first command creates a library called SOURCE with a text description of:

```
'AS/400 source               code'
```

The second command creates a library called SOURCE with a text description of:

```
'AS/400 source code'
```

Continuation characters can be specified only within compiled CL programs. However, examples in this text follow this convention whenever a command string is forced to wrap to an additional line.

PARAMETER VALUES

The most difficult aspect of using CL commands may be the syntax rules for parameters and their values. Common areas of misunderstanding include the use of parameter keywords, how to use parentheses, and the use of apostrophes—often referred to as quotes. Quoted strings in commands use the single quote or apostrophe (') character on the keyboard, not the double quotation (") character.

Parameter values may be specified as literal values, as CL program variables, as expressions that resolve to a value, or as predefined values. *Predefined values* are the CL version of reserved words. Predefined values can be easily identified because they always begin with an asterisk. For example, to direct the output of a DSPJOB (Display Job) command to the printer, the following command can be used:

```
DSPJOB     OUTPUT(*PRINT)
```

The value *PRINT, specified for the OUTPUT parameter, is a predefined value that, in this case, causes the output from the DSPJOB command to be sent to a printed report. The predefined values for any parameter can be displayed by prompting the command, and then prompting the parameter itself.

Parameters may be entered either in keyword form or in positional form. When entering command parameters in keyword form, the parameter value must be surrounded by parentheses and must immediately follow the keyword. For example, the following command illustrates the keyword form of parameter entry:

```
DSPMSG   MSGQ(QSYSOPR)
```

On parameters entered in positional form, the keyword is omitted and the parentheses are optional unless required to satisfy some other syntax rule. The following command illustrates the positional form of command entry:

```
DSPMSG   QSYSOPR
```

When parameters are specified positionally, they must be entered in the order they are defined to the command. Each command has a MAXPOS (Maximum Positional Parameters) attribute that limits the number of allowable positional parameters.

The keyword form and positional form can be specified on the same command. However, once a keyword is specified, all subsequent parameters also must be in keyword form. For example:

```
ADDPFM    QCLSRC  EXMPL10
```

The previous command is valid because it contains two positional parameter values. If the command were specified as follows, it would be invalid:

```
ADDPFM   FILE(QCLSRC) EXMPL10
```

The FILE parameter is specified in the keyword form but the member parameter is not. The proper specification would be as follows:

```
ADDPFM   FILE(QCLSRC) MBR(EXMPL10)
```

Default Values

Command parameters that are not required are referred to as *optional parameters*. All optional parameters have default values that are used when no value is specified by the user. The default value for any command parameter is displayed when the command is prompted.

The default value for any optional parameter can be specified positionally by using the null value (*N). The null value (*N) indicates a parameter position for which no value is specified.

To illustrate the use of null values, consider the command MONMSG (Monitor Message). MONMSG has the following three parameters, all of which are allowed positionally:

- MSGID (Message Identifier).
- CMPDTA (Comparison Data).
- EXEC (Command to Run).

By using the null value for the second (and virtually never used) parameter, the third parameter can be specified positionally. The commands shown in Figure 1.2 are equivalent.

```
MONMSG     MSGID(CPF9999)                  EXEC(GOTO ERROR)
MONMSG     CPF9999                         EXEC(GOTO ERROR)
MONMSG     CPF9999      CMPDTA(*NONE)       EXEC(GOTO ERROR)
MONMSG     CPF9999      CMPDTA(*N)          EXEC(GOTO ERROR)
MONMSG     CPF9999      *N                  GOTO ERROR
```

Figure 1.2: Specifying positional parameters.

Qualified Values

Many parameters allow the use of qualified values. For example, most OS/400 objects may be qualified by library. Qualifiers, if used, must precede the object or other value and must be separated with a slash ("/"). In the following DSPPFM command, the file named MYFILE is qualified to the library named TEST.

```
DSPPFM     FILE(TEST/MYFILE)
```

Lists of Parameter Values

Some parameters can contain simple, mixed, or complex lists of values. The LIBL (Library List) parameter of the CHGLIBL (Change Library List) command is an example of a simple list. For example, on the following CHGLIBL command, each element of the list for the LIBL parameter is the name of a library:

```
CHGLIBL    LIBL(QTEMP QGPL DATALIB PGMLIB)
```

Each element of the list must be separated from the other elements by one or more blanks, and the entire list must be enclosed in parentheses—even if specified without the keyword.

The LOG (Message Logging) parameter of the CHGJOB (Change Job) command is a mixed list of related values. Each element of the list has a different meaning. For example:

```
CHGJOB     LOG(4 00 *MSG)
```

Again, elements of the list are separated by one or more blanks.

The POOLS (Storage Pools) parameter of the CHGSBSD (Change Subsystem De-scription) command is an example of a complex list. In other words, it's a list of lists. Each major element of the list contains its own mixed list.

```
CHGSBSD    QINTER  POOLS((1 *BASE) (2 *INTERACT))
```

Elements of each sublist are separated by one or more blanks, and the sublist is enclosed in parentheses. The entire complex list also must be enclosed in paren-theses. Blanks are not required between parentheses.

Expressions

The CL language supports expressions similar to most other high-level lan-guages. The three types of expressions CL supports are:

- Character-string expressions.
- Arithmetic expressions.
- Logical expressions.

Character-string expressions can be simple or complex. Simple character-string expressions include those shown in Figure 1.3.

```
CHGVAR    VAR(&ADDRESS)  VALUE('123 Main Street')
CHGVAR    &HEADLINE      'Dana and Ian shoot hoops.'
CHGVAR    &OBJECT        VALUE(PROG1)
```

Figure 1.3: Examples of simple character-string expressions.

The first simple character-string expression is an example of a quoted character string, with embedded blanks. When blanks are included in the character string, they must be enclosed in single quotation marks or apostrophes. The second exam-ple is similar to the first, but avoids the use of keywords. Because the third example contains no special characters or embedded blanks, it doesn't require quotation marks.

Complex character-string expressions can be used only in CL programs and are made up of more than one value or a portion of a value. Figure 1.4 shows examples.

```
CHGVAR      &ADDRESS      VALUE(&CITY *BCAT &STATE)
CHGVAR      VAR(&LIB)     VALUE(%SST(&NAME 11 10))
CHGVAR      VAR(&NAME)    VALUE(&LIB *TCAT '/' *CAT 'PROG1')
```

Figure 1.4: Examples of complex character-string expressions.

The first example concatenates two character variables together. The second example retrieves a subset (i.e., substring) of the &NAME CL variable. The third example concatenates CL variables with a quoted literal value.

Arithmetic expressions are specified free-form. They can include addition, subtraction, multiplication, and division operations (i.e., + - * /), as well as parentheses. Figure 1.5 shows some examples.

```
CHGVAR      VAR(&RETAIL)   VALUE(&WHLSLS + (&WHLSLS * &PERCENT))
CHGVAR      VAR(&AMOUNT)   VALUE(((&A - 8) * 128) + &B)
CHGVAR      &SIZE          1024
```

Figure 1.5: Examples of free-form arithmetic expressions.

The first example calculates the value of the CL variable &RETAIL using only other CL variables. The second uses both CL variables and numeric literal values to calculate the value for the CL variable &AMOUNT. The third example assigns the value 1,024 to the CL variable &SIZE.

Logical expressions produce a value that results in a logical *true* or *false* ('1' or '0'). They can be specified on the IF command and the CHGVAR command in a CL program. See Figure 1.6 for some examples.

```
IF          (&A = &B)      THEN(CHGVAR &MSG VALUE('A equals B'))
IF          (&IN03)        THEN(CHGVAR &MSG VALUE('F3 pressed'))
CHGVAR      VAR(&EQUAL)    VALUE(&A = &B)
```

Figure 1.6: Examples of logical expressions.

The logical expression in the first example is the most common form and is referred to as a *relational expression*. The variable &A is compared (using the = operator) to variable &B. If the condition test is true, a logical '1' is returned and the command specified for the THEN parameter is performed. The second example tests the logical variable &IN03. If the variable is true (i.e., equal to '1') then the command specified for the THEN parameter is performed. The third example assigns a '1' or '0' to the CL variable &EQUAL. The CL variable &EQUAL must be declared as a logical variable.

Quoted Values

As mentioned earlier, character-string expressions often require that they be enclosed in apostrophes (') or single quotes. For example, the TEXT parameter of the CRTPF (Create Physical File) command normally is quoted as follows:

```
CRTPF    FILEA RCDLEN(100) TEXT('This is a sample file')
```

If the TEXT parameter value weren't quoted, the command analyzer would attempt to interpret it as a simple list with five elements, thus causing an error. In the following command, the value for the TEXT parameter need not be quoted because it contains neither special characters nor embedded blanks:

```
CRTPF    FILEB RCDLEN(100) TEXT(Samplefile)
```

Note, however, that in this example, the text will be converted to uppercase. Non-quoted text strings are always translated to uppercase characters. This is one reason that many programmers develop the habit of quoting all character strings.

Any quoted value is passed to the command-processing program as a character literal. This is especially important to understand when coding the CALL command. CALL has two parameters, PGM (Program to Call) and PARM (Parameter List). PARM accepts a list of parameters that can have various attributes. The use of apostrophes is crucial to the proper interpretation of each element in the list. The following command passes four parameters to the CL program XMPL201:

```
CALL     XMPL201    PARM('NBR-1' string2 '3' 4)
```

The first parameter must be quoted because of the hyphen character (–). The second parameter is correctly interpreted as a character literal, but is translated to uppercase characters ('STRING2'). Because the third parameter is quoted, it is passed as a single character '3' while the unquoted fourth parameter is passed as a packed decimal value of 4. Parameter passing in CL programs is covered in more detail in chapter 5.

USING CL COMMANDS

CL commands can be run in several environments. They can be run interactively by entering them in any of the three standard command entry interfaces. The first of these is the Command Line, an input-capable field at the bottom of many system displays and menus. Second is the Command Entry display, a screen designed specifically for entering commands. The Command Entry display can be displayed by calling the system-supplied program QCMD or by pressing F10 from one of various system menus. Third is a Command Line Window that allows commands to be entered by a user from within user-written programs. A command window can be invoked within Source Entry Utility (SEU) by pressing F21 or within a user-written application by calling the system program QUSCMDLN.

CL commands also can be run as batch jobs by submitting them to a batch subsystem with the SBMJOB (Submit Job) command. For example, the following SBMJOB command submits a CPYF (Copy File) command to batch. The job is named RUN202.

```
SBMJOB   CMD(CPYF ARTRANS TOFILE(ARHIST) MBROPT(*ADD)) +
           JOB(RUN202)
```

Batch Job Stream

A seldom-used method of running commands on the AS/400 is using a batch job stream made up of independent CL commands. With this technique (sometimes called *batch mode*), the commands may be supplied as records in a source-file member, a diskette file, or a Remote Job Entry (RJE) communications file. A special job called a *spooled reader* processes the records, places a batch job on a job queue and converts the records to commands to be run by that job. The function supported by batch CL is roughly analogous to that of System/3 OCL procedures or JCL. Batch CL doesn't support branching, conditioning, error handling, or program variables.

Additionally, and most importantly, CL commands can be compiled into CL programs. Compiled CL remedies all of the shortcomings of batch CL and adds the advantage of better performance.

Command Environment (Entry Codes)

You can control the environments in which a command can be run through the command's entry codes. Entry codes are specified on the ALLOW (Where Allowed to Run) parameter of the CHGCMD (Change Command) command. If *BATCH is one of a command's entry codes, the command is valid in a batch input stream, external to a compiled CL program. Commands specified with *INTERACT are valid when run interactively, external to a compiled CL program.

> **NOTE:** REXX is the SAA (Systems Application Architecture) general-purpose procedure language and is interpreted by the AS/400 REXX Interpreter. The REXX language is not detailed in this text.

The *BPGM option specifies that the command can be included in a compiled CL program that runs in batch. *IPGM denotes that the command can be included in a compiled CL program that runs interactively. The values *BMOD and *IMOD indicate that the command can be used in a batch CL ILE program or interactive CL ILE program, respectively. The values *BREXX and *IREXX indicate that the command can be used in a REXX procedure run in a batch or interactive job, respectively. Commands with the *EXEC entry code can be passed as a parameter to the system program QCMDEXC.

The restrictions that are imposed by the entry codes usually make good sense. For example, the DSPPFM (Display Physical File Member) command is not allowed to run in a batch job or a batch program because it uses a display file. The DCL (Declare Variable) command has entry codes for only *BPGM, *IPGM,

*BMOD, and *IMOD because CL program variables are only supported in CL programs and procedures.

The entry codes for any command can be determined by using the DSPCMD (Display Command) command.

Some AS/400 installations have changed the entry codes on certain commands, such as CRTCBLPGM (Create COBOL Program), to prevent programmers from running interactive compiles. Such changes are specified on the ALLOW parameter of the CHGCMD (Change Command) command and require that the user making the change has authority to change the command.

The mode in which commands are valid also is restricted. One or more of three possible modes are specified for each command. If *PROD is specified, the command is valid in the production mode. Debugging commands other than STRDBG (Start Debug) have only *DEBUG specified, but most commands are valid in both the production and debugging mode. A few commands, such as ENDSRVJOB, have only *SERVICE specified and are valid only in the service mode. There should never be a need to change the valid mode for a system command that was shipped with the operating system. The valid modes for any command can be determined by using the DSPCMD command.

The Command Processor

In addition to running commands within compiled CL programs, commands also may be syntax checked and run from within *high-level language* (HLL) programs. The three system *Application Program Interfaces* (APIs) that provide this function are:

1. QCMDEXC—Processes any command passed to it as a character string.

2. QCMDCHK—Syntax checks any character string passed to it for proper command syntax.

3. QCAPCMD—A more complex API that combines and adds to the functions of QCMDCHK and QCMDEXC. This generally is used only when more sophisticated command analyzer functions are required.

Calling QCMDEXC or QCMDCHK is simple; the command string and the length of the command string are passed as parameters. For example:

```
CALL    QCMDEXC PARM('STRPRTWTR DEV(PRT01)' 20)
```

This sample code would run the STRPRTWTR command. Normally, the command string is stored in a CL variable of not more than 9,999 characters. The length is specified as a literal or a decimal variable with a length of 15 digits with 5 decimal positions. See Figure 1.7.

```
DCL       &CMD       TYPE(*CHAR)  LEN(1000)
CHGVAR    VAR(&CMD)  VALUE('STRPRTWTR DEV(PRT01)')
CALL      QCMDEXC    PARM(&CMD 20)
```

Figure 1.7: Example of calling QCMDEXC with a variable as the parameter.

The syntax is the same for QCMDEXC and QCMDCHK. QCMDCHK, however, doesn't run commands. Instead, QCMDCHK syntax checks, prompts, and returns a completed command string to the CL variable. The intent of QCMDCHK is to allow commands to be entered and syntax checked before they are run with QCMDEXC.

Some examples of CL commands that are commonly processed by QCMDEXC are the override file commands OVRDBF (Override with Database File) and OVRPRTF (Override with Print File, etc.). In an OPM environment, overrides are typically no longer in effect after the issuing program ends. Consequently, calling a CL program to perform overrides from another HLL is not usually a workable solution. However, because QCMDEXC treats commands as though they were run by its calling program, the overrides remain in effect after QCMDEXC returns.

In a CL program, QCMDEXC also is useful when a command must be dynamically linked (in other words, when the command to be run is not known at compile-time). This technique allows commands to be stored in and retrieved from a database file, a message file, or some other storage medium.

The Command Prompter

Whether a CL command is typed on a command line, on the command entry display, or in a source member through SEU, prompting support is available by pressing F4. The prompter is a powerful aid that will make almost any command easier to type. The prompter lists the parameters and their attributes as well as the valid choices for each parameter, and it offers on-line help for the command and each parameter.

One of the greatest advantages of using the prompter is that you don't need to remember keywords or the order of parameters. If you are just becoming familiar with CL commands, the prompter can be extremely valuable.

USES OF CL PROGRAMS

AS/400 CL is an operator control language, a job control language, and is considered by some to be a high-level programming language. CL can be compiled, it can perform device file I/O, and it can be called recursively.

Each command, with a few special exceptions, invokes a program referred to as its Command Processing Program (CPP). User-written commands usually have a CL program or some other language program as their CPP. OS/400 commands, often called System Commands, call OS/400 system programs to perform their work.

It is important to understand that the nature of CL restricts the usefulness of CL programs to less than that of full-function business application programs. CL programs generally serve to:

- Simplify or control operations.
- Support applications.
- Perform system management functions.

A single CL program typically performs one or more of the preceding tasks.

CL Programs for Operations Control

As an operator control language, CL programs are used to establish or modify a job's work environment. Examples are changing the delivery mode of the user's message queue or adjusting the job's use of resources for better runtime performance. CL programs are also often used as menus. Menus for end-users are popular because they inform the workstation operator of the options available, and menus can restrict the users to those tasks. In addition, menus reduce typing and the potential for errors. In short, menus allow commonly used CL commands to be prepared in advance by a programmer and selected by an operator.

There are several alternatives to menus written in CL. The AS/400 supports a menu object that functions similarly to a System/36 menu. Commercial menu systems also are available. Additionally, any high-level language can be used to process menu options.

Whether integrated within a CL program, embedded in a menu object, or acting as a stand-alone program, compiled CL programs provide distinct benefits to system operators. This is especially true when several commands are run in a sequence. In this regard, CL programs serve the same purpose as batch files under PC-DOS and OCL "procs" on the System/36.

CL Programs for Application Support

As a batch-job control language, CL commands may be run either as part of a CL program or as a batch-job stream of independent CL commands. However, the second approach, referred to as batch mode, is seldom used. When used to control the steps of a job, a compiled CL program submitted to batch with SBMJOB offers better flexibility, function, and performance than batch-job streams.

A CL application program that runs in batch typically is used to call HLL programs in a specific sequence. For example, a batch CL program can:

- Summarize the data.
- Organize the data.
- Print a report using the data.

CL commands and programs can be used to directly manipulate the database. For example, files can be copied, sorted, cleared, and deleted using CL commands. Also, CL programs commonly override printer files in order to change output attributes (such as number of copies, output queue, or type of form) of the reports.

However, CL programs that support interactive applications, as a rule, should not include commands that perform long-running functions such as copying or sorting large files. One function frequently used in interactive CL programs is to "pre-open" database files before running other high-level language programs. This allows application programs to avoid the relatively lengthy process of opening a file.

Both batch and interactive CL programs can include commands to override database files so that files other than those referenced by the HLL program can be opened. Also, OS/400 message and system-error handling, required by any application, is almost always performed in a CL program.

CL Programs for System Functions

There are times when a CL program can be used by itself to add a valuable feature to the operating system. Such a CL program could be a general utility program or a program to provide a complex operator function. A CL program is often required because CL provides the only high-level language access to certain system functions and values. In addition, job and object management functions can be performed easily with CL.

Most CL commands have no corresponding function in other high-level languages. Although more and more API functions are provided with each new release of OS/400, many functions are available only in CL.

REVIEW QUESTIONS

1. AS/400 CL is a set of commands used to request _____ _____; it is comparable to _____ and _____.

2. Parameters may be entered either in _____ form or in _____ form.

3. Parameter values that are specified as _____ or _____ must be enclosed in parentheses.

4. Character string values that contain special characters or embedded blanks are called _____ _____ and must be enclosed in _____, or single quotes.

5. CL commands can be run in several environments: _____, _____, _____, _____, or _____.

2

CL PROGRAM STRUCTURE

CL programs can be stored in source file members. AS/400 SEU can be used to create or edit CL statements. To start SEU for a specific source-file member, run the command shown below. This command starts the AS/400 editor for the source file member AGING. If AGING doesn't exist, SEU creates a new member with that name.

```
STRSEU SRCFILE(QCLSRC) SRCMBR(AGING) TYPE(CLP)
```

Usually, Programming Development Manager (PDM) is used for the edit/compile/debug cycle of application development. PDM supports CL program source members as well as all other OS/400 source types.

To start PDM, run the STRPDM command, and select Option 3 (Work with Members Using PDM). This will provide you with a prompt requesting the name of the source file, library, and member list you prefer to work with. Type in QCLSRC as the name of the source file and leave the source member name and type set to *ALL.

When you press the Enter key, a list of members within QCLSRC is displayed. You can edit any of the members by typing the Edit option (Option 2) next to the member name. To create a new member, press the Create function key (F6).

Once editing is completed for a CL program, use the PDM compile option (Option 14) to create the CL program object. Once the CL program is compiled, it is ready to be called.

CREATING CL PROGRAMS

Before a CL program can be run, it must be compiled using the CRTCLPGM (Create CL Program) command. Creating ILE modules and programs is described in chapter 13. The CRTCLPGM command has several parameters that affect the manner in which the program is created and the way the compiled program runs. For the most part, compiling a CL program, requires only a few keywords and values. For example:

```
CRTCLPGM   PGM(mylib/myclpgm) SRCFILE(QCLSRC)
SRCMBR(*PGM)
```

This CRTCLPGM command compiles the CL program named MYCLPGM, and stores it in the library named MYLIB. The PGM parameter is all that is really needed. The SRCFILE and SRCMBR parameters that are shown are the default values. Therefore, they aren't even necessary.

CRTCLPGM Parameters

The PGM (Program) parameter is required, and it determines the name of the compiled CL program and the library in which it is created. If the library is specified as the predefined value *CURLIB, the program is created in the current library of the job in which the CRTCLPGM command is run.

The SRCFILE (Source File) and SRCMBR (Source Member) parameters identify the qualified name of the source file and the name of the member that contains the source for the CL program. The OPTION (Source Listing Options) parameter accepts a list of options that control the source listing:

- Whether a source listing is produced.
- Whether a cross-reference of variables and labels is produced.
- Whether a compiled program object is created.
- The level of compiler error message text that is produced.

A similar parameter, GENOPT (Generation Options), accepts a list of options that control the generation of object code:

- Whether a listing of the intermediate representation of the program and the machine instructions is produced.
- Whether a cross-reference of variables in the intermediate representation is produced.

The USRPRF (User Profile) parameter determines whether the CL program runs with the authority of the user or the combined authority of the user and the owner of the program. The owner of the program initially is the user profile that created the program. The owner of the program can be changed with the CHGOBJOWN (Change Object Owner) command.

The LOG (Write Commands to the Job Log) parameter specifies whether the commands appear in the job log. The default LOG(*JOB) means that the LOGCLPGM (Log CL Program Commands) job attribute will determine whether or not the CL commands are written to the job log. If LOG(*YES) or LOG(*NO) is specified, then this value overrides any value specified by the LOGCLPGM job attribute.

The source for a CL program can be retrieved from the program object with the RTVCLSRC (Retrieve CL Source) command and placed in a source member. This capability is controlled by the ALWRTVSRC (Allow Retrieve Source) parameter.

The REPLACE (Replace Program) parameter controls whether a new program will replace an existing CL program. If a program is replaced, the USRPRF and AUT parameters are ignored and the respective values of the previously existing program are used.

By specifying the TGTRLS (Target Release) parameter, a CL program can be created to run on a previous release of the operating software.

The level of authority to the CL program that is given to users who have no specific authority granted is determined by the AUT (Authority) parameter.

The TEXT parameter can contain up to 50 characters of descriptive text that will be part of the compiled program's description. The default, *SRCMBRTXT, indicates that the text of the source member is used.

The attributes of a CL (or any other) program can be displayed or printed using the DSPPGM (Display Program) command. Of the attributes determined by parameters of the CRTCLPGM command, SRCFILE, SRCMBR, USRPRF, LOG, ALWRTVSRC, and TEXT may be displayed. Other statistical and performance-related information also may be displayed.

THE CL PROGRAM OBJECT

A CL program is a permanent OS/400 object of the type *PGM, with the attribute CLP. It is created by compiling a group of CL commands from a source-file member with type CLP.

HLL program objects contain object code generated by a compiler. CL program objects, however, contain object code and "tokenized" CL commands. At runtime, the commands are processed by the command analyzer. The values of any CL variables are replaced with data at runtime. Because compiled CL commands must be processed by the command analyzer at runtime, CL program performance is relatively slow compared to other HLL programs. However, compiled CL programs run much faster than interactive CL commands or commands run with QCMDEXC.

The performance advantage that compiled CL has over interpreted CL is attributable to two factors. First, interpreted CL is syntax checked, or *parsed*, at runtime and CL programs are parsed at compile time. Also, the process of passing a command to the command analyzer is much faster from a CL program than from interactive CL.

A few commands, called *in-line commands*, actually are compiled into object code. In-line commands include PGM, ENDPGM, DCL, DCLF, MONMSG, CALL, TFRCTL, SNDF, RCVF, SNDRCVF, GOTO, DO, ENDDO, CHGVAR, IF, and ELSE. All in-line commands have several characteristics in common. First, they have no command processing program (CPP). The DSPCMD (Display Command)

command shows a value for the CPP, but the CPP doesn't actually exist. Second, most in-line commands are never written to the job log, even if *YES is specified for the LOG parameter when the CL program is created. The exceptions are CALL, TFRCTL, RCVF, SNDF, and SNDRCVF. Additionally, with the exception of CALL, in-line commands can be run only in a CL program.

Some commands, other than in-line commands, are permitted only in CL programs. For example, any command having a parameter that requires a CL variable for its value can only be run in a CL program. Such commands only have entry codes of *IPGM, *BPGM, *IMOD, or *BMOD.

ANATOMY OF A CL PROGRAM

If you are familiar with COBOL or RPG, you know that these languages provide distinct areas or *sections* in the language for specific functions. For example, in RPG file description specifications, files are declared to the RPG program. In COBOL, files are declared in the FILE-SECTION.

While the divisions of a CL program are not nearly as structured as those of COBOL and RPG, CL does enforce, in a limited way, the concept of sections. For purposes of this discussion, there are four definable sections of a CL program. They are the:

1. Program Identification section.
2. Declarative section.
3. Global Error Monitor section.
4. Procedure section.

While not explicitly described by IBM, these four sections are defined by their function and by the order in which they must be coded in the CL program.

Program Identification Section

The program identification section of a CL program is not formally supported by the language and exists only due to programming conventions. It is composed of a standardized block of comments placed before any CL commands in the program and is used to identify the program's name, author, and purpose and to provide a place to log modifications to the program.

Declarative Section

The beginning of the declarative section is earmarked by the PGM (Program) command. The PGM command identifies the start of the CL program and specifies any parameters that are to be received by the program. Although the PGM command is not required unless parameters are received, it is normally included in every CL program. Many programmers also include the name of the CL program in a label on the PGM command. I prefer to put the name of the program in a block of comments at the beginning of the program.

Variables used in CL programs are defined in the declarative section, following the PGM command. There are two CL commands that are used to define or declare CL variables. The DCL (Declare CL Variable) command is used to define CL program variables. The DCLF (Declare File) command is used to define a file to the CL program. The compiler uses the DCLF command to reference the external description of the file and declares a CL variable for each field defined in the file.

Call Message Queue:
Programmers who have worked on the AS/400 for some time may be more familiar with the term program message queue. *This terminology has adapted to the advent of the Integrated Language Environment (ILE). For a further discussion of this topic, see chapter 13.*

Global Error Monitor Section.

The global error monitor section determines, at a global (or program) level, how errors are to be handled. *Exceptions* (or errors) may be signaled to a CL program by other programs that it calls. Called programs include the command-processing programs that support each system command. A called program signals an exception by sending an "escape" message to a special message queue called the *call message queue* (or *program message queue*) of the calling program.

If an exception is signaled to a CL program that doesn't have an error monitor, the program receiving the exception fails, and a default error-handler is called. The default error-handler sends a message to the workstation operator or the system operator. For interactive jobs, invoking the default error-handler is generally considered to be an inadequate solution. Although the workstation operator is prompted to supply one of several possible responses, the prompts are crude, at best, and often are confusing to users. More importantly, this condition is perceived (and rightfully so) as a "bug" by most users. Good design dictates that such exceptions be trapped and handled by the application.

Handling errors in CL is accomplished by monitoring for exception messages using the MONMSG (Monitor Message) command. The MONMSG command may be used at either a command level or a program level. A command-level MONMSG monitors only for exceptions caused directly by the command that immediately precedes it in the program. A program-level, or global, MONMSG monitors for exceptions throughout the entire invocation of the program.

Error handling is discussed in more detail in chapter 7. For now, just keep in mind the relevance of error handling to program structure. All global MONMSG commands must be coded in a global-error monitor section following the declarative section and before any other commands.

Procedure Section

The procedure section in CL is analogous to the COBOL procedure division and RPG calculation specifications. It contains the functions to be performed by the program and the logic that controls the functions. The procedure section ends with the ENDPGM (End Program) command. As its name implies, the ENDPGM command identifies the end of the CL program source. In addition to being a CL compiler directive, the ENDPGM command forces a running CL program to terminate and return control to its caller.

Interestingly enough, none of the sections of a CL program are mandatory. In fact, a CL program can be successfully compiled from a CL source member with absolutely no records. The compile takes much longer than one would expect, but the created CL program runs quite quickly.

REVIEW QUESTIONS

1. CL is a high-level programming language that is used for
    _____, _____, and
    _____.

2. A CL program is a permanent AS/400 _____ that contains executable object
    code and _____ _____.

3. There are four definable sections of a CL program: the _____
    section, the _____ section, the _____
    section, and the _____ section.

4. All _____ and _____ used in a CL program must be declared at the
    beginning of the program in the declarative section.

5. Errors signaled to a CL program may be trapped by either a _____ level
    MONMSG command or a _____ level MONMSG coded in the global-error
    monitor section.

3

CL PROGRAM
VARIABLES AND EXPRESSIONS

Many features of AS/400 CL make it a powerful job control language as well as a useful language for accessing system functions. One of the most important features is the use of CL program variables. Chapter 2 describes how CL program variables must be defined or declared to the CL program, either explicitly, with the DCL (Declare CL Variable) command, or implicitly, with the DCLF (Declare File) command. Let's examine CL's two declarative commands more closely.

THE DCL COMMAND

The DCL command has four parameters:

1. VAR (Variable Name).
2. TYPE (Data Type).
3. LEN (Length of Variable).
4. VALUE (Initial Value).

The VAR parameter is used to name the CL variable being declared. CL variable names begin with an ampersand (&) and can be from two to 11 characters (including the ampersand). The 10 characters following the ampersand must adhere to the rules for a simple OS/400 name. The characters can begin with A–Z, $, #, or @ and can be followed by up to nine additional characters. The remaining characters can be A–Z, 0–9, $, #, @, or underscore (_).

The TYPE parameter is required and determines the data type of the variable. CL supports three data types: *CHAR (Character), *DEC (Numeric or Decimal), and *LGL (Logical). Logical variables are often referred to as *switches, flags*, or *indicators*.

Unlike some programming languages, CL provides no capability for defining program variables dynamically. Although this constraint might be considered a handicap, explicitly defined variables force a pragmatic approach to data usage and data typing, often reducing programmer confusion.

For character and logical variables, the LEN parameter is specified as an integer. For decimal variables, LEN is specified as a pair of integers, separated by one or more blanks, that represent the full length of the variable and the number of decimal positions, respectively. If the second integer is omitted for a decimal variable, the number of decimal positions will be 0. If the LEN parameter is omitted entirely, a default size for the specified data type is used. Table 3.1 lists the default sizes for each CL data type.

Table 3.1: CL Variable Data Type Size Limits.

Data Type	Default Length	Range Min/Max
*CHAR	32	1 to 9,999
*DEC	(15 5)	(1 0) to (15 9)
*LGL	1	1 to 1

The maximum size of a CL variable depends on its type. Character variables may be up to 9,999 bytes in length, and decimal variables may be up to 15 digits in length with up to 9 decimal positions. Logical variables are always 1 byte. The VALUE parameter may be used to specify the initial value for a CL variable when the program starts. If VALUE is omitted, character variables are initialized to blanks, decimal variables to zero, and logical variables to a logical false or '0'.

The size of the variable &MESSAGE1 is 10 characters, and it is initialized to the value 'Hello', followed by blanks. The size of the &MESSAGE2 variable will default to 32 characters, and it is initialized to the value 'World', followed by blanks. The size of the variable &NAME is specified as 35 characters, and it is initialized to blanks.

The size of the &GROSS variable is 7 digits with 2 decimal positions, and it is initialized to 00123.00. The size of the &NET variable is 15 digits with 5 decimal positions, and it is initialized to the value 0000000123.00000. The size of the variable &TOTAL is declared as 7 with 0 decimal positions, and it is initialized to zero (0). Figure 3.1 illustrates various examples of specifying the DCL command.

```
DCL     &MESSAGE1   TYPE(*CHAR) LEN(10)   VALUE('Hello')
DCL     &MESSAGE2   TYPE(*CHAR)           VALUE('World')
DCL     &NAME       *CHAR           35
DCL     &GROSS      TYPE(*DEC)  LEN(7 2) VALUE(123)
DCL     &NET        TYPE(*DEC)            VALUE(123)
DCL     &TOTAL      *DEC            7
DCL     &ON         TYPE(*LGL)            VALUE('1')
DCL     &OFF        *LGL
```

Figure 3.1: Examples of using the DECLARE command.

The variables &ON and &OFF are logical variables with a length of 1. The variable &ON is initialized to '1' and &OFF is initialized to '0'.

THE DCLF COMMAND

The DCLF (Declare File) command specifies a file and formats used by the CL program. The importance of this to a discussion of CL variables is that the compiler uses the DCLF command to reference the external description of the file and implicitly declares a CL variable for each field defined in the file. Fields that are externally defined as character or hexadecimal are declared as character variables. Fields externally defined as packed decimal, zoned decimal, or binary are declared as decimal variables. Floating point fields are not supported in CL.

The name used for each CL variable brought in from the file description is the same as the field name in the file, prefixed with an ampersand. Thus, if a "part master" file contains a field named PARTNO, the compiler will declare a CL variable named &PARTNO having the same attributes as PARTNO.

Indicators used in a display file that is declared in a CL program are declared as logical variables named &INnn. For example, indicator 03 is implicitly declared as &IN03.

VALUES OF VARIABLES

The six possible ways to set or change the value of a CL variable are:

1. A CL variable can be initialized to a specific value by including the VALUE parameter on the DCL command.

2. If a CL variable is an input field on a file declared to the program, its value is set whenever a record from the file is read.

3. If a CL variable is specified in the parameter list on the PGM command, its value is already set when the CL program is called.

4. If a CL variable is a parameter passed to another program, it can be altered by the called program.

5. If a CL variable is specified as a *return variable parameter* on a command, its value is set by that command. (Return variables parameters are command parameters that specify a CL variable in which to return information to the CL program.)

6. A new value can be assigned to any CL variable using the CHGVAR (Change Variable) command.

THE CHGVAR COMMAND

The CHGVAR (Change Variable) command is used to assign a value to any CL variable, regardless of the data type. CHGVAR supports free-form arithmetic expressions, yet its arithmetic capability is somewhat restricted. For example, CHGVAR supports no direct function for computing a square root, no MODULA function (division yielding a remainder), and neither exponent nor trigonometric functions. The character string operations of CHGVAR include a substring function and concatenation.

The CHGVAR command has two parameters: VAR (CL Variable Name), which identifies the CL variable to be changed, and VALUE (New Value), which contains the value to be assigned to the variable. The VALUE parameter can contain a literal, a CL variable, or an expression. Because all data types can be handled by this single command, it is important to exercise care in performing the CHGVAR operation. To avoid problems using CHGVAR, you'll need to learn a few elementary guidelines for specifying the VALUE parameter.

ASSIGNING VALUES TO CHARACTER VARIABLES

The guidelines for assigning a character value to a character variable are as follows:

- The value is left justified and completely replaces the variable. In other words, the value is padded with blanks to the right of the data.

- Character string literal values must be quoted when they contain special characters. Specifically, characters other than A–Z, 0–9, $, #, or @.

- Lowercase, unquoted character string literal values are translated to uppercase characters.

- To include an apostrophe (') in a literal, you must double the apostrophe and quote the string.

- A quoted string of all numeric digits is treated as alphanumeric characters.

One common source of problems is the incorrect use of apostrophes when specifying literal values. Recall that character literal values can be either quoted or unquoted strings. The following commands illustrate the correct use of quoted strings:

```
CHGVAR     VAR(&GREETING)  VALUE('HELLO!')
CHGVAR     VAR(&GREETING)  VALUE('HI THERE')
```

The first CHGVAR example must use quotes because it contains a special character (!). The second CHGVAR example must use quotes because it contains an embedded blank. Omitting the quotes in either example would cause a syntax error.

In the CL program XMPL301 (see Figure 3.2), &CITY is initialized to the value 'St. Paul'.

```
 1.00 /*************************************************************/
 2.00 /* Program Name: XMPL301 - Quoted character strings       */
 3.00 /*************************************************************/
 4.00
 5.00 PGM
 6.00    DCL         &CITY    TYPE(*CHAR) LEN(15) VALUE('St. Paul')
 8.00
 9.00    CHGVAR      &CITY    VALUE(Chicago)
10.00
11.00 ENDPGM
```

Figure 3.2: Specifying quoted character strings.

The result of the CHGVAR command assigns the value 'CHICAGObbbbbbbbb' to &CITY. There are three important things to notice here. First, the value is left justified in the variable. Second, the value is padded with blanks to the right of the data, overlaying the original value entirely. Third, because the string is unquoted, the value is translated to uppercase characters. To include lowercase characters in the result, the CHGVAR command should be coded using a quoted string value as follows:

```
CHGVAR     &CITY  VALUE('Chicago')
```

The following command demonstrates how to specify a literal apostrophe in a character string:

```
DCL       &ADVERTISE   *CHAR     12
CHGVAR    &ADVERTISE   VALUE('Eat at Joe''s')
```

In this example, the value Eat at Joe's is assigned to &ADVERTISE. To include the special character ('), the apostrophe in the literal is doubled and the string is quoted. Note that even though &ADVERTISE is 12 characters, the value is specified as a string of 13 characters, including the doubled apostrophe. Sometimes, character literal values can contain all numeric digits, as in the following example:

```
DCL       &ADDRESS   *CHAR     10
CHGVAR    &ADDRESS   VALUE('3046')
```

After the preceding CHGVAR, the value of &ADDRESS is '3046bbbbbb'. Using a quoted string causes the numbers to be treated as characters. Notice that the resulting value is left justified and blank padded in the variable. The surrounding quotes are required to distinguish a character literal from a numeric literal.

It is not necessary for the data type of the value to always match that of the CL variable. If you want to be able to predict the results of a CHGVAR operation, however, you should understand the subtleties of mismatching data types. The guidelines for assigning a numeric value to a character variable are as follows:

- The result is right justified and zero filled.

- If the value is negative, the sign is placed into the first position of the result.

- If there are decimal positions in the value, the decimal point is placed into the result.

- The character variable should be large enough to contain all the digits, the sign, and the decimal point.

In the following examples, literal values are used for the sake of clarity only. It is far more common, however, to specify CL variables or expressions rather than literal values for the VALUE parameter—especially when the data types don't match.

If numbers are not quoted, they are treated as numeric literal values. Consider the examples shown in Figure 3.3.

```
DCL       &TEXT    TYPE(*CHAR)  LEN(10)
CHGVAR    &TEXT    VALUE('123')
CHGVAR    &TEXT    VALUE(123)
```

Figure 3.3: Examples of literal values.

The first CHGVAR assigns the value '123bbbbbbb' to &TEXT. When the apostrophes are removed, as in the second CHGVAR, &TEXT is changed to '0000000123'. The following command assigns the value '-0000012.3' to &TEXT:

```
CHGVAR    &TEXT   VALUE(-12.3)
```

You can see that the sign and decimal point are placed into the result. If the character variable is not large enough to contain all the digits, the sign, and the decimal point, the compile-time error CPF0819 ("Variable or substring of variable too small to hold result") is generated.

ASSIGNING VALUES TO DECIMAL VARIABLES

Using CHGVAR with decimal variables also has its own set of guidelines. The guidelines for assigning a numeric value to a decimal variable follow:

- The value may contain only the digits 0 through 9, the decimal point (.), and the plus sign (+) or minus sign (-).

- If no sign is specified, the value is a positive number.

- If no decimal point is specified, the value is an integer.

- Truncation of overflow high-order digits generates a runtime error.

- Truncation of overflow low-order digits occurs without generating a runtime error.

Using CHGVAR with decimal variables has its own set of pitfalls. But before discussing potential problems, let's see how CHGVAR deals with numbers. The following example uses a 5,2 decimal variable:

```
DCL        &NUMBER    *DEC      LEN(5 2)
CHGVAR     &NUMBER    VALUE(1)
```

The preceding CHGVAR command assigns the value 001.00 to &NUMBER, which should not surprise anyone. Because CL programs store all decimal variables in packed format, &NUMBER is stored internally as X'00100F'. Because neither a sign nor a decimal point is specified, the result is a positive integer.

Specifying negative numeric literal values requires that the value be preceded by a minus sign. If the CHGVAR command is specified as follows, the value of &NUMBER becomes -000.20 or X'00020D':

```
CHGVAR     &NUMBER    VALUE(-.2)
```

The following example illustrates that CHGVAR will not passively truncate extra high-order digits:

```
DCL        &NUMBER    *DEC      LEN(5 2)
CHGVAR     &NUMBER    VALUE(12345)
```

When included in a CL program, the preceding CHGVAR command would satisfy the syntax-checking of both the Source Entry Utility (SEU) and the compiler. At program runtime, however, this command generates the error message MCH1210 (Receiver value too small to hold result).

Although it might seem that a five-digit number should fit into a CL variable with a length of five, only three of the five digits are used for the integer portion. The largest possible value for &NUMBER, therefore, is 999.99.

Many RPG programmers take advantage of a flaw in RPG III when they use the technique of multiplying a date in month-day-year (MDY) order by 10000.01 (or 10000.0001 for 8-digit dates) to convert it to year-month-day (YMD) order. The technique works in RPG III only because RPG III ignores high-order truncation.

For this reason, errors related to truncation of a high-order digit in an RPG III program are often difficult to diagnose.

In RPG IV, a runtime error can optionally be generated when numeric overflow is detected. Although one could argue that the use of "gimmicky" techniques such as this is poor practice, CL can employ this device. CL program XMPL302 (shown in Figure 3.4) receives a MDY formatted date as a parameter and returns a date in YMD format. This example (Figure 3.4) is Y2K compliant.

```
 1.00 /*******************************************************/
 2.00 /* Program Name: XMPL302 - Convert numeric date        */
 3.00 /*******************************************************/
 4.00
 5.00 PGM          PARM(&MMDDYYYY &YYYYMMDD)
 6.00
 7.00   DCL        &MMDDYYYY *DEC      (8 0)
 8.00   DCL        &YYYYMMDD *DEC      (8 0)
 9.00
10.00   CHGVAR     &YYYYMMDD VALUE(&MMDDYYYY * 10000.0001)
11.00              MONMSG   MSGID(MCH1210)
12.00
13.00 ENDPGM
```

Figure 3.4: Numeric date conversion.

By monitoring for the message MCH1210, the high-order overflow condition can be ignored.

This technique is not the only, nor necessarily the best, way to convert from one date format to another. The system command, CVTDAT (Convert Date), also performs date conversion. If there is an advantage to using the multiplication approach, it is that it works with numeric variables. The CVTDAT command works only with character variables.

The CHGVAR command ignores extra low-order digits in the value. For example, the value specified in the following CHGVAR command has more decimal positions than can fit into the CL variable, &NUMBER:

```
DCL          &NUMBER  *DEC  LEN(5 2)
CHGVAR       &NUMBER  VALUE(12.345)
```

The preceding CHGVAR command yields a result for &NUMBER of 012.34 without generating a runtime error. Like RPG and most other HLLs, CHGVAR will cause extra low-order decimal positions to be automatically truncated without generating an error. Unlike RPG, however, there is no built-in mechanism, such as "half adjust," for rounding.

A simple technique can be used when rounding is necessary. CL program XMPL303 (shown in Figure 3.5) will round a CL variable with two decimal positions to an integer variable.

```
 1.00 /**************************************************/
 2.00 /* Program Name: XMPL303 - Half adjust (rounding)       */
 3.00 /**************************************************/
 4.00
 5.00 PGM        PARM(&AMOUNT &WHOLE$)
 6.00
 7.00   DCL      &AMOUNT     *DEC    (7 2)
 8.00   DCL      &WHOLE$     *DEC    (5 0)
 9.00
10.00   IF       (&AMOUNT *GE 0)   CHGVAR &WHOLE$ (&AMOUNT + .5)
11.00   ELSE     CHGVAR &WHOLE$    (&AMOUNT - .5)
12.00
13.00 ENDPGM
```

Figure 3.5: Decimal rounding.

In the example shown in Figure 3.5, if &AMOUNT is 123.4999, &WHOLE$ will be 123. If &AMOUNT is 123.5000, &WHOLE$ will be 124.

The code shown in Figure 3.5 is not generic, but it is easily modified to handle any number of decimal places in the rounded number. Just remember that the amount to add or subtract is half the value that is being rounded.

Provided the character value adheres to the rules for numeric data, a character value can be assigned to a decimal variable. Several earlier examples illustrate changing a character variable to a numeric value. The converse situation, supplying a character value for a decimal variable, is handled equally as well by CHGVAR in the following example:

```
DCL        &NUMBER  *DEC     LEN(5 2)
CHGVAR     &NUMBER  VALUE('-123.45')
```

The CHGVAR command assigns the value -123.45 to &NUMBER, which is internally represented as X'12345D'. However, rather than use a character literal as the CHGVAR value for a decimal variable, you would probably just specify a numeric literal. There are many times, though, that you might want to assign the value of a character CL variable or expression to a decimal variable, and the same rules apply: only the digits 0 through 9, the decimal point, and the plus and minus signs are allowed in the value of the character variable. Extra integer positions will cause a runtime error and extra decimal positions are truncated.

ASSIGNING VALUES TO LOGICAL VARIABLES

Using the CHGVAR command to assign values to a logical variables requires that the value specified for the VALUE parameter equate to true or false (i.e., logical '1' or '0' respectively.) The VALUE parameter can contain a logical literal value, a logical variable, or a logical expression. The examples shown in Figure 3.6 demonstrate how CHGVAR can be used to assign a value to a logical variable.

```
DCL     &YES    *LGL     VALUE('1')
DCL     &ERROR  *LGL
DCL     &X      *DEC  3  VALUE(99)

CHGVAR  &ERROR  '1'
CHGVAR  &ERROR  &YES
CHGVAR  &ERROR  (&X = 99)
```

Figure 3.6: Assigning values to logical variables.

All three CHGVAR commands assign a true condition to the &ERROR CL variable. The first CHGVAR command assigns a logical literal to the CL variable &ERROR. The second CHGVAR command assigns the value of the logical variable &YES to the logical variable &ERROR. The third CHGVAR illustrates a shortcut for changing a logical variable to true or false based on a logical expression. The logical expression is evaluated and results in a true or false value. That value is then assigned to the CL variable &ERROR in the previous example.

EXPRESSIONS

The capability to work with variable data in CL programs is augmented by the use of expressions. Actually, all CL variables and constants are simple expressions. But for purposes of this text, the term *expression* generally means complex expression.

- Character string expressions.
- Arithmetic expressions.
- Logical expressions.

Character String Expressions

Character string expressions are particularly versatile. They can be used in CL programs for any parameter defined with EXPR(*YES) on any CL command. (Almost all command parameters allow expressions.) A character-string expression performs an operation on two or more character operands as defined by one or more character-string operators. Character operands may be character variables, character literal values, substrings of character variables, or other character-string expressions.

There are three character-string operators: *CAT, *TCAT, and *BCAT. Each of the operators may also be specified symbolically using the symbols ||, |<, and |> respectively.

*CAT concatenates the operands on either side of it. For example, presume a CL program includes the following commands:

```
DCL     &FIRSTNAME  *CHAR  LEN(10)  VALUE('Wayne')
DCL     &FULLNAME   *CHAR  LEN(20)
CHGVAR  &FULLNAME   VALUE(&FIRSTNAME *CAT 'Evans')
```

The preceding CHGVAR command will assign the value 'WaynebbbbbEvans' to &FULLNAME. There are five spaces between 'Wayne' and 'Evans' because the last five characters of &FIRSTNAME are blanks.

It is often necessary to concatenate without leaving the spaces between the operands. *TCAT concatenates the two operands with trailing blank truncation of the first operand. For example, the following command changes the value of &FULLNAME to 'WayneEvans':

```
CHGVAR  &FULLNAME  VALUE(&FIRSTNAME *TCAT 'Evans')
```

The five spaces between 'Wayne' and 'Evans' are gone, but the result is probably still not what you want. When dealing with names or words, the *BCAT operator is used most often. *BCAT concatenates the operands on either side of it with trailing blank truncation of the first operand, inserting one space between the first and second operand. For example, the following command changes the value of &FULLNAME to 'WayneьEvans':

```
CHGVAR  &FULLNAME  VALUE(&FIRSTNAME *BCAT 'Evans')
```

In addition to the character-string operators, CL provides a built-in substring function, which operates on a character variable and produces a string that is a subset of the string contained by the variable. The syntax for the function is %SUBSTRING (&var x y) or the more common %SST(&var x y), where *&var* is a character CL variable name, and *x* and *y* are literal integers or decimal CL variables containing integer values. The substring function returns a character string whose value is a subset of *&var* beginning with the *x* position for a length of *y*. For example, consider a CL program that includes the commands shown in Figure 3.7.

```
DCL     &ALPHABET  *CHAR  26 VALUE('ABCDEFGHIJKLMNOPQRSTUVWXYZ')
DCL     &ANSWER    *CHAR  2
DCL     &START     *DEC   3 VALUE(14)

CHGVAR  &ANSWER    %SST(&ALPHABET &START 2)
```

Figure 3.7: Substring example.

Because &START is an integer equal to 14, &ANSWER is changed to the two characters in &ALPHABET beginning in position 14, or 'NO'.

The substring function also works nicely with the Local Data Area (LDA), the Group Data Area (GDA), and the Program Initialization Parameter Data Area (PDA).

For example, an interactive program might place the date '12231997' in positions 101 through 108 of the LDA and then submit a batch job. A CL program in the batch job can easily retrieve the date from the LDA, as in the following example:

```
DCL     &DATE  *DEC     8
CHGVAR  &DATE  %SST(*LDA 101 8)
```

This is an excellent example of assigning the value of a character string expression to a decimal variable.

> **NOTE:** The LDA is a 1,024-byte data area automatically created for each job and is private to the job. Because the LDA of a batch job is initialized with the value of the submitting job's LDA, it is commonly used as a vehicle for passing data to a batch job.
>
> The GDA is a 512-byte data area automatically created when an interactive job becomes a group job. The GDA is shared by all jobs in the group but is private to the group. The concepts of group jobs are not discussed in this text.
>
> The PDA is a 2,000-byte data area automatically created for each "prestart" job when the job is started.

Besides being used in the VALUE parameter of CHGVAR, SUBSTRING can be used in the VAR parameter to assign a new value to a subset of a character CL variable, as in the following example:

```
DCL     &BESTFRIEND   *CHAR  10  VALUE('computer')
CHGVAR  %SST(&BESTFRIEND 3 4)    VALUE('work')
```

The preceding CHGVAR command replaces the four characters in &BESTFRIEND beginning in the third position, or 'mput', with the characters 'work', changing the value of &BESTFRIEND from 'computer' to 'coworker'.

Substring and concatenation can be combined in complex character-string expressions. CL program XMPL304 (shown in Figure 3.8) illustrates using a combination of both character-string operations in a single expression to generate a full name in the last-name, first-name, middle-initial format.

```
 1.00 /***********************************************************/
 2.00 /* Program Name: XMPL304 - Complex char string expression */
 3.00 /***********************************************************/
 4.00
 5.00 PGM
 6.00
 7.00    DCL  &FIRSTNAME  *CHAR  LEN(10)  VALUE('Wayne')
 8.00    DCL  &LASTNAME   *CHAR  LEN(15)  VALUE('Evans')
 8.00    DCL  &FULLNAME   *CHAR  LEN(30)
 9.00    DCL  &ALPHABET   *CHAR   26 +
10.00           VALUE('ABCDEFGHIJKLMNOPQRSTUVWXYZ')
11.00
12.00    CHGVAR  &FULLNAME   VALUE(&LASTNAME *TCAT ',' +
13.00             *BCAT &FIRSTNAME +
15.00             *BCAT %SST(&ALPHABET 15 1) +
16.00             *CAT '.')
12.00 ENDPGM
```

Figure 3.8: Complex character string expression example.

The CHGVAR in the preceding example produces a value of 'Evans, Wayne O.' for the &FULLNAME CL variable. A similar technique can be used to modify a portion, or substring, of a character CL variable. The example shown in Figure 3.9 replaces a single character in a variable.

```
DCL    &FULLNAME *CHAR   30 VALUE('Wayne Z. Evans')

CHGVAR VAR(%SST(&FULLNAME 7 1))   VALUE ('O')
```

Figure 3.9: Example of using %SST in the VAR parameter of the CHGVAR command.

The CHGVAR command (shown in Figure 3.9) changes the value of &FULLNAME from 'Wayne Z. Evans' to 'Wayne O. Evans' .

Coding and Interpreting Complex Character-String Expressions

For CL programmers, complex string expressions often causes confusion. A few simple techniques can make this area easier to understand. When trying to code one of these expressions, it is often helpful to start by writing out an example of how the *value* produced by the expression should look. For example, suppose the result of an expression should be:

```
O'Leary says, 'Aye Laddie'
```

Presume that the entire value is a literal with the exception of the phrase [Aye Laddie], which is supplied in a CL variable named &PHRASE. (Square brackets are used here in place of quotation marks to avoid confusion. They are not part of the value.) The expression must be made up of the variable &PHRASE concatenated between two character literals, [O'Leary says, '] and the trailing [']. The expression can be built in steps. Start by writing the first literal, some space, the variable name, some more space, and the second literal:

```
O'Leary says, '    &PHRASE    '
```

Then, double each single quote (apostrophe):

```
O''Leary says, ''    &PHRASE    ''
```

Next, place single quotes around each complete literal:

```
'O''Leary says, '''    &PHRASE    ''''
```

Next, insert the appropriate concatenation symbols between the operands (literals and variables) and surround the expression with parentheses:

```
('O''Leary says, '''  *CAT  &PHRASE  *TCAT  '''')
```

To interpret this expression, the process is approximately reversed. First, identify the literals. They begin and end with single quotes. The quotes that surround literals are always immediately

1. Within the parentheses.
2. Before or after a concatenation symbol.

Write the expression without the surrounding parentheses and quotes:

```
O''Leary says, ''  *CAT  &PHRASE  *TCAT  ''
```

Then, wherever there are two quotes together, eliminate one:

```
O'Leary says, '  *CAT  &PHRASE  *TCAT  '
```

Next, replace the variable with any value that seems reasonable:

```
O'Leary says, '  *CAT  Follow the rainbow.  *TCAT  '
```

Next, apply the concatenation operators:

```
O'Leary says, 'Follow the rainbow. '
```

Here are three tips to keep in mind when interpreting complex character string expressions:

1. Four quotes in a row ('' '') always represents a single, literal apostrophe standing by itself;

2. Three quotes in a row always represents a single apostrophe at the beginning or end of a literal;

3. Two quotes in a row can never be the beginning or ending of the literal.

Arithmetic Expressions

Another type of expression, the arithmetic expression, performs an operation on two or more numeric operands (decimal variables, numeric literal values, or other arithmetic expressions) as defined by one or more arithmetic operators.

There are four arithmetic operators supported by CL: (+) for addition, (-) for subtraction, (*) for multiplication, and (/) for division. Arithmetic expressions in CL are coded and resolved using standard algebraic notation rules. In other words, expressions are resolved left to right, multiplication and division are resolved before addition and subtraction, and if parentheses are nested, innermost parenthetical expressions are resolved first. Consider the example shown in Figure 3.10.

```
DCL     &X   *DEC    3  VALUE(5)
DCL     &Y   *DEC    3

CHGVAR  &Y   VALUE(&X * 2 - 3)
CHGVAR  &Y   VALUE((-3 * &Y + 36) / 3)
```

Figure 3.10: Arithmetic operations.

Substituting 5 for &X in the first arithmetic expression, the value of &Y becomes 7.

$$(5 * 2 - 3) = 7$$

Substituting 7 for &Y in the second expression, the new value of &Y is 5.

$$\frac{(-3 * 7 + 36)}{3} = \frac{15}{3} = 5$$

%BIN Built-in Function

Support for converting binary to decimal or decimal to binary in CL is provided by the binary built-in function. The syntax for the function is %BINARY(&var [x y]) or the more common %BIN(&var [x y]), where &var is a character CL variable name, and x and y are integers. The binary function returns a character string containing a binary number of length y with a value beginning with the x position of &var.

The length and starting position are optional and can be integer literals or variables. If specified, the length must be 2 or 4, corresponding to a 2-byte or 4-byte binary value. If the length is not specified, an entire 2- or 4-byte character variable must be used. For example, consider a CL program that includes the commands as shown in Figure 3.11.

```
DCL      &BIN2    *CHAR    2
DCL      &STRING  *CHAR    512
DCL      &COUNT   *DEC     (5 0)
DCL      &START   *DEC           VALUE(1)

CHGVAR  %BIN(&BIN2)  VALUE(512)

CHGVAR  %BIN(&STRING &START 2) VALUE(32)

CHGVAR  &COUNT     %BIN(&BIN2)
```

Figure 3.11: A %BIN example.

The first CHGVAR assigns the binary representation of 512 (X'0200') to the character variable &BIN2. The second CHGVAR assigns the binary representation of 32 (X'0020') to the first two positions of &STRING. The third CHGVAR converts the binary value stored in &BIN2 (512) to packed decimal format and assigns it to &COUNT.

The most common uses of the binary function occur in command-processing programs (discussed in chapter 14) and in CL programs that call APIs that receive or return binary parameters. An example of the latter is the program DAYOFWEEK shown in chapter 13 (see Figure 13.5).

REVIEW QUESTIONS

1. CL supports three data types: _____, _____, and _____.

2. Character-string expressions may be used in CL programs for the _____ parameter of a CHGVAR command and for most command parameters.

3. _____ _____ may be used in CL programs for most numeric command parameters.

4. Arithmetic expressions are resolved using _____ _____ _____ rules.

4

CL Program Logic Control

The power of any programming language is determined in part by how well the structured programming constructs are supported, and the ease and clarity with which program logic can be expressed. Compared with most high-level languages on the AS/400, CL rates rather poorly in this respect. CL lacks direct support for any iterative constructs such as DO-WHILE and DO-UNTIL.

To be fair, CL should be compared to other control languages. The logic and structure support in compiled CL greatly exceeds that of either S/370 JCL or System/3 OCL. And its DO group support gives CL a significant edge over System/36 OCL. In one regard—in the use of complex, parenthetical, logical expressions—CL is stronger than RPG III. The tools used to implement control and structure in CL programs are as follows:

- Relational and logical expressions.
- The IF and ELSE commands.
- The GOTO command.
- DO groups.

RELATIONAL EXPRESSIONS

A relational expression is a special type of logical expression that represents a relationship between two values, called *operands*. The two operands may be literal values, variables, or other expressions. Expressions used as relational operands may be character, arithmetic, logical, or even other relational expressions. The type of relationship evaluated is determined by a relational operator. See Table 4.1.

Table 4.1: Relational Expression Operators.

Relational Operator	Relational Symbol	Description
*EQ	=	Equal to
*GT	>	Greater than
*LT	<	Less than
*GE	>=	Greater than or equal to
*LE	<=	Less than or equal to
*NE	¬=	Not equal to
*NG	¬>	Not greater than
*NL	¬<	Not less than

Even if the information in Table 4.1 is somewhat foreign to you, the concepts should sound familiar. For example, the relational operators supported in CL are the same as those supported by RPG and many other languages. Notice that each of the CL relational operators listed above can be specified as a reserved word or as a symbol.

Table 4.2: Examples of Relational Expressions.

(&NUM *GT 10)	Compares a decimal CL variable to a numeric literal.
((5 * &NUM) *LE &MAX)	Compares an arithmetic expression to a decimal variable.
(%SST(&OBJ 1 9) *EQ '*ALL')	Compares a character string expression to a character literal
(&IN03 = '1')	Compares an indicator (logical variable) to a logical literal.

The operands on either side of the operator must have the same data type—numeric, character or logical. Numeric operands are compared algebraically. That means that each side of the expression is resolved to a number using standard algebra rules, and the resulting numbers are compared in value. Character operands are compared in accordance with the EBCDIC collating sequence. For logical operands, true, or '1', is greater than false, or '0'. Table 4.2 contains several examples of relational expressions.

In each of the previous examples, the relationship expressed by the relational operator will result in true or false, depending on the resolved values of the two operands.

LOGICAL EXPRESSIONS

Logical expressions evaluate logical variables, relational expressions, and other logical expressions. By definition, they always resolve to a true or false condition. In other words, the result, or resolved value, of any logical expression is always either '1' (true) or '0' (false).

Table 4.3: Boolean CL Operators.

Reserved Word	Symbol	Description
*AND	&	Expression is true when both operands are true.
*OR	|	Expression is true when either operand is true.
*NOT	¬	Negates the expression. If it would normally result in true, *NOT would make it false.

Logical expressions themselves may be used as operands that are combined by logical operators forming complex logical expressions. The logical, or Boolean, operators shown in Table 4.3 can be specified as either reserved words or symbols.

The operator *NOT is evaluated before *AND and *OR, and up to five levels of parentheses may be used to control the order of evaluation. Figure 4.1 contains several examples of logical expressions.

```
1.  (&IN01)
2.  (&IN01 *AND &IN02)
3.  (*NOT &IN01 *AND &IN02)
4.  (*NOT (&IN01 *AND &IN02))
5.  ((*NOT &IN01) *OR (*NOT &IN02))
6.  (&NUM *GT 10 *OR &NAME *EQ 'Wayne')
```

Figure 4.1: Examples of logical expressions.

Example 1 [(&IN01)], a logical variable, is the simplest form of a logical expression. In example 2 [(&IN01 *AND &IN02)], the expression logically ANDs two logical variables. If indicator 01 and indicator 02 are both on, the expression is true. In example 3, [(*NOT &IN01 *AND &IN02)], the *NOT is evaluated first and negates &IN01 only. The expression is true only if indicator 01 is off and indicator 02 is on.

Parentheses used in example 4 [(*NOT (&IN01 *AND &IN02))] cause the *NOT to negate the entire parenthetical expression (&IN01 *AND &IN02). This expression is true if it is not the case that both indicator 01 and indicator 02 are on. In other words, the expression is true if either (or both) indicator 01 or indicator 02 are off.

Example 5 [((*NOT &IN01) *or (*NOT &IN02))] is an equivalent and, perhaps, a clearer way to code the same expression. The inner parentheses here are not required, and their removal would not change the value of the expression. Their inclusion, however, can make the expression easier to decipher. Again, the expression is true if either (or both) indicator 01 or indicator 02 are off.

Remember that all relational expressions are, by definition, also logical expressions. In example 6 [(&NUM *GT 10 *OR &NAME *EQ 'WAYNE')], a relational expression comparing numeric operands is logically OR'ed to a relational expression comparing character operands. While this sounds like it could present a compatibility problem with regard to data type, it doesn't. Both operands of the *OR operator are relational expressions, which resolve to either '1' or '0'. If either or both of the relational expressions are true, the entire logical expression is also true.

CONDITIONED ACTIONS

Given the limited arsenal of CL commands that support structure and logic, each of them is bound to see heavy action. The workhorse of CL logic implementation is the IF command, along with its faithful sidekick, ELSE. The IF command tests a condition and performs an action based on that condition being true.

The IF Command

Having only two parameters, the syntax for IF is simple. The first parameter, COND (Condition), is used to specify the condition that must be met for the action to be performed. The value for the COND parameter must be a logical expression. The syntax for IF sometimes appears extremely complicated because logical expressions can be far more complex than the examples examined so far. On the other hand, the condition tested is most often a simple relational expression such as (&OPTION *EQ 5).

The second parameter, THEN, specifies a command to be run if the condition is true. Any command except PGM, ENDPGM, DCL, DCLF, MONMSG, ENDDO, and ELSE may be conditioned using IF. An example of a typical IF command is the following:

```
IF    COND(&OPTION *EQ 5)  THEN(CALL PGMA)
```

The preceding IF command evaluates the relational expression (&OPTION *EQ 5). If it resolves to true—that is, if the value of &OPTION is 5—then the CALL command is run. If the expression is false, control passes to the next statement in the CL program. Remember that expressions are always enclosed in parentheses, even when specified positionally, as follows:

```
IF    (&OPTION *EQ 5)  CALL PGMA
```

Although there are many times when IF stands alone, it is often used in conjunction with ELSE. The ELSE command must always immediately follow an IF command or the ENDDO command of a DO group that was conditioned by IF. The ELSE command has a single parameter, CMD, that specifies the command to run when the tested condition on the related IF is false. Together, IF and ELSE provide the support for the structured IF-THEN-ELSE. The following example illustrates IF-THEN-ELSE in CL:

```
IF    (&USRCLS = '*USER')  THEN(DSPJOB)
ELSE  CMD(WRKJOB)
```

The preceding IF command evaluates the relational expression (&USRCLS = '*USER'). If it resolves to true ('1'), then the DSPJOB (Display Job) command is run and control passes to the next statement in the CL program following the ELSE. If the expression is false, the WRKJOB (Work with Job) command is run.

Nested IF and ELSE Commands

CL allows up to 10 levels of nested IF commands. A program's logic begins to get complicated in any language when structured constructs are nested. In order to avoid problems with overly complicated code, you should understand the various ways that IF and ELSE can be nested in CL.

As mentioned earlier, virtually any command can be used as the THEN parameter of the IF command. That includes another IF command! When IF commands are nested directly—that is, when the THEN parameter for an IF contains another IF—the logic, especially when multiple ELSE commands follow the IF commands, can become difficult to decipher. It is important to remember that each ELSE refers to the innermost unmatched-paired IF. The exception to this rule is that an IF within a DO group cannot be paired with an ELSE that is outside of the DO group. The CL program shown in Figure 4.2 illustrates nested IF statements with their ELSE statements.

As a demonstration of how nested logic affects complexity, study the code shown in Figure 4.2, and try to determine the resulting value of &EASTWOOD. If possible, type the source code into a source member and compile the program. When you run the program, the final value of &EASTWOOD is displayed in a message.

```
 1.00 /************************************************************/
 2.00 /* Program Name: XMPL401 - Nested IF/ELSE                   */
 3.00 /************************************************************/
 4.00
 5.00 PGM
 6.00    DCL        &A        *DEC    VALUE(20)
 7.00    DCL        &B        *DEC    VALUE(15)
 8.00    DCL        &C        *DEC    VALUE(27)
 9.00    DCL        &D        *DEC    VALUE(99)
10.00    DCL        &E        *DEC    VALUE(99)
11.00    DCL        &EASTWOOD *CHAR   5  VALUE('Clint')
12.00
13.00    IF         (&A = 10) THEN(IF (&B = &C) THEN(IF (&D <= &E) +
14.00               THEN(CHGVAR &EASTWOOD VALUE('Good'))))
15.00    ELSE       CMD(CHGVAR &EASTWOOD VALUE('Bad'))
16.00    ELSE       CMD(CHGVAR &EASTWOOD VALUE('Ugly'))
17.00
18.00    SNDMSG     MSG('Eastwood is' *BCAT &EASTWOOD) TOUSR(*REQUESTER)
19.00
20.00 ENDPGM
```

Figure 4.2: Nested IF statements.

The correct answer is "Clint"—the value of &EASTWOOD remains unchanged. If &A is not equal to 10, nothing happens at all. The two ELSE commands are paired with the two innermost IF statements, but there is no ELSE paired with the outer-most IF.

As the level of nesting expands, the complexity of IF statements increases, while the readability decreases. This complexity is often compounded when various programming styles and techniques are applied. CL does not warrant complex programming styles. Unlike some high-level languages, such as C or COBOL, reducing the number of lines of code adds little or no benefit to the performance of a CL program.

For example, the following alternative to the preceding example in Figure 4.3 uses two additional lines of code, yet generates object code that is equivalent to the original "nested IF statements" illustration. It makes use of indentation and positionally coded parameters to make the code more readable.

```
 1.00 /***********************************************************/
 2.00 /* Program Name: XMPL402 - Indented IF/ELSE                */
 3.00 /***********************************************************/
 4.00
 5.00 PGM
 6.00    DCL        &A          *DEC     VALUE(20)
 7.00    DCL        &B          *DEC     VALUE(15)
 8.00    DCL        &C          *DEC     VALUE(27)
 9.00    DCL        &D          *DEC     VALUE(99)
10.00    DCL        &E          *DEC     VALUE(99)
11.00    DCL        &EASTWOOD *CHAR    5  VALUE('Clint')
12.00
13.00    IF         (&A = 10) +
13.01               IF    (&B = &C) +
13.02                     IF    (&D <= &E) +
14.00                           CHGVAR &EASTWOOD VALUE('Good')
15.00                     ELSE  CHGVAR &EASTWOOD VALUE('Bad')
16.00               ELSE  CHGVAR &EASTWOOD VALUE('Ugly')
17.00
18.00    SNDMSG     MSG('Eastwood is' *BCAT Eastwood) TOUSR(*REQUESTER)
19.00
20.00    ENDPGM
```

Figure 4.3: Nested IF statements.

As with the THEN parameter of the IF command, virtually any command can be used as the CMD parameter of the ELSE command. A nested IF-THEN-ELSE structure is formed when that command is an IF. The examples shown in Figure 4.4 illustrate the nested IF-THEN-ELSE structure. Although the examples are identical in function, the second uses positional parameters to make the code more readable.

```
      IF        COND(&USRCLS = '*PGMR') THEN(CALL INLPGMR)
      ELSE      CMD(IF (&USRCLS = '*SECOFR') THEN(CALL INLSEC)
      ELSE      CMD(CALL INLUSER)
or:
      IF        (&USRCLS = '*PGMR')    CALL INLPGMR
      ELSE IF   (&USRCLS = '*SECOFR')  CALL INLSEC
      ELSE                            CALL INLUSER
```

Figure 4.4: Nested IF-THEN-ELSE.

When IF-THEN-ELSE structures are nested, that is, when the CMD parameter for an ELSE contains an IF, the IF tests are mutually exclusive. In other words, the IF conditions are tested in order until one is true. Once a condition is true, the THEN action is performed and no other conditions are tested. This is typical of nested IF-THEN-ELSE logic supported by most programming languages.

CL program XMPL403, shown in Figure 4.5, receives a test score in the range 0–100 and uses a series of nested IF-THEN-ELSE structures to determine a letter grade.

```
 1.00 /******************************************************/
 2.00 /* Program Name: XMPL403 - Nested IF-THEN-ELSE        */
 3.00 /******************************************************/
 4.00
 5.00 PGM         PARM(&SCORE)
 6.00   DCL       &SCORE    *DEC
 7.00   DCL       &GRADE    *CHAR   1
 8.00
 9.00   IF        (&SCORE > 95)  CHGVAR  &GRADE   'A'
10.00   ELSE  IF  (&SCORE > 87)  CHGVAR  &GRADE   'B'
11.00   ELSE  IF  (&SCORE > 75)  CHGVAR  &GRADE   'C'
12.00   ELSE  IF  (&SCORE > 67)  CHGVAR  &GRADE   'D'
13.00   ELSE                     CHGVAR  &GRADE   'F'
14.00
15.00   SNDMSG    MSG('Grade is' *BCAT &GRADE) TOUSR(*REQUESTER)
16.00
17.00 ENDPGM
```

Figure 4.5: Nested IF-THEN-ELSE.

If all the ELSE commands were omitted from the example above, any and all values for &SCORE would yield a value of 'F' for &GRADE. Each IF command would run independently of the others, and the very last command to run would determine the value of &GRADE.

Because of the nested IF-THEN-ELSE structures, however, once one of the conditions is found to be true, no other conditions are tested. For example, if &SCORE has a value of 90, the first condition tested (&SCORE > 95) is false. Therefore, the following ELSE runs the second IF, testing the condition (&SCORE > 87). Because this condition is true when &SCORE equals 90, &GRADE is changed to 'B' and control passes to the statement following the final ELSE (in this case the SNDMSG command).

Notice that the CMD parameter on the final ELSE command is not another IF command. Often, a series of nested IF-THEN-ELSE structures ends with a "catch-all" ELSE command. If none of the conditions on the preceding IF commands is true, the command specified on the CMD parameter of the catch-all ELSE will run.

BRANCHING IN CL

The CL command GOTO is used to branch to a different point in a CL program. It has a single parameter, CMDLBL (Command Label), which designates the target of the branch. While CMDLBL must be a valid label in the CL program, the colon (:) it delimits is not included as part of the CMDLBL parameter. Figure 4.6 shows an example.

```
TOP:
   .
   .
   GOTO   CMDLBL(TOP)

or, positionally:
   GOTO   TOP
```

Figure 4.6: Example of branching in CL.

Because CL doesn't support commands for iteration looping or subroutines, GOTO takes its place alongside IF and ELSE as one of the commands required for implementing structure and logic in CL programs. The most common forms of the iterate construct are DO-WHILE and DO-UNTIL, each of which performs a "loop" while or until some condition is true. A "correct" DO-WHILE tests the condition at the top of the loop. A "correct" DO-UNTIL tests the condition at the bottom of the loop and, consequently, always performs the loop at least once. Because CL supports neither loop directly, IF and GOTO must be used to implement the DO-WHILE and DO-UNTIL constructs.

CL program XMPL404, shown in Figure 4.7, uses a DO-UNTIL style loop to replace each period (.) in a 20-byte character variable with a slash (/).

```
 1.00 /******************************************************/
 2.00 /* Program Name: XMPL404 -  Replace '.' with '/' (do 20 tms) */
 3.00 /******************************************************/
 4.00
 5.00 PGM          PARM(&NAME)
 6.00   DCL        &NAME  *CHAR  20
 7.00   DCL        &COUNT *DEC  /* counter for loop */
 8.00
 9.00 DO_AGAIN:
10.00   CHGVAR     &COUNT   VALUE(&COUNT + 1)
11.00   IF         (%SST(&NAME &COUNT 1) = '.') +
12.00              CHGVAR  %SST(&NAME &COUNT 1)    VALUE('/')
13.00
14.00   IF         (&COUNT *LT 20)  GOTO DO_AGAIN
15.00
16.00   SNDMSG     MSG('Name is' *BCAT &NAME) TOUSR(*REQUESTER)
17.00
18.00 ENDPGM
```

Figure 4.7: An example of a DO-UNTIL loop.

The label DO_AGAIN: begins the loop. It is a correct DO-UNTIL loop because the function is always performed at least once, and the condition (&COUNT *LT 20) is tested at the bottom of the loop. If the condition is true, the GOTO command is used to branch to the top of the loop.

Although it is possible to build a "correct" DO-WHILE loop in CL, it is often more convenient to code a hybrid loop, with the condition tested somewhere inside the loop. CL program XMPL405, shown in Figure 4.8, illustrates a commonly used hybrid loop. The program displays a menu and processes the selected option.

```
 1.00 /*********************************************************/
 2.00 /* Program Name: XMPL405 - Process menu options (do-while)*/
 3.00 /*********************************************************/
 4.00
 5.00 PGM
 5.00    DCLF      MENUDSPF
 6.00
 7.00 DISPLAY:
 8.00    SNDRCVF   RCDFMT(MENU)
 9.00    IF        &IN03    GOTO QUIT
10.00
11.00    IF        (&OPTION = 1)  TFRSECJOB
12.00    ELSE IF   (&OPTION = 2)  ENDRQS
13.00    ELSE IF   (&OPTION = 3)  WRKJOB
14.00
15.00    GOTO      DISPLAY
16.00
17.00 QUIT:
18.00 ENDPGM
```

Figure 4.8: Common display processing loop example.

The label DISPLAY: begins the loop; the condition of indicator 03 is set by the SNDRCVF command and then tested. Assume that F3 is used as an exit key in the display file MENUDSPF and that it sets indicator 03 on. (For more information about using display files in CL programs, see chapter 9.) If the condition is true—that is, if indicator 03 is on—the GOTO command is used to exit from the loop. This loop functions as a DO-WHILE because the condition is tested near the top of the loop. Therefore, it is possible that the function within the loop—running menu optionsm—may never be performed at all.

Do Groups

DO and ENDDO are two structured CL commands that are always paired. They delineate a group of commands to be treated as a complete unit of code. Commands that are included between a DO and an ENDDO command are referred to as a DO group.

The real power of DO groups becomes apparent when they are conditioned by an IF, ELSE, or MONMSG command. For that matter, there is no reason for using a DO group in any other way. A common use for DO groups is to reduce the complexity caused by nested IF commands. You may recognize the example shown in Figure 4.9 as another alternative to the original nested-IF-commands illustration. It makes use of indentation, positionally coded parameters, comments, and DO groups to make the code easier to read.

```
 1.00 /*******************************************************/
 2.00 /* Program Name: XMPL406 - Nested DO groups           */
 3.00 /*******************************************************/
 4.00
 5.00 PGM
 6.00    DCL      &A          *DEC   VALUE(20)
 7.00    DCL      &B          *DEC   VALUE(15)
 8.00    DCL      &C          *DEC   VALUE(27)
 9.00    DCL      &D          *DEC   VALUE(99)
10.00    DCL      &E          *DEC   VALUE(99)
11.00    DCL      &EASTWOOD   *CHAR   5   VALUE('Clint')
12.00
13.00    IF       (&A = 10) DO
13.01             /*  A=10 so Eastwood is good, bad or ugly */
13.02             IF   (&B = &C) DO
14.00                  IF     (&D <= &E)  CHGVAR &EASTWOOD VALUE('Good')
15.00                  ELSE    CHGVAR &EASTWOOD VALUE('Bad')
15.01                  ENDDO
15.02
16.00             ELSE CHGVAR &EASTWOOD VALUE('Ugly')
16.01
16.02             ENDDO  /* A=10, Eastwood is good, bad or ugly */
16.03
16.04    ELSE     /* A *NE 10, so do nothing */
17.00
18.00    SNDMSG   MSG('Name is' *BCAT &NAME) TOUSR(*REQUESTER)
19.00
20.00    ENDPGM
```

Figure 4.9: Nested DO group example.

Although the use of DO and ENDDO in the preceding example is optional, there are many cases where this dynamic duo is required. The reason DO groups are so important to structured CL is that the IF statement's THEN parameter, the ELSE statement's CMD parameter, and the MONMSG statement's EXEC parameter each accept only a single CL command. DO groups can greatly augment the power of the IF, ELSE, and MONMSG commands. When you want to run a group of commands, based on a condition, you have only three options:

1. Condition each command in the group with a separate IF.

2. Use GOTO to branch to a routine in another part of the CL program and then return using another GOTO.

3. Specify the DO command as the single command to run conditioned by an IF, ELSE, or MONMSG.

All commands within the DO group will be run based on the condition.

The CL program in Figure 4.10, XMPL407, displays a menu and processes the selected option. Unlike example XMPL405, each option runs several commands.

```
 1.00 PGM             /* XMP1407 */
 2.00   DCLF          MENUDSPF
 3.00   DCL           &MBRNAME  *CHAR  10  /* Member name  */
 4.00   DCL           &RPY      *CHAR   1  /* MSG reply    */
 5.00   DCL           &USER     *CHAR  10  /* User profile */
 6.00
10.00 DISPLAY:
12.00   SNDRCVF       MENU
13.00   IF            (&IN03)  GOTO QUIT
14.00
15.00   IF            (&OPTION = 1)   +
16.00                 DO    /* Submit payroll report */
17.00                 CALL  GETMBRCL  &MBRNAME
18.00                 ADDPFM  DATEFILE  MBR(&MBRNAME)
19.00                 OVRDBF  DATEFILE  MBR(&MBRNAME)
20.00                 CALL  GETDTERG
21.00                 SBMJOB  PAYROLLRPT  CMD(CALL PRB199RG) +
22.00                           JOBD(PAYROLL)
23.00                 ENDDO   /* End Submit payroll report */
24.00
25.00   ELSE IF       (&OPTION = 2) +
26.00                 DO    /* Submit p/r backup */
27.00                 SNDUSRMSG  ('Daily or weekly (D W)?') +
28.00                         VALUES(D W) MSGRPY(&RPY)
29.00                 IF        (&RPY = D) +
30.00                     SBMJOB  PRBKPDAILY CMD(CALL PRB900CL) +
31.00                         JOBD(PAYROLL)
```

Figure 4.10: CL DO groups in a menu (part 1 of 2).

```
32.00                  ELSE       SBMJOB PRBKPWEEK  CMD(CALL PRB910CL) +
33.00                             JOBD(PAYROLL)
34.00                  ENDDO      /* Submit p/r backup */
35.00
36.00    ELSE          DO         /* Invalid option */
37.00                  RTVJOBA    USER(&USER)
38.00                  CALL       DUMBKEYSTR  PARM(&USER)
39.00                  ENDDO      /* Invalid option */
40.00
41.00    GOTO          DISPLAY
42.00
43.00 QUIT:
44.00    ENDPGM
```

Figure 4.10: CL DO groups in a menu (part 2 of 2).

A DO command is specified for the positionally coded THEN parameter on each IF command that tests the value of &OPTION (lines 15.00–16.00 and 25.00–26.00). Also, a DO command is used for the CMD parameter on the catch-all ELSE command (line 36.00).

DO groups provide the same kind of support for the MONMSG command as they do for IF and ELSE. That is, they allow more than a single command to be run based on an error message. The example in Figure 4.11 demonstrates how multiple commands may be conditioned by a MONMSG command.

```
DCL        &RPY   *CHAR   1  /* Reply */

STRPRTWTR  LASER  OUTQ(LASER)  MSGQ(LASER)
   MONMSG  CPF3310 EXEC(DO)  /* Writer already started */
           SNDUSRMSG  MSG('LASER is already started. +
               Ignore, Go, or Cancel (I G C)') VALUES(I G C) +
               DFT(C) TOMSGQ(QSYSOPR) MSGRPY(&RPY)

           IF         (&RPY = I)   GOTO BYPASS
           ELSE IF    (&RPY = C)   RETURN
           ELSE IF    (&RPY = G)   CHGWTR  LASER OUTQ(LASER)
           ENDDO                   /* Writer already started */
BYPASS:
```

Figure 4.11: Multiple commands conditioned by a MONMSG.

As shown in Figure 4.11, if the STRPRTWTR command generates a CPF3310 error message, the entire routine in the DO group will run.

One more use for DO and ENDDO is in a work-around to a very common coding error. Assume that, if a particular argument is true, you want to create a physical file in the QTEMP library. Because you know the file might already exist, you follow the CRTPF command with a generic MONMSG command to ignore the exception. Look at the example shown in Figure 4.12. What's wrong with this code?

```
IF      (&ARGUMENT = &TRUE) +
        CRTPF    QTEMP/WORKFILE    RCDLEN(80)
        MONMSG   CPF0000
```

Figure 4.12: Example of invalid use of MONMSG.

The SEU CL syntax checker won't detect an error in the code shown in Figure 4.12, but the compiler will notify you that MONMSG is not valid for an IF command. The MONMSG command in this example is invalid because the CRTPF command is actually a parameter on the IF command. This fact is disguised slightly because the THEN parameter is coded positionally on a separate line from the IF command. (The "+" continuation character is the tip-off!) In the version of the example shown in Figure 4.13, a DO group is used to correct the problem.

```
IF      (&ARGUMENT = &TRUE)   DO
        CRTPF    QTEMP/WORKFILE    RCDLEN(80)
        MONMSG   CPF0000
        ENDDO
```

Figure 4.13: Example of using DO group in correctly coding MONMSG.

REVIEW QUESTIONS

1. A _____ _____ evaluates a relationship between two values, called

    _____.

2. Operands may be _____, _____, or _____ _____.

3. Relational expressions are a subset of _____ _____.

4. Logical expressions evaluate _____ _____, _____ _____, and _____ _____ _____.

5. The IF command tests a _____ and performs an action based on that test.

6. The ELSE command specifies a _____ ____ ____ when the tested condition on the related IF is false.

7. GOTO can be used to implement _____ _____, not directly supported in CL, such as DO-WHILE and DO-UNTIL.

8. DO and ENDDO are always paired and delineate a group of commands to be treated as a _____ ____ __ ____ , and called a ____ _____.

5

CALL/PARM PROCESSING

Call/Parm processing has two primary elements: program-to-program control and parameter passing. After describing the options for navigating among CL programs and other high-level language (HLL) programs, this chapter focuses on the inner workings of AS/400 parameter passing and how it relates to CL programming. Because CL programs are most often used for job control and application support, it is crucial that you understand the basic concepts of program-to-program control. CL program navigation is accomplished using five commands:

- CALL
- PGM
- RETURN
- ENDPGM
- TFRCTL

THE CALL COMMAND

The CALL command is used to invoke another CL program or any other type of program. The first of two parameters, PGM, is used to specify the name of the program to call. If parameters are to be passed to a called program, the second parameter, PARM, is used to specify the parameter list.

The use of the terms *PARM* and *parameter* can be confusing. Parameters can be classified as command parameters or program parameters. Command parameters are the parameters of a CL command, and program parameters are used to pass data between programs. Program parameters do not have keywords and are always specified positionally. PARM is used as the keyword of a command parameter of the CALL, TFRCTL, and PGM commands. In the example shown in Figure 5.1, the PARM parameter of the CALL command contains a list of three program parameters to be passed to PGMA:

```
DCL    &ERROR  *LGL
.
.
CALL   PGM(PGMA)   PARM('ABC Company' 911231 &ERROR)
```

Figure 5.1: Example of CALL command passing parameters.

Up to 40 program parameters can be specified for the PARM parameter of the CALL command. They can be any combination of character string literal values, numeric literal values, logical literal values, hexadecimal literal values, floating point literal values, and CL program variables. The three parameters being passed in the previous example are a character string literal, a numeric literal, and a CL program variable.

When another program is called, the calling program is suspended while the called program runs. Then, when the called program ends, control returns to the statement following the CALL command, and processing continues.

THE PGM COMMAND

A CL program starts with the PGM (Program) command. The PGM command may be preceded by comments and blank source-statement lines. If parameters are to be received by a CL program, the PGM command is used to specify the parameter list. PGM has one parameter, PARM, that corresponds to the PARM parameter on the CALL command. It can be used to specify a list of up to 40 program variables into which parameters are received. As shown in Figure 5.2, the PGM command receives three parameters into CL program variables. Parameter passing is discussed in detail later in this chapter.

```
PGM     PARM(&COMPANY &DATE &ERROR_FLG)
DCL     &COMPANY     *CHAR    35
DCL     &DATE        *DEC    (6 0)
DCL     &ERROR_FLAG  *LGL
```

Figure 5.2: Receiving parameters on the PGM command.

THE RETURN COMMAND

The RETURN command may be used at any point in a CL program to return control to its caller—that is, to return control to the program that called the CL program in question. The caller may be another CL program or any other type of program. Unlike some other HLLs, a returning CL program always terminates. It is removed from the *call stack* (sometimes referred to as the program invocation stack), and its storage is freed. Another call to the same CL program reloads the program and reinitializes any CL variables the program uses.

The preceding is one reason why repeated calls to CL programs from other HLLs should be avoided whenever possible. Much of the initialization overhead associated with repeated calls to an RPG program, for example, can be avoided by returning from the program with the last record indicator (LR) off. Unfortunately, CL programs offer no such option.

> **Call Stack:** Programmers who have worked on the AS/400 for some time might be more familiar with the term program invocation stack. *This terminology has adapted to the advent of the Integrated Language Environment (ILE). For a further discussion of this topic, see chapter 13.*

THE ENDPGM COMMAND

The ENDPGM (End Program) command is generally used to designate the end of a CL program. ENDPGM functions primarily, as a compiler directive, to stop compiling. Consequently, any commands following the ENDPGM command are ignored by the CL compiler. You can make use of this feature when testing various coding alternatives by moving large sections of a CL program after the ENDPGM command instead of deleting them or commenting them out.

The role of ENDPGM in CL program navigation is that it carries with it an implied RETURN. In other words, when the ENDPGM command is encountered in a CL program, the program ends precisely as though a RETURN command were issued. In fact, many CL programmers code a label (usually ENDPGM:) on the ENDPGM command and use the command GOTO ENDPGM in place of a RETURN. Although from a style standpoint, this technique cannot be recommend, there is nothing wrong with it technically.

THE TFRCTL COMMAND

The TFRCTL (Transfer Control) command is a program-control option that is unique to CL. TFRCTL has parameters identical to the CALL command (PGM and PARM) and, like CALL, is used to invoke another program. There is, however, a very significant difference in the way the two commands operate. Unlike CALL, TFRCTL removes the transferring CL program from the call stack and frees its associated storage. When the called, or *transferred-to* program ends, control returns to the caller of the program that performed the TFRCTL.

For example, a CL program named PGMA is called (see Figure 5-3.) When PGMA begins to run, it is added to the call stack. At the point when

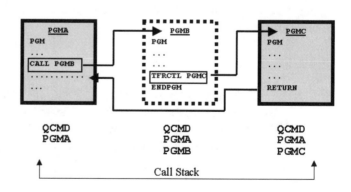

Figure 5.3: An example using TFRCTL.

PGMA issues a call to PGMB, PGMA is suspended and PGMB is added to the call stack. The last thing PGMB does is transfer control to PGMC, causing PGMB to be removed from the call stack. PGMC is added to the call stack. When PGMC ends, control returns to PGMA (not PGMB as with CALL).

There are two performance benefits in using TFRCTL. One benefit is that, when files are opened, each invocation in the stack must be checked for file overrides. Because TFRCTL leaves the call stack a little smaller, all file opens run slightly faster.

The second advantage is a result of freeing the associated program storage. With the storage freed, the virtual storage (memory) required by the job or, more specifically, the *process access group* (PAG), will be smaller. A smaller PAG translates to more efficient use of virtual storage.

There is a rather subtle restriction on the TFRCTL command that may prohibit its use in some situations. Because parameters are passed by reference, not by value, and the storage associated with a CL program issuing a TFRCTL is freed, all parameters specified on the PARM list of a TFRCTL command must be CL variables that were previously passed to the transferring CL program by a program that is still active. The CL program shown in Figure 5.4 illustrates the use of parameters by the TFRCTL command.

```
 1.00 /*************************************************************/
 2.00 /* Program Name: XMPL501  - Transfer control with parameters */
 3.00 /*************************************************************/
 4.00
 5.00 PGM          PARM(&FILE)
 6.00    DCL       &FILE  TYPE(*CHAR) LEN(10)
 7.00
 8.00    OVRDBF    PGMFILE  TOFILE(&FILE)
 9.00    TFRCTL    PGM(XMPL501B) PARM(&FILE)
10.00
11.00 ENDPGM
```

Figure 5.4: Transfer control with parameters.

At line 9.00 in Figure 5.4, CL program XMPL501 transfers control to program XMPL501B, passing one parameter. The parameter is valid because it is a CL variable that is received by XMPL501 (line 5.00). When XMPL501B ends, control passes to the caller of XMPL501.

If a CALL command had been used in place of TFRCTL, control would return to XMPL501. The next command is the ENDPGM command. Therefore, CL program XMPL501 would immediately end, returning control to its caller. By using TFRCTL, the PAG is smaller and file opens are faster.

TFRCTL is the only CL command that is not allowed in an ILE CL procedure. (See chapter 13.) As a general rule, however—if there is no need to return to an OPM CL program and no need to pass parameters that were not previously received—TFRCTL is a good alternative to the CALL command.

MORE ABOUT PROGRAM PARAMETERS

Although parameter passing in OS/400 is standardized across all programming languages, a study of CL would not be complete without a discussion of the topic. This section focuses on the inner workings of, and addresses the potential problems associated with, passing parameters in CL programs.

Parameters are passed by reference (not value). In other words, a pointer to the location of the data, rather than a copy of the data, is passed from the caller to the called program. CL program variables and literal values are stored in an area of virtual storage called the *program automatic storage area* (PASA). CL variables and literal values passed as parameters are stored in the PASA of the program in which they were originally defined.

The called program references the parameter by defining a parameter of its own (literal values passed as parameters are always received into CL variables), and the parameters of both the calling and called programs address the same location in storage. Consequently, if the value of a parameter is changed in one program, it is also changed in all other programs in which it is referenced. Because the programs address parameter variables by address rather than variable name, the calling and called programs can use different CL variable names for the same parameter. Figure 5.5 illustrates passing parameters in CL programs.

```
 1.00 /**********************************************************/
 2.00 /* Program Name: XMPL502 - Pass score, get grade         */
 3.00 /**********************************************************/
 4.00
 5.00 XMPL502: PGM
 6.00    DCL        &LETTER  *CHAR   1
 7.00
 8.00    CALL       XMPL503  PARM(85 &LETTER)
 9.00
10.00    SNDMSG     MSG('Grade is' *BCAT &LETTER) TOUSR(*REQUESTER)
11.00
12.00 ENDPGM
     /*********** End of CLP Source ***************/

 1.00 /**********************************************************/
 2.00 /* Program Name: XMPL503 - Get score, return grade       */
 3.00 /**********************************************************/
 4.00
 5.00 PGM        PARM(&SCORE &GRADE)
 6.00    DCL        &SCORE   *DEC LEN(15 5)
 7.00    DCL        &GRADE   *CHAR   1
 8.00
 9.00    IF         (&SCORE > 95)  CHGVAR  &GRADE  'A'
10.00    ELSE  IF   (&SCORE > 87)  CHGVAR  &GRADE  'B'
11.00    ELSE  IF   (&SCORE > 75)  CHGVAR  &GRADE  'C'
12.00    ELSE  IF   (&SCORE > 67)  CHGVAR  &GRADE  'D'
13.00    ELSE                      CHGVAR  &GRADE  'F'
14.00
15.00 ENDPGM
     /*********** End of CLP Source ***************/
```

Figure 5.5: Passing parameters between CL programs.

Program XMPL502 declares one CL variable, &LETTER, and calls XMPL503 passing two parameters: the numeric literal 85 and the CL variable &LETTER. As shown in Figure 5.5, XMPL503 receives two parameters into the CL variables &SCORE and &GRADE. Although the number and order of parameters, their data-type, and their length must all match, the names of CL variables need not be the same in the calling and called programs.

The values for the literal, 85, and the CL variable, &LETTER, are located in storage associated with CL program XMPL502. Because the parameters passed to XMPL503 contain pointers to that data, the CL variables &SCORE and &GRADE in XMPL503 address the same storage associated with XMPL502. After XMPL503 changes the value of &GRADE and ends, the value of &LETTER in XMPL502 also is changed.

PARAMETER PASSING RULES

There are several idiosyncrasies associated with passing parameters between CL programs that, if not observed, can be the source of unpredictable results and program runtime errors. By observing the following simple rules for passing and receiving data, parameter passing can be accomplished without problems. A further explanation of some of the rules follows the complete list.

1. The parameter lists of the calling and called programs must correspond in number of parameters and order of specification.

2. Program variables that are passed as parameters should have the same size and attributes in both the calling and called programs.

3. Character string literal values less than 32 bytes in length always allocate 32 bytes of storage for the literal. Positions to the right of literal data (within the 32 bytes) are padded with blanks.

4. Character-string literal values that are 32 bytes or longer allocate storage equal to the actual length of the literal.

    ➢ Corollary 1: Character literal values longer than 32 bytes are not padded with blanks to the length expected by the receiving program.

    ➢ Corollary 2: If a CL variable into which a character-string parameter is received is defined as more than 32 bytes, the passed literal should be the same length as the variable in the called program.

5. Logical literal values are passed as character-string literal values.

6. Numeric values passed as character literal values must be quoted.

7. Numeric literal values are converted to packed decimal values with a length of 15 digits with 5 decimal positions.

    ➢ Corollary 1: If numeric literal values are passed, the receiving CL program must declare the decimal variable as LEN(15 5)

8. Floating-point literal values are passed with a length of 8 bytes.

9. All parameters passed on a CALL through a SBMJOB command, whether CL variables or literal values, are treated as literal values.

Rules 1 and 2

Rule 1 states that the parameter lists of the calling and called programs must correspond in number of parameters and order of specification. The exception is that parameters may be omitted on calls to ILE CL procedures. This is discussed further in chapter 13.

Rule 2 states that program variables that are passed as parameters must have the same size and attributes in both the calling and called programs.

In Figure 5.6, the example programs show how parameters are passed between two CL programs. The first program, XMPL508, calls the other program, XMPL509, and XMPL509 calls a high-level language program.

```
  1.00 /*****************************************************/
  2.00 /* Program Name: XMPL508  - Example calling program w/3 parms*/
  3.00 /*****************************************************/
  4.00
  5.00 PGM
  6.00    DCL       &EMPLNO  TYPE(*CHAR) LEN(3)
  7.00    DCL       &SALARY  TYPE(*DEC)  LEN(7 2)
  8.00    DCL       &CANCEL  TYPE(*LGL)
  9.00
 10.00    CALL      XMPL509  PARM(&EMPLNO &SALARY &CANCEL)
 11.00    IF        &CANCEL  RETURN
 12.00
 13.00    /* Now call the RPG program to do the DB work */
 14.00    CALL      XMPL508RG   PARM(&EMPLNO &SALARY)
 15.00
 16.00 ENDPGM
```

```
  1.00 /*****************************************************/
  2.00 /* Program Name: XMPL509  - Example called program w/3 parms */
  3.00 /*****************************************************/
  4.00
  5.00 PGM          PARM(&EMP# &PAY$ &ERROR)
  6.00    DCL       &EMP#   TYPE(*CHAR) LEN(3)
  7.00    DCL       &PAY$    TYPE(*DEC)  LEN(7 2)
  8.00    DCL       &ERROR   TYPE(*LGL)
  9.00
 10.00    CALL      XMPL509RG  PARM(&EMP# &PAY$)
 11.00
 12.00    IF        (&EMP# = '000')  CHGVAR &ERROR '1'
 13.00
 14.00 ENDPGM
```

Figure 5.6: An example of a CL-to-CL call with CL variables as parameters.

In Figure 5.6, at line 10.00 of XMPL508, the CALL to XMPL509 specifies three parameters, the same number that is received by XMPL509. The data type and size of the CL variables passed by XMPL508 correspond exactly to those in XMPL509. Note that the CL variable names can be different in each program.

Rule 3

Rule 3 states that character-string literal values shorter than 32 bytes are blank padded and passed with a length of 32. To appreciate the impact of this rule, you must recall that parameters are actually passed as pointers and not as data. Consider CL program XMPL504 (shown in Figure 5.7) that is written to receive a 10-character parameter containing the name of a file.

```
 1.00 /*******************************************************/
 2.00 /* Program Name: XMPL504  - Receive character parm      */
 3.00 /*******************************************************/
 4.00
 5.00 PGM          PARM(&FILE)
 6.00   DCL        &FILE  TYPE(*CHAR) LEN(10)
 7.00
 8.00   OVRDBF     PGMFILE  TOFILE(&FILE)
 9.00   CALL       XMPL504RG
10.00
11.00 ENDPGM
```

Figure 5.7: CL Receiving a character parameter.

If you call the CL program, passing the literal 'TEMPFILE', the passed value takes up 8 bytes of storage in the PASA. Yet, the called program references 10 bytes of data!

It might seem that the 2 bytes of storage in the PASA following the file name could contain almost anything. If those 2 bytes contained zeros, for example, you might expect the called program to use 'TEMPFILE00' for the file name. But, as shown by the following, this is not the case :

```
CALL  XMPL504  PARM('TEMPFILE')
```

The value of &FILE in CL program XMPL504 will be 'TEMPFILE𝖇𝖇'. Rule 3 ensures that the storage following the literal 'TEMPFILE' contains blanks. As long as the length of the CL variable receiving the parameter doesn't exceed 32 bytes, it is blank padded. Many programmers have taken advantage of the third precept without ever realizing the problems it was helping them avoid.

Rule 4

The second corollary to Rule 4 states that, if a CL variable into which a character-string parameter is received is defined as more than 32 bytes, the passed literal should be the same length as the CL variable in the called program. In Figure 5.8, the example illustrates a technique for padding a long character literal parameter to the length expected by the CL program. The CL program XMPL505 receives a 35-character parameter.

```
                    *...v....1....v....2....v....3....v
    CALL   XMPL505  ('San Francisco                      ')
```

Figure 5.8: Example of padding a character literal.

This CALL command will pass the value 'San Francisco' padded with blanks to 35 positions to the program XMPL505. Because of this padding, all 35 positions of the CL program variable &CITY contain valid data. See Figure 5.9.

```
 1.00 /****************************************************/
 2.00 /* Program Name: XMPL505  - Receive  L-o-n-g character parm  */
 3.00 /****************************************************/
 4.00
 5.00 PGM         PARM(&CITY)
 6.00   DCL       &CITY    TYPE(*CHAR) LEN(35)
 7.00
 8.00   CALL      XMPL505RG PARM(&CITY)
 9.00
10.00   SNDPGMMSG ('Location is' *BCAT &CITY) TOUSR(*REQUESTER)
11.00
12.00 ENDPGM
```

Figure 5.9: Sending padded parameters to CL programs.

The technique shown in Figure 5.9 could become tedious when very long parameters are used, but you don't need to count the blanks exactly. Just be sure there are at least enough blanks to fill up the CL variable. Extra blanks will be truncated.

Rule 5

Rule 5 is self-explanatory.

Rule 6

Rule 6 states that numeric values passed as character literal values must be quoted. If a CL program receives a parameter into a character variable, the principles for assigning a numeric value to a character variable with CHGVAR do not apply. The CL program XMPL506 receives a character parameter. To pass a numeric value to the program, the numeric value must be quoted. For example:

```
CALL     XMPL506   ('369')
```

This CALL command passes the value '369' to the program XMPL506 (see Figure 5.10.) Because &DEPT is a three-character CL variable, quoting is required for the numeric value.

```
 1.00 /****************************************************************/
 2.00 /* Program Name: XMPL506  - Receive num value in char parm    */
 3.00 /****************************************************************/
 4.00
 5.00 PGM        PARM(&DEPT)
 6.00   DCL      &DEPT  TYPE(*CHAR) LEN(3)
 7.00
 8.00   CALL     XMPL506RG PARM(&DEPT)
 9.00
10.00   SNDPGMMSG  ('Department is' *BCAT &DEPT) TOPGMQ(*SAME)
11.00
12.00 ENDPGM
```

Figure 5.10: Passing a numeric value to a character CL variable.

Rule 7

The seventh rule states that numeric literal values are passed in packed format with the default length of 15,5. Consequently, the receiving program must declare the decimal variable with LEN(15 5). Figure 5.11 shows how to define a numeric CL variable that is used as a parameter that could be passed as a literal.

```
 1.00 /*************************************************************/
 2.00 /* Program Name: XMPL507    - Receive numeric parm          */
 3.00 /*************************************************************/
 4.00
 5.00 PGM         PARM(&OPTION)
 6.00 DCL         &OPTION TYPE(*DEC) LEN(15 5)
 7.00
 8.00 IF          (&OPTION = 1) CALL XMPL507R1
 9.00
10.00 ELSE IF     (&OPTION = 2) CALL XMPL507R2
11.00
12.00 ELSE        SNDPGMMSG ('Invalid Option')
13.00
12.00 ENDPGM
```

Figure 5.11: Numeric parameters In CL programs.

The following CALL command passes a numeric literal to the CL program XMPL507.

```
CALL    XMPL507   PARM(2)
```

The command analyzer converts all unquoted numerical literal values to packed decimal. It uses the default length of 15 digits with 5 decimal positions. As a result of this CALL, the CL variable &OPTION receives a value of X'000000000200000F'.

Rule 8

Rule 8 is self-explanatory.

Rule 9

For the implications of Rule 9, see this chapter's discussion under the subheading Passing Numeric Parameters with SBMJOB.

PARAMETER PASSING PITFALLS

The remainder of this chapter approaches parameter passing with an emphasis on potential hazards and their circumvention. Most of the problems associated with passing character-string parameters can be attributed to overlooking the corollaries to the fourth rule. Those corollaries state that character literal values longer than 32 bytes are not blank padded and for CL variables longer than 32 bytes, passed literal values must be at least as long as the variable.

In Figure 5.12, the CL program XMPL510 shows the typical problems related to passing long, literal, character-string parameters:

```
 1.00 /*************************************************************/
 2.00 /* Program Name: XMPL510  - Receive 2 char parms, 1st long   */
 3.00 /*************************************************************/
 4.00
 5.00 PGM         PARM(&CITY &STATE)
 6.00   DCL       &CITY   TYPE(*CHAR) LEN(35)
 7.00   DCL       &STATE  TYPE(*CHAR) LEN(15)
 8.00
 9.00   SNDPGMMSG ('Location is' *BCAT &CITY  *TCAT ',' +
10.00               *BCAT &STATE *TCAT '.') +
11.00               TOUSR(*REQUESTER)
11.00 ENDPGM
```

Figure 5.12: Passing long, literal, character string parameters.

The CL program XMPL510 receives two character parameters, &CITY and &STATE, with lengths of 35 and 15 bytes, respectively. Notice the value of &CITY if XMPL510 is called with the literal parameters 'San Francisco' and 'California' (Figure 5.13).

```
CALL    XMPL510  PARM('San Francisco' 'California')

                        *...v....1....v....2....v....3....v
Value of &CITY  is: 'San Francisco                   Cal'
Value of &STATE is: 'California        '
```

Figure 5.13: Receiving long, literal, character string parameters.

The last three bytes (positions 33–35) of the &CITY CL variable contain the characters 'Cal'. This anomaly can be particularly difficult to uncover because there are no error- handling techniques that detect this condition. To illustrate the phenomenon, a portion of the PASA is shown in Figure 5.14.

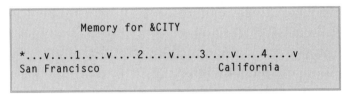

Figure 5.14: Literal, character-string parameters in memory.

The value 'San Francisco' is padded with blanks to a length of 32 bytes and is loaded into storage beginning in position 1. The value 'California' also is padded with blanks and loaded into storage, beginning with the very next available byte (position 33). The pointer to the starting position of the first value is passed to XMPL510, which uses it to address 35 bytes of data for the CL variable &CITY. Consequently, &CITY contains the value 'San Francisco' padded with blanks to a length of 32, followed by the first 3 bytes of 'California'.

Exactly the same thing would happen if the first parameter were passed as a variable having a length of 32 bytes. If the parameter being passed is a CL variable, however, the problem can be easily corrected by ensuring that both the calling and called programs declare the same size for the variable. If the parameter must be passed as a literal, the solution is to blank pad the character literal to the length of the CL variable in the called program.

Passing Numeric Literal Parameters

The most perplexing obstacles to passing parameters are those that pertain to numeric literal values. Virtually all problems related to passing numeric literal parameters can be attributed to a misunderstanding of Rule 7. As shown in Figure 5.15, CL program XMPL511 is a typical example of a program with potential for this type of problem.

```
 1.00 /**********************************************************/
 2.00 /* Program Name: XMPL511  - Receive non-std  numeric parm    */
 3.00 /**********************************************************/
 4.00
 5.00 PGM          PARM(&AMOUNT)
 6.00   DCL        &AMOUNT  TYPE(*DEC)  LEN(7 2)
 7.00
 8.00   CHGVAR     &AMOUNT  VALUE(&AMOUNT / 100)
 9.00
10.00 ENDPGM
```

Figure 5.15: Receiving literal, decimal parameters.

CL program XMPL511 receives a numeric parameter into a CL variable (&AMOUNT) declared as 7,2. Assume that the program is intended to be called by another program that passes the parameter correctly. However, if the programmer has just completed the first successful compile and is eager to test the program, he or she might type the following command from the Command Entry display and, consequently, would receive the function check message:

```
CALL   XMPL511  PARM(12345.67)
Function check. MCH1202 unmonitored by XMPL511 at stmt 800.
```

Because MCH1202 indicates a decimal data error, the nature of the problem is not readily apparent. Certainly, 12345.67 is a valid number that fits into a 7,2 variable just fine! This is a perfect example of being smitten by a misunderstanding of Rule 7, which states that numeric literal values are passed in packed format with a length of 15,5.

Figure 5.16 is a representation of a part of the PASA that illustrates what happens when XMPL511 is passed as a numeric literal:

```
Position:   *...v....1....v....2....v....3..
Zone:       00024600
Digit:      0013570F

                    &AMOUNT
```

Figure 5.16: Literal, decimal parameters in memory.

The value 12345.67 is zero-filled to a size of 15,5 and packed, and is loaded into storage beginning in position 1. The positive sign "F" is written to the digit portion of the low-order (right-most) byte. The pointer to position 1 is passed to XMPL511, which addresses the first 4 bytes (7 digits, packed) for the CL variable &AMOUNT. The variable &AMOUNT then contains the hexadecimal (hex) value X'00000123'.

The preceding value obviously isn't the value that was intended to be passed. And, because there is no sign in the low-order position, it is not valid numeric data and, consequently, causes the decimal data error.

Fortunately, there are several solutions to this problem. One popular approach is to place the numeric data in the *local data area* (LDA) and retrieve it into CL variables in the program. However, this chapter is about passing parameters, and several approaches to successfully passing the required parameter are explored.

One way to circumvent the obstacle is to pass the literal as something other than a pure numeric value. The key to this method is knowing what the called program needs to receive. Because all decimal variables in CL are stored in packed format, the program stores a 7-digit number in 4 bytes. You can pass the exact data and length that you need by specifying the parameter value as a hexadecimal (hex) literal (as shown in Figure 5.17).

> **NOTE:**
>
> *Hexadecimal values are denoted by an "x" followed by a quoted string of hexadecimal values. Each hex value comprises a pair of characters in the ranges 0–9 or A–F. Each pair represents the zone and digit portions of 1 byte of data. For data in the packed decimal format, each byte contains two numeric digits. Consequently, when hex values represent packed decimal data, the zone and digit portions of each byte except the last must contain only the digits 0 through 9. The digit portion of the low-order byte must contain a valid sign: "F" or "D". (Note: "F" is the positive sign and "D" is the negative sign.)*

```
CALL      XMPL511   PARM(X'1234567F')

          Value of &AMOUNT is:   12345.67

or:

          CALL      XMPL511   PARM(X'1234567D')

          Value of &AMOUNT is:  -12345.67
```

Figure 5.17: Specifying the parameter value as a hexadecimal (hex) literal.

Specifying the hex value X'1234567F' for the program parameter correctly maps 12345.67 into a 7,2 CL variable. To make the number negative, it would be passed as X'1234567D'. In Figure 5.18, the representation of a portion of the PASA illustrates what happens when a parameter is passed as a hexadecimal literal.

```
CALL    XMPL511   PARM(X'1234567F')

Position:     *...v....1....v....2....v....3..
Zone:         1357
Digit:        246F

                Value of &AMOUNT is 12345.67
```

Figure 5.18: Hex literal, decimal parameters in memory.

Two other points should be kept in mind when passing numeric values as hexadecimal literal values. You must be sure to include enough places for the full size of the CL variable, whether the digits are significant or not. Specifically, to pass the value 1 for a 7,2 CL variable, the literal is X'0000100F'. Also, if the variable has an even number of digits, precede it with one additional leading zero. For example, to pass the value 12 for a 2,0 variable, the literal is X'012F'.

This approach is reasonable for occasional testing of program modules. However, if a program is going to be called frequently and requires a numeric literal parameter, a more permanent solution would be to create a simple command to call the program. The command interpreter provides a convenient front-end for running programs that accept parameters.

A user-written command can be thought of as a "call" interface that is customized for a specific program. Because the more generic CALL command must make assumptions about the attributes of literal values, it is possible that the data is passed in a manner that is incompatible with the called program. But, because command parameters are defined with the correct size and attributes, the command interpreter doesn't need to make assumptions and, hence, can place the data in the PASA appropriately. For more detail on creating commands, see chapter 14.

In Figure 5.19, the command definition specifications are for the command RUN511, which can be used to run the CL program XMPL511.

```
  1.00  /*************************************************************/
  2.00  /* Command Name: RUN511      - Run pgm w/ non-std parm      */
  2.00  /* CPP.........: XMPL511     - Receive non-std numeric parm */
  3.00  /*************************************************************/
  4.00
  5.00    CMD          PROMPT('Run XMPL511')
  6.00
  7.00    PARM         KWD(AMOUNT) TYPE(*DEC) LEN(7 2) +
  8.00                   PROMPT('Enter Amount')
  9.00
 10.00  /***********   End of CMD source   *****************/
```

Figure 5.19: Command for passing decimal parameters.

Notice that the PARM statement defines the AMOUNT parameter as a 7,2 numeric value. Armed with this knowledge of the command processing program's requirements, the command interpreter places the parameter data in the PASA so that it can be correctly interpreted by XMPL511. The command shown in Figure 5.20 demonstrates using a user-written command to correctly pass numeric data to a program.

```
RUN511     AMOUNT(75)


Position:    *...v....1....v....2....v....3..
Zone:        0050
Digit:       070F

              Value of &AMOUNT is 75.00
```

Figure 5.20: Decimal parameters in memory.

Passing Numeric Parameters with SBMJOB

Perhaps the most common cause of frustration related to passing parameters is passing numeric parameters to a submitted job. In Figure 5.21, the CL program XMPL512 submits a batch job that calls XMPL511.

```
 1.00 /**********************************************************/
 2.00 /* Program Name: XMPL512  - Example pgm to submit w/num parm */
 3.00 /**********************************************************/
 4.00
 5.00 PGM
 6.00   DCL        &AMOUNT  TYPE(*DEC)  LEN(7 2)
 7.00
 8.00   CHGVAR     &AMOUNT  VALUE(12345.67)
 9.00   SBMJOB     JOB(TEST#1) CMD(CALL XMPL511 PARM(&AMOUNT))
10.00
11.00 ENDPGM
```

Figure 5.21: SBMJOB with decimal parameters.

Program XMPL512 declares a CL variable, &AMOUNT, as 7,2 and uses it in the CMD parameter of the SBMJOB command. Because XMPL511 and XMPL512 both declare the passed parameter &AMOUNT as 7,2, it appears that this code should work correctly. But it doesn't!

One of the tasks the SBMJOB command performs is to create a special message queue—called the Job Message Queue—for the submitted job. SBMJOB then resolves any CL variables in the command specified on the CMD parameter and places the resulting command string in a request message on the job message queue for the batch job. When the submitted job runs, it receives the request message and runs the command.

By the time the batch job receives that request message, there are no longer any links to CL variables in the submitting job. It treats the command precisely as though it were entered on the command entry display. In other words, OS/400 treats the parameter as a numeric literal. Therefore, the value is passed as 15,5, but the variable in the CL program is defined as 7,2. Once again, a decimal data error (MCH1202) is generated.

The solutions previously offered for passing numeric literal values—passing hexadecimal parameters and creating user-written commands—both work well in a SBMJOB environment, as does the technique of loading the data into the LDA and extracting it in the submitted job. However, another way to address passing numeric literal parameters merits serious consideration.

The corollary to Rule 7 states that if numeric literal values are passed, the receiving CL program must declare the decimal variable as LEN(15 5). If you know you will need to pass numeric literal values as parameters, you should declare the receiving CL variable as 15,5. It makes sense to take advantage of the fact that OS/400 is going to assume that numeric literal values are all 15,5. In Figure 5.22, the CL program XMPL513 is identical to XMPL512 except that it submits a batch job to call XMPL511B instead of XMPL511.

Like XMPL512, XMPL513 declares a 7,2 CL variable named &AMOUNT, which it incorporates in the CMD parameter of the SBMJOB command. The important difference is the distinction between XMPL511 and XMPL511B. Program XMPL511B receives the parameter into a CL variable called &AMOUNT_IN, which is declared as 15,5.

The numeric literal 12345.67 maps correctly into the &AMOUNT_IN CL variable (see Figure 5.23). The CHGVAR command is used to copy that value to the &AMOUNT CL variable.

```
 1.00 /*******************************************************/
 2.00 /* Program Name: XMPL513  - Example pgm to submit w/dec parm */
 3.00 /*******************************************************/
 4.00
 5.00 PGM
 6.00   DCL       &AMOUNT  TYPE(*DEC)  LEN(7 2)
 7.00
 8.00   CHGVAR    &AMOUNT  VALUE(12345.67)
 9.00   SBMJOB    JOB(TEST#2) CMD(CALL XMPL511B PARM(&AMOUNT))
10.00
11.00 ENDPGM


 1.00 /*******************************************************/
 2.00 /* Program Name: XMPL511B  - Example submitted program    */
 3.00 /*******************************************************/
 4.00
 5.00 PGM         PARM(&AMOUNT_IN)
 6.00   DCL       &AMOUNT_IN TYPE(*DEC)  LEN(15 5)
 7.00   DCL       &AMOUNT    TYPE(*DEC)  LEN( 7 2)
 8.00
 9.00   CHGVAR    &AMOUNT    VALUE(&AMOUNT_IN)
10.00
11.00   CHGVAR    &AMOUNT    VALUE(&AMOUNT / 100)
12.00
13.00 ENDPGM
```

Figure 5.22: Correct SBMJOB with decimal parameters.

```
Position:   *...v....1....v....2....v....3..
Zone:       00024600
Digit:      0013570F

                          Value of &AMOUNT_IN is 12345.67
```

Figure 5.23: Decimal parameters in memory.

REVIEW QUESTIONS

1. CL program navigation is accomplished using five commands: _____, _____, _____, _____, and _____.

2. A returning CL program always terminates. It is removed from the _____ _____ and its storage is _____.

3. TFRCTL is used to invoke another program and is similar to CALL except that it _____ and _____.

4. Because parameters are passed by _____, if the value of a parameter is changed in one program, it is also changed in all others.

5. SBMJOB places the submitted command on the ___ _____ _____ of the submitted job. Parameters on a submitted CALL command are always treated as _____.

6. If you know you will need to pass numeric literals as parameters, declare the receiving CL variable as _____, _____.

6

INTRODUCTION TO
MESSAGE HANDLING

It has been said about the AS/400 that "the entire operating system is driven by messages." Of course, this statement is too global to go unchallenged, but it contains a great deal of truth. Messages seem to pervade the system. Error conditions are signaled by messages; job logs are made up of messages; the diagnostics at the end of a compile listing are messages; the commands run by the system request menu are found in a message; even the options on AS/400 menus are messages.

The most common use of messages, however, is as a form of data used for communication. Unlike data stored in a database, each message can be unique in format, content, and meaning. Messages are used to communicate between and among users, programmers, system operators, programs, jobs, and the system history log.

The OS/400 message-handling function is supported by a single facility, the Generalized Message Handler, that is responsible for managing all message-handling functions. Two object types, a message file (MSGF) and a message queue (MSGQ), are provided to support the message handler.

MESSAGE FILES

The content of a message may be supplied dynamically as an *immediate message* (sometimes referred to as an *impromptu message*). One of the strengths of OS/400's message-handling capability, however, is that the content of a message also may be predefined partially or in full in a message description. Message descriptions are stored in a message file. OS/400 includes several message files, including one for

- General system messages, QCPFMSG.
- Each program product.

All of the message files can be displayed through the WRKMSGF (Work with Message Files) command.

The name of the general system message file, QCPFMSG, is a remnant from the IBM System/38 computer, the precursor to the AS/400. QCPFMSG was named for Control Program Facility (CPF), the operating system of the System /38. For compatibility, QCPFMSG was not renamed in OS/400.

In addition to the system-supplied message files, it is customary to create at least one message file for user-defined messages using the CRTMSGF (Create Message File) command. The following command creates a user message file named USERMSG in the general-purpose library:

```
CRTMSGF  MSGF(QGPL/USERMSG) TEXT('User-defined messages')
```

User-defined message descriptions can be added to USERMSG and maintained using the following commands:

- WRKMSGD (Work with Message Descriptions)
- ADDMSGD (Add Message Description)
- CHGMSGD (Change Message Description)
- RMVMSGD (Remove Message Description)
- DSPMSGD (Display Message Description)

MESSAGE DESCRIPTIONS

Because users and programs have different requirements for message information, predefined message descriptions often include both natural-language message text for human users and a data format that a program can easily decipher. The definition of a message in a message file includes:

- A message identifier (MSGID), used for referencing the message.
- The message text.
- Additional text called second level text.
- The format for substitution data, which can be inserted into the text.
- Other miscellaneous attributes.

If you were to type "see spot run" (without the quotes) on the command entry display and press enter, the following messages would be generated:

```
> see spot run
  Command SEE in library *LIBL not found.
  Error found on SEE command.
```

Although not complete sentences, the messages are intended to be informative. In addition, each message refers to the context in which it is generated. In other words, each message refers to the command named "SEE" (which doesn't exist). By positioning the cursor on the second message and pressing the help key, additional information about the message is displayed. Included in the information displayed is the message identifier (CPF0001) as well as additional text for the message, often including the cause and suggestions for recovery.

You can display the description for message identifier CPF0001 using the DSPMSGD (Display Message Description) command:

```
DSPMSGD  CPF0001
```

The Display Formatted Message Text display, (option 1 on the DSPMSGD menu) displays the first-level and second-level text of the message. Also, the positions for substituted text are identified through message data fields. Message data fields are identified by an ampersand (&) followed by the numbers 1 through 99. Message fields allow the substitution of message data to make the final text of the message specific to the context and, hence, more meaningful. For example, the message "Error found on SEE command" is far more explicit than the generic "Error found on command."

Message CPF0001 contains a single message data field identified as &1. The locations of the message field in the message text determines where the command name is placed when the message is sent.

The Display Field Data display (option 2 on the DSPMSGD menu) displays the format of each message data field for the message identifier. The sole message field for CPF0001 is &1. It is defined as a *CHAR data type with a length of 10. There is no meaningful description for message data fields included in the message description itself. The meaning of a message data field can be determined only by observing how it is used in the message.

MESSAGE QUEUES

Messages are sent to and received from an object called a message queue (MSGQ). There are various classes of message queues. User message queues can be created with the CRTMSGQ (Create Message Queue) command. Some message queues are shipped with the system, such as the System Operator Message Queue (QSYSOPR) and the System Log Message Queue (QHST).

Other message queues, such as workstation message queues and user-profile message queues, are created automatically by the operating system. A workstation message queue is created for each display device description. A user profile message queue is created for each user profile on the system unless an existing workstation or user message queue is assigned as the user-profile message queue.

A job can allocate a user message queue, a workstation message queue, or QSYSOPR by using the DLVRY (Delivery Mode) parameter of the CHGMSGQ (Change Message Queue) command. Delivery modes that allocate a message queue are *BREAK and *NOTIFY.

Also, OS/400 automatically creates a special message queue called a *job message queue* for each job. Much of the error handling done in CL programs involves sending and receiving messages to and from the job message queue. Consequently, understanding the structure of the job message queue is a prerequisite to writing CL programs that include error-handling logic.

The job message queue can be thought of as a job's internal mailroom. In some ways, it is a lot like the wall full of message boxes that various departments in a company might have used to distribute memos before the e-mail era. It is a vehicle for programs to communicate with each other. Figure 6.1 depicts the job message queue and illustrates the relationship between the job message queue and the call stack. The job message queue is logically partitioned into an *external message queue* for the job and a *call message queue* for each program or procedure invocation in the job. The external message queue is used by programs to communicate with a job's user.

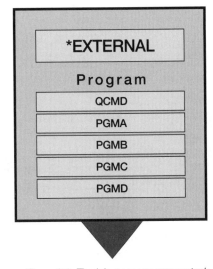

Figure 6.1: The job message queue stack.

Sending Messages

Five commands are available for sending messages to message queues. Table 6.1 lists the CL commands that send messages. Table 6.1 also specifies the following for each command:

- Whether predefined messages may be sent.
- The kinds of message queue to which a message may be sent.
- The message types that may be sent.

Table 6.1: Message Sending Commands.

Command Name	Description	MSGID Allowed	MsgQ Type	Message Type
SNDMSG	Send Message	No	Non-PGM	*INFO *INQ
SNDBRKMSG	Send Break Message	No	WRKSTN	*INFO *INQ
SNDPGMMSG	Send Program Message	Yes	All	All
SNDUSRMSG	Send User Message	Yes	Non-PGM	*INFO *INQ
SNDRPY	Send Message Reply	No	N/A	*RPY

Legend:
Non-PGM — Not a call message queue
WRKSTN — Workstation device message queue
N/A — Not applicable

SNDMSG (Send Message) and SNDBRKMSG (Send Break Message) are limited, message-sending commands that are generally used by users and the system operator to send immediate informational and inquiry messages to other users. Informational messages are usually used for communication among users. Inquiry messages are used when a reply is desired. A message using the SNDBRKMSG command causes the workstation's interactive job to be suspended while the message interrupts or "breaks into" the job and is displayed on the screen. Figure 6.2 demonstrates some of the capabilities of the SNDMSG and SNDBRKMSG commands.

```
(1)  SNDMSG    MSG('Please sign off NOW!  ') TOUSR(*ALLACT)
(2)  SNDMSG    MSG('3 more minutes please!') TOMSGQ(QSYSOPR)
(3)  SNDMSG    MSG('I''m making history.  ') TOMSGQ(QHST)
(4)  SNDBRKMSG MSG('How about lunch?       ') TOMSGQ(DSP09) +
               MSGTYPE(*INQ) RPYMSGQ(AARONV)
```

Figure 6.2: Examples of SNDMSG and SNDBRKMSG commands.

In Figure 6.2, the first command sends the informational message 'Please sign off NOW!' to all users who are currently signed on to the system. The messages might or might not break into the users' interactive jobs, depending on the delivery mode of their user message queue. The second command sends the informational message '3 more minutes please!' to the system operator message queue. The message will break into a job that has put the QSYSOPR message queue in break delivery mode.

The third command places the entry 'I'm making history.' on the system history log. The message can be viewed by running the DSPLOG (Display History Log) command. Notice the doubled apostrophe in the word 'I''m' (I'm).

The fourth command, a SNDBRKMSG command, sends the inquiry message 'How about lunch?' to the workstation message queue DSP09. A sender's copy of the message is sent to AARONV, the reply message queue. If any user is signed on to device DSP09, the message will break into the interactive job, and the user can provide a reply to the message. The reply is appended to the sender's copy of the message in AARONV. If the AARONV message queue has been placed in *BREAK delivery mode by an interactive job, the reply will break into that job. Otherwise, the reply can be viewed by running the command DSPMSG AARONV.

SNDUSRMSG (Send User Message) is a very useful command in application CL programs. If it is used to send an inquiry message, the command parameters to receive the reply are built into the SNDUSRMSG command. Additionally, parameters are included for specifying validation criteria for the reply. The following command gives the system operator an opportunity to continue processing or cancel a task:

```
SNDUSRMSG  MSG('Go or Cancel? (G C)') VALUES(G C) +
             TOMSGQ(QSYSOPR) MSGRPY(&RPY)
```

Only the values G and C are accepted as a reply; however, lowercase responses are automatically translated to uppercase. The sending CL program remains suspended until the operator responds to the message. At that time, the CL variable &RPY will contain the operator's reply and the program logic can be based on its value.

The most versatile command for sending messages is SNDPGMMSG (Send Program Message). It can be used to send any type of message to any type of message queue and can send either immediate or predefined messages. SNDPGMMSG is equipped with numerous parameters that provide options for sending messages.

SNDPGMMSG Parameters

The MSG (Message) parameter accepts up to 3,000 characters of message text for an immediate message (512 if you are prompting). Alternatively, MSGID (Message Identifier) and MSGF (Message File) can be used to specify a predefined message. Any substitution data required by a predefined message is supplied through the MSGDTA (Message Data) parameter. For example, if message identifier CPF0001 (Error found on &1 command.) in QCPFMSG is sent, the value "SEE" could be supplied as message data, causing the final message text to be "Error found on SEE command."

The MSGTYPE (Message Type) parameter defaults to *INFO but allows all of the message types to be sent. For inquiry and notify messages, the RPYMSGQ (Reply Message Queue) parameter is used to specify the message queue to which the reply should be sent.

Three parameters—TOPGMQ (To Call Stack Entry Message Queue), TOMSGQ (To Non-Program Message Queue), and TOUSER (To User Profile)—are used to direct the message to the desired message queue. If either TOMSGQ or TOUSER is specified, the message is sent to the indicated non-program message queue.

TOPGMQ is specified as a list of two values, *relationship entry* (or *offset entry*) and *call stack entry*. The first value, relationship, can be specified as *SAME (use the entry in the second value) or *PRV (use the caller or the requester of the entry in the second value). Additionally, the single value *EXT can be specified for TOPGMQ, indicating that the message should be sent to the job's external-message queue. The external message queue is used by programs in a job to communicate with the workstation operator of an interactive job. Messages sent to the job's external message queue are displayed on the Program Messages display.

The second value (the call stack entry) can be the name of an OPM program that is currently in the job's call stack or the default, predefined value '*' (the * implies the name of the OPM program sending the message). The use of the call stack entry and additional special values in the ILE environment is discussed in chapter 13. The remainder of this discussion is strictly from an OPM perspective.

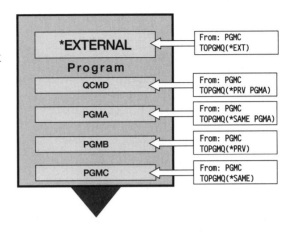

Figure 6.3: The target of Sent Program Messages.

The permissible values for the relationship portion of TOPGMQ reflect that inter-program communication flows in just one direction—up. Because programs are always suspended while other programs that they call are running, the active program with control is always the lowest program in the stack, and hence it cannot send messages to a program below itself. Using the TOPGMQ parameter of SNDPGMMSG, a CL program can thus send a message to any of the following:

- Itself.
- Its caller.
- Any named program in the stack.
- Any named program's caller.
- The external message queue.

Figure 6.3 illustrates the ways in which the TOPGMQ parameter can be specified. The example assumes that the call stack consists of QCMD, PGMA, PGMB, and PGMC. PGMC is the active program with control. It uses the SNDPGMMSG command to send messages, as in the following example:

```
SNDPGMMSG MSG('All OK?') TOPGMQ(*EXT) MSGTYPE(*INQ)
```

The preceding command sends the inquiry message, 'ALL OK?', to the job's external message queue. The job is interrupted while the program messages are displayed. After the workstation operator responds to the message, control returns to PGMC. Inquiry and notify messages sent to the external message queue give the workstation operator the opportunity to reply to the message.

Informational, completion, and diagnostic messages sent to the external message queue are displayed until the operator presses the Enter key. Status messages sent to the external message queue are displayed on the message line of the current display panel without interrupting the job. Escape messages cannot be sent to the external requester.

Request messages can be sent to the external message queue, but they are not displayed. They remain on the job message queue as a "pending request" until and unless they are received by a program. If a command entry screen is displayed, pending requests are received and treated as commands to be run. Also, request messages can be retrieved by pressing the F9 key on a command line or command-entry screen.

The following command sends an informational message to the caller of PGMA (QCMD). It isn't necessary to know the name of a program's caller to send it a message. The message 'ALL OK' will appear in the job log:

```
SNDPGMMSG MSG('All OK') TOPGMQ(*PRV PGMA) MSGTYPE(*INFO)
```

In the preceding example, the MSGTYPE parameter may be omitted because *INFO is the default.

The following command sends an escape message to PGMA, collapsing the call stack. Both PGMC and PGMB will be terminated, and PGMA will be sent an exception:

```
SNDPGMMSG MSGID(CPF9897) MSGF(QCPFMSG) MSGDTA('Not OK!') +
          TOPGMQ(*SAME PGMA) MSGTYPE(*ESCAPE)
```

Because a predefined message is required for exception messages, the MSGID and MSGF parameters are necessary in the preceding command. In this example, the general error message identifier CPF9897 incorporates the character string supplied in the MSGDTA parameter to send the error message 'NOT OK!'. Many programmers are more familiar with using CPF9898. The difference is that the message text for CPF9898 includes a period after the substitution variable ('&1.'). If CPF9898 were specified in the prior example, the message 'NOT OK!.' Would be sent.

The following command sends the completion message 'ALL OK' to the sender's caller (PGMB):

```
SNDPGMMSG MSG('All OK') TOPGMQ(*PRV) MSGTYPE(*COMP)
```

An equivalent method of specifying the to-message-queue as the sender's caller is TOPGMQ(*PRV *). Or, because (*PRV *) is the default, the TOPGMQ parameter could be omitted entirely.

If the value of a character CL variable &ORD# is '001738', the following command sends the informational message 'ORD# = 001738' to the sender's call message queue:

```
SNDPGMMSG MSG('Ord# =' *BCAT &ORD#) TOPGMQ(*SAME) MSGTYPE(*INFO)
```

By reviewing the job log, you can tell that Order number 001738 is processed by the job.

When the SNDPGMMSG command is used to send a message, the Message Reference Key (MRK, pronounced "mark") can be returned to the sending program. The MRK is a unique string of characters that identifies a particular instance of a message in a queue. To receive the MRK, a CL program variable must be named on the KEYVAR parameter of SNDPGMMSG. The MRK may be referenced at a later point in the CL program to receive, move, reply to, re-send, or remove the message. For example, after the following SNDPGMMSG command, the message reference key of the message is stored in the CL variable &MRK:

```
SNDPGMMSG MSG('Save my key.') KEYVAR(&MRK)
```

Types of Messages

One attribute of a message is its type, which is determined by the MSGTYPE (Message Type) parameter of the message-sending command. Each message type has its own unique characteristics and is treated differently by the system. Some types of messages are limited as to the type of message queue to which they may be sent and whether they may reference predefined message descriptions or use impromptu message text.

The valid message types are as follows: *INFO, *INQ, *COMP, *DIAG, *ESCAPE, *NOTIFY, *STATUS, and *RQS. Table 6.2 contains a list describing the message types that can be used in CL programs. The table also specifies the kinds of message queue to which each message type may be sent and whether a message identifier is required.

Table 6.2: Types of Messages.

Message Type	Description	Target Message Queue	MSGID Required	Notes
*INFO	Informational	Any	No	
*INQ	Inquiry	Non-Program	No	1
*COMP	Completion	Any	No	
*DIAG	Diagnostic	Any	No	2
*ESCAPE	Escape	Any	Yes	2, 3
*NOTIFY	Notification	Any	Yes	2
*STATUS	Status	External (*EXT)	Yes	4
*RQS	Request	Any	No	2, 5

Notes:

1. Inquiry messages may be sent to the external (*EXT) message queue.
2. These types of messages are usually sent to a call message queue.
3. Escape messages cannot be sent to the external (*EXT) message queue.
4. Status messages sent to a call message queue function similar to *NOTIFY messages.
5. Predefined messages cannot be sent as Request (*RQS) messages.

Informational (*INFO) and inquiry (*INQ) messages are the most commonly used message types and are ordinarily used for communication among users. Informational messages simply convey information and inquiry messages require a reply.

Completion messages differ from informational messages only in their use. Completion messages usually are sent to the requester of a task once the task has successfully completed its function. Usually, completion messages are sent by a program to the call message queue of its caller. Completion messages also are sent to the submitter of a batch job to indicate whether the job completed successfully or terminated abnormally.

Unresolvable errors are communicated through two types of messages, diagnostic (*DIAG) and escape (*ESCAPE). Diagnostic messages are similar to informational messages but usually they contain specific information about a problem and are sent to the call message queue of the requester of a task that has encountered a problem. Normally, one or more diagnostic messages are followed by an escape message.

The escape message contains more general information about the error and often refers to "previous messages in the job log." Escape messages inform the calling program that a requested function could not be performed and that the task program has aborted.

When an escape message is sent, it causes the sending program to terminate. Moreover, it immediately terminates all programs that are currently called, either directly or indirectly, by the target program. (The target of a message is the call message queue to which the message is sent.) In other words, sending an escape message collapses the entire call stack below the target of the message.

Although notify (*NOTIFY) messages are used extensively by OS/400, they are seldom employed in user-written CL programs. Like inquiry messages, notify messages require a reply. Furthermore, a notify message sent to an interactive job's external message queue acts like an inquiry message: the workstation operator supplies a reply, which may be received by the program sending the notify message.

A notify message sent to a call message queue, however, functions more like a "warning" message. If the program to which a notify message is sent monitors for the message, control returns to the target program and the call stack is collapsed as though the message were an escape message. If the message is not monitored for or if it is sent to the external message queue of a batch job, the default reply for the message is sent and control returns to the sending program.

Status (*STATUS) messages usually contain information about the status of a long-running task or function. When they are sent to an interactive job's external message queue, the message is displayed on the message location line of the current display panel. (The message location line is determined by the MSGLOC DDS keyword and is usually the last line on the display.) For more information on sending status messages, see chapter 12.

No message information for a status message is stored in the message queue to which it is sent. This unique characteristic gives status messages the phantom-like quality of vanishing if ever sent to any message queue other than the job's external message queue. A status message, like a notify message, functions as a "warning" if sent to a call message queue. If it is monitored for, it is treated like an escape message. Otherwise, the sending program continues processing.

Escape, notify, and status messages are called *exception messages*, and they can be monitored for in a CL program. Because the MONMSG command requires a message identifier to be specified, all three types of exception messages must use predefined message descriptions. CPF9897 and CPF9898 in the QCPFMSG message file are general-purpose message descriptions that can be used in CL programs to send exception messages with impromptu message text.

Request (*RQS) messages generally contain a CL command: they represent the primary method of requesting work on the AS/400. Request messages have unique qualities that allow them to play an important role in a special type of program called a Request Processing Program (RPP). QCMD is the best known and most important RPP in OS/400. Request messages must be immediate and are sent to call message queues or the job's external message queue. Examples of RPPs are discussed in chapter 9 and chapter 11.

Other types of messages that are not accessible through CL exist, but they are of no real importance to CL programming and are not discussed here.

RECEIVING PROGRAM MESSAGES

Until a program message is received, it is like a letter in a mailbox. It has been delivered by the message handler but the missive hasn't been taken from the mailbox and opened. It is not necessary, however, for every message to be received. In fact, most messages are never received. Some messages are just not very important. Other messages can have an impact without ever being received. An escape message, for example, signals an exception to the target program whether or not the message is received.

The command used to receive a message is RCVMSG (Receive Message). The primary purpose for receiving a message is to return information about the message to the program receiving it. RCVMSG supports 15 parameters that specify CL variables into which the message information can be returned. Parameters that specify a CL variable in which information is returned to the CL program are referred to as *return variable parameters*.

RCVMSG Parameters

Some of the more useful return variable parameters are:

- MSG—the complete first-level text of the message.
- MSGID—the message identifier of the message.
- MSGDTA—the substitution values, or message data.
- MSGF—the message file where the message is defined.
- SNDMSGFLIB—the library containing the message file.

For example, a CL program that receives message identifier CPF0001 ("Error found on &1 command.") could determine the name of the command that failed by retrieving it from the message data. See Figure 6.4.

Other important return variable parameters include:

- KEYVAR—the MRK of the message received.
- SENDER—a formatted character string containing information about the sender of the message.
- RTNTYPE—a two character code that identifies the type of message sent.

```
DCL          &MSGDTA  *CHAR  512
DCL          &MSGID   *CHAR  7
DLC          &MSGKEY  *CHAR  4
DCL          &PGM     *CHAR  10
MONMSG       MSGID(CPF0000)  EXEC(GOTO ERROR)

DSPDTAARA    DTAARA(QTEMP/TEMPDATA)

/* additional user code goes here... */
RETURN
/*-----------------------------------------------------------*/
ERROR:
RCVMSG       MSGID(&MSGID) MSGDTA(&MSGDTA)

IF           &MSGID = 'CPF0001') DO
             CHGVAR  VAR(&PGM)  VALUE(%SST(&MSGDTA 1 10))
             /* Now you've got the command that failed! */
             ENDDO
```

Figure 6.4: Extracting Information from message data.

Table 6.3 lists the values that can be received into the CL variable specified on the RTNTYPE parameter.

RCVMSG supports six parameters that provide numerous options for receiving messages. One of two parameters, PGMQ (Call Stack Entry Message Queue) or MSGQ (Message Queue), determines the message queue from which a message is to be received. If MSGQ is specified, a message is received from the indicated non-program message queue.

PGMQ is specified identically to the TOPGMQ parameter of SNDPGMMSG. It is entered as a list of two values: relationship and program. The single value *EXT can be specified, indicating that a message should be received from a job's external message queue.

A program cannot receive messages from the call message queue of another program that it called because, when a called program ends, it is removed from the call stack. Using the PGMQ parameter of RCVMSG, a CL program can only receive messages from its own call message queue, the call message queue of its caller, a named program in the stack, a named program's caller, or the external message queue.

The WAIT parameter indicates the maximum time that the CL program will wait for a message from a non-program message queue. If PGMQ is specified, the WAIT parameter must be 0.

When a message is received, it is, by default, removed from the message queue. The RMV (Remove) parameter can be used to stipulate that the message should not be removed. If RMV(*NO) is specified, the message remains on the message queue, and its status is changed from "new" to "old."

Table 6.3:
Message Return Code Descriptions.

Return Code	Type of Message
01	Completion
02	Diagnostic
04	Information
05	Inquiry
08	Request
10	Request with prompting
14	Notify
15	Escape
21	Reply, not checked for validity
22	Reply, checked for validity
23	Reply, message default used
24	Reply, system default used
25	Reply, from system reply list

The new or old status of a message affects how it can be received. When receiving messages sequentially, only "new" messages are received. For example, the following command receives the first new message on the call message queue without removing it:

```
RCVMSG  PGMQ(*SAME) RMV(*NO)
```

Because the status of the received message is changed to old, a subsequent RCVMSG command will receive the next new message on the queue.

Performing this operation in a loop constitutes sequential processing of a message queue. As shown in Figure 6.5, the short CL program, XMPL601, receives new messages from a user-profile message queue sequentially in first-in-first-out (FIFO) order:

```
 1.00 /****************************************************************/
 2.00 /* Program Name: XMPL601 - Receive NEW messages sequentially */
 3.00 /****************************************************************/
 4.00
 5.00 PGM
 6.00    DCL       &MSG  *CHAR  512
 7.00    DCL       &MSGQ *CHAR   10
 8.00
 9.00    RTVUSRPRF MSGQ(&MSGQ)
10.00
11.00 TOP:
12.00    RCVMSG    MSGQ(&MSGQ)  WAIT(*MAX)   RMV(*NO) MSG(&MSG)
13.00
14.00    IF        (&MSG = 'QUIT')  RETURN
15.00
16.00    GOTO      TOP
17.00
18.00 ENDPGM
```

Figure 6.5: Receiving new messages sequentially.

The name of the user-profile message queue is obtained through the RTVUSRPRF (Retrieve User Profile) command and is stored in the CL variable &MSGQ at line 9.00. The message text is received into the CL variable &MSG. If the text of the message is 'QUIT', the CL program ends. Otherwise, it branches to the top of the loop and attempts to receive another message.

Messages also can be received randomly by MRK. To receive a message randomly, the MSGKEY (Message Key) parameter must specify the name of a CL variable containing the MRK of a message. An example follows:

```
SNDPGMMSG   MSG('Save my key.') TOPGMQ(*SAME) KEYVAR(&MRK)
RCVMSG      PGMQ(*SAME) MSGKEY(&MRK)
```

After the SNDPGMMSG command above, the message reference key of the message is stored in the CL variable &MRK. The message is received later in the CL program using the RCVMSG command. Much of the versatility of the RCVMSG command is provided by the MSGTYPE (Message Type) parameter. Except for *NOTIFY, *ESCAPE, and *STATUS, any of the message types available on the SNDPGMMSG command can be specified on the RCVMSG command. As shown in

Figure 6.6, XMPL602 receives only new diagnostic messages from a call message queue sequentially in FIFO (first-in, first-out) order.

```
 1.00 /******************************************************/
 2.00 /* Program Name: XMPL602 - Receive NEW diag msgs sequentially/
 3.00 /******************************************************/
 4.00
 5.00 PGM
 6.00    DCL          &MSG  *CHAR  512
 7.00
 8.00 TOP:
 9.00    RCVMSG       PGMQ(*PRV) MSGTYPE(*DIAG) RMV(*NO) MSG(&MSG)
10.00
11.00    IF           (&MSG = ' ')  RETURN
12.00
13.00    GOTO         TOP
14.00
15.00 ENDPGM
```

Figure 6.6: Receiving new diagnostic messages only.

The message text is received into the CL variable &MSG. If there are no new diagnostic messages on the call message queue, &MSG will contain blanks. Consequently, if the value of &MSG is blank, the loop and the CL program ends. Otherwise, it branches to the top of the loop and attempts to receive another diagnostic message.

Additional pre-defined values for MSGTYPE provide special functions. For example, *ANY is the default and doesn't denote any particular type of message. If the default of *ANY is accepted and MSGKEY is not specified, the first new message of any type, except a sender's copy of an inquiry message, is received. If a MRK is specified on the MSGKEY parameter, any message with the specified MRK, except for a sender's copy of an inquiry message, is received. To receive the sender's copy of an inquiry message, specify *COPY for the MSGTYPE parameter.

If *EXCP is specified for MSGTYPE, the last new exception message is received. Because exception (escape and notify) messages are received in last-in, first-out (LIFO) order, it is easy to receive an escape message immediately after the error is trapped by way of the MONMSG command. The example shown in Figure 6.7 demonstrates a technique for removing an unwanted escape message from the job log.

```
CRTDTAARA    QTEMP/TEMPDA  TYPE(*CHAR) +
             TEXT('Temporary Data Area')
MONMSG       CPF1023 EXEC(RCVMSG MSGTYPE(*EXCP) RMV(*YES))
```

Figure 6.7: Removing an escape message from the job log.

If the data area TEMPDA already exists in QTEMP, the error is trapped, the escape message is removed, and processing continues. Although RMV(*YES) is the default, it is coded in this example to more clearly express the intent of the RCVMSG command. A reply to an inquiry message can be received in a CL program by specifying MSGTYPE(*RPY). The example shown in Figure 6.8 sends an inquiry message and waits for a reply.

```
SNDPGMMSG  MSG('Go or Cancel?') TOMSGQ(QSYSOPR) +
           MSGTYPE(*INQ) KEYVAR(&MRK)
RCVMSG     MSGTYPE(*RPY) MSGKEY(&MRK) WAIT(*MAX) RMV(*NO) +
           MSG(&REPLY)
```

Figure 6.8: Example of sending an inquiry message and waiting for a reply.

An inquiry message and its reply share the same message reference key. The MRK of the inquiry message must be captured using the KEYVAR parameter so that it can be supplied as the value for MSGKEY on the RCVMSG command. WAIT(*MAX) ensures that the CL program will wait until there is a reply to the inquiry.

The values *FIRST or *LAST can be specified for MSGTYPE to receive the first or the last message respectively, on the message queue, whether it is new or not. The actual message type that can be received follows the rules for MSGTYPE(*ANY). The following command receives the last message on the workstation message queue for DSP09:

```
RCVMSG     MSGQ(DSP09) MSGTYPE(*LAST) RMV(*NO)
```

The value *NEXT can be specified for MSGTYPE in conjunction with the MSGKEY parameter to receive the next message on the queue following the message with the indicated MRK. MSGTYPE(*PRV) can likewise be used to receive the previous message. Message types *NEXT and *PRV can receive old and new messages sequentially in a loop.

The MRK of each received message must be returned in the KEYVAR parameter and used as the MSGKEY on a subsequent RCVMSG. To begin this chain with the first or last message on the message queue, specify MSGTYPE as *FIRST or *LAST one time. As shown in Figure 6.9, CL program XMPL603 uses a combination of MSGTYPE(*FIRST) and MSGTYPE(*NEXT) to receive both old and new messages sequentially in FIFO order.

```
 1.00 /************************************************************/
 2.00 /* Program Name: XMPL603 - Receive ALL messages sequentially */
 3.00 /************************************************************/
 4.00
 5.00 PGM
 6.00    DCL        &MSG   *CHAR   512
 7.00    DCL        &MRK   *CHAR   4
 8.00
 9.00    RCVMSG     PGMQ(*SAME)  MSGTYPE(*FIRST) +
10.00               RMV(*NO)  KEYVAR(&MRK)  MSG(&MSG)
11.00
12.00 LOOP:
13.00    RCVMSG     PGMQ(*SAME)  MSGTYPE(*NEXT)  MSGKEY(&MRK) +
14.00               RMV(*NO)  KEYVAR(&MRK)  MSG(&MSG)
15.00
16.00    IF         (&MSG = ' ')  RETURN
17.00
18.00    GOTO       LOOP
19.00
20.00 ENDPGM
```

Figure 6.9: Receiving ALL messages sequentially.

The RCVMSG command at line 9.00 receives the first message on the call message queue. The text of the message and the message reference key are returned in the CL variables &MSG and &MRK, respectively. The MRK of the first message is then used in the RCVMSG command at line 13.00 within the loop. With

MSGTYPE(*NEXT) specified and MSGKEY containing the MRK of the first message, the second message on the queue is received.

Note that the CL variable &MRK is used both as the value for the MSGKEY parameter and as the return variable on the KEYVAR parameter. As each message is received in the loop, &MRK is changed to contain the MRK of the message just received. This CL program could have been written to receive all the messages in LIFO (last-in-first-out) order by specifying MSGTYPE(*LAST) on the first RCVMSG command and MSGTYPE(*PRV) on the RCVMSG in the loop.

Messages also can be received sequentially by message type. To receive messages sequentially by message type, specify a message type or *ALL for the MSGTYPE parameter. Using this technique, "new" messages only are received in FIFO order. However, if *EXCP is specified for MSGTYPE, exception (*ESCAPE and *NOTIFY) messages are received in LIFO order.

Using the command SNDRPY (Send Reply), a CL program can send an immediate (i.e., impromptu) reply to an inquiry message that it has received. The reply is linked to the inquiry message via the message queue and the message reference key. The example in Figure 6.10 demonstrates receiving an inquiry message and sending a reply in a CL program:

```
RCVMSG  MSGQ(QSYSOPR) MSGTYPE(*INQ) KEYVAR(&MRK) +
          WAIT(*MAX)  RMV(*NO) MSG(&MSG)

SNDRPY  MSGKEY(&MRK)  MSGQ(QSYSOPR) RPY('C') RMV(*NO)
```

Figure 6.10: Receiving a message and sending a reply.

This example is similar to sending an inquiry and waiting for a reply in that an inquiry message and its reply share the same message reference key. The MRK of the inquiry message must be captured using the KEYVAR parameter of RCVMSG so that it can be supplied as the value for MSGKEY on the SNDRPY command.

Note that the MSGQ parameter of the SNDRPY command references the message queue of the inquiry message and not the message queue to which the reply is sent. The RPYMSGQ parameter of the various SNDxxxMSG commands specifies the message queue to which the reply is sent.

When *NO is specified for the RMV parameter, the inquiry message and its reply can be displayed or received again. However, the inquiry message can be replied to only once. If RMV(*YES) is specified, both the message and the reply are removed from the message queue when the reply is sent. Nevertheless, a sender's copy is kept.

REMOVING MESSAGES

The RMVMSG (Remove Message) command removes (deletes) a message or group of messages from a message queue. The PGMQ, MSGQ, and MSGKEY parameters are analogous to their counterparts on the RCVMSG command. The CLEAR parameter determines which messages to remove and accepts values of *BYKEY, *ALL, *OLD, *NEW, and *KEEPUNANS.

For example, the following command removes a message with a specific MRK from the call message queue of the caller of a program named APDRIVER:

```
RMVMSG  PGMQ(*PRV APDRIVER) MSGKEY(&MRK) CLEAR(*BYKEY)
```

To remove all but unanswered inquiries on a user-defined message queue named HELPDESK, you could run the following command:

```
RMVMSG  MSGQ(HELPDESK) CLEAR(*KEEPUNANS)
```

A special value for the PGMQ parameter, *ALLINACT, allows you to clear the call message queues for all inactive programs. Removing all messages for programs that have completed can help keep the size of the job log small. To trim the job log in a long running job, periodically run the following command:

```
RMVMSG  PGMQ(*ALLINACT)  CLEAR(*ALL)
```

REVIEW QUESTIONS

1. Messages are a form of data used for _____. The _____ _____ _____ manages all message-handling functions.

2. Predefined messages are stored in an object type called a _____ _____.

3. The message file that contains system messages is named _____.

4. Predefined messages include both natural language message text and a defined format for _____ _____ _____.

5. The job message queue is logically partitioned into an _____ message queue for the job and a _____ message queue for each program or procedure invocation in the job.

6. The external message queue is used to communicate with the _____'s _____.

7. Unresolvable errors are communicated using _____ and _____ messages.

8. Diagnostic messages contain _____ information about a problem and escape messages contain more _____ information about the error.

9. Sending an escape message _____ the entire call stack below the target of the message.

10. Escape, notify, and status messages are called _____ messages. They can be monitored for in a CL program.

11. Using the _____ parameter of SNDPGMMSG, a CL program can send a message to: _____, _____, _____, _____, or _____.

12. The RCVMSG command supports 15 parameters, referred to as _____ _____ parameters, that specify CL variables into which information about a message can be returned.

13. The _____ command removes a message or group of messages from a message queue or program message queue.

7

ERROR HANDLING

I f there is one aspect of programming that is often overlooked (other than documentation, of course), it is error handling. Unfortunately, few, if any, programmers consistently produce "bug-free" code and, some bugs usually manage to slip through even the most rigorous testing. Even a perfectly bug-free program can fail if a referenced object has been changed or deleted. Consequently, programs sometimes produce unanticipated results.

An *exception* is a condition that occurs when the system attempts to do something that it cannot do. For example, if you run the command DLTPGM XMPL700 and the program XMPL700 doesn't exist, an exception is generated. Because error conditions, or exceptions, are usually signaled with messages, understanding exception handling requires at least an elementary grasp of OS/400 message handling. Before reading this chapter, you might want to review chapter 6.

MONITORING FOR EXCEPTIONS

CL programs are informed of unresolvable conflicts by lower level OS/400 components. When a low-level component is unable to perform its task, it signals an exception to its requester. In other words, it sends an escape message to its calling program's message queue. In a CL program, the MONMSG (Monitor Message) command is used to monitor for exceptions.

The MONMSG command may be used at either a program level or a command level. A program level (also called global) MONMSG remains in effect for the duration of the CL program and must be coded immediately after any declarative commands.

A command level MONMSG supersedes a global MONMSG but applies only to the specific command that it follows in the CL program. Command level MONMSG commands may follow any command other than PGM, ENDPGM, DO, ENDDO, IF, ELSE, GOTO, and RETURN.

MONMSG has three parameters: MSGID, CMPDTA, and EXEC. The MSGID parameter is used to specify as many as 50 message IDs. All message IDs begin with three alphanumeric characters, followed by four numbers. (The four numbers can be any hexadecimal digits 0–9 or A–F.)

The messages to monitor can be denoted specifically or generically by using pairs of zeros in the number portion of the MSGID. The easiest way to explain this is by example. Table 7.1 lists several MONMSG examples.

Table 7.1: Receiving All Messages Sequentially.	
MONMSG MSGID(CPF0000)	Monitors for all messages beginning with "CPF".
MONMSG MSGID(CPF3700)	Monitors for messages that begin with "CPF37"; i.e., CPF3700 through CPF37FF.
MONMSG MSGID(CPF3709)	Monitor for message CPF3709 only.

You can use the optional EXEC parameter to run a command if the monitored exception occurs. If you leave EXEC blank, the exception is ignored and processing continues. The EXEC parameter for a global MONMSG must be a GOTO command or must be omitted. Figure 7.1 shows examples.

```
PGM
   MONMSG     MSGID(CPF3709)
   MONMSG     MSGID(CPF0000)  EXEC(GOTO ERROR)

   CRTPF      QTEMP/TEMP      RCDLEN(100)
     MONMSG   MSGID(CPF7302)  EXEC(CLRPFM FILE(TEMP))
```

Figure 7.1: Example of correct use of EXEC.

The MONMSG for CPF3709 causes CPF3709 errors to be ignored globally. The generic MONMSG for CPF0000 causes a branch to the ERROR label globally for all errors other than CPF3709 or any errors monitored by a command level MONMSG. The command level MONMSG for CPF7302 (File &1 not created in library &2) supersedes the global, generic MONMSG. If the file TEMP cannot be created in QTEMP, the CLRPFM (Clear Physical File Member) command runs. Note that if the CLRPFM command fails, the global, generic monitor causes a branch to ERROR.

The optional CMPDTA parameter is seldom used. CMPDTA accepts up to 28 characters of compare data text that may be used to further restrict the messages to be monitored. If a message arrives on the call message queue that matches the MSGID, and CMPDTA is specified, the compare data must exactly match an equal number of characters of the message data for the message to be monitored. Consider example XMPL701 as shown in Figure 7.2.

```
 1.00 /****************************************************/
 2.00 /* Program Name: XMPL701 - MONMSG using CMPDTA      */
 3.00 /****************************************************/
 4.00
 5.00 PGM
 6.00     MONMSG    CPF7306     CMPDTA('KEEP')
 7.00
 8.00     ADDPFM    FILE(WORK)  MBR(WORK01)
 9.00     ADDPFM    FILE(WORK)  MBR(KEEP02)
10.00     ADDPFM    FILE(WORK)  MBR(WORK03)
11.00     ADDPFM    FILE(WORK)  MBR(KEEP04)
12.00
13.00     CALL      PGMA
14.00     CALL      PGMB
15.00
16.00     RMVM      FILE(WORK)  MBR(WORK01)
17.00     RMVM      FILE(WORK)  MBR(WORK03)
18.00
19.00 ENDPGM
```

Figure 7.2: Using MONMSG compare data.

CL program XMPL701 contains a global MONMSG for CPF7306. Running the DSPMSGD (Display Message Description) command, you can see that the first level message text for CPF7306 is as follows:

```
Member &1 not added to &2 in &3.
```

117

It is apparent that &1 is replaced by the member name, which means that the member name is contained in the first 10 characters of message substitution data.

Notice that there are four ADDPFM (Add Physical File Member) commands in the CL program. If the member cannot be added for any reason, the error message CPF7306 is sent. Looking back at the global MONMSG for CPF7306, the 4-byte character string 'KEEP' is specified for the CMPDTA parameter, and the EXEC parameter has been omitted. Consequently, any CPF7306 message for a member whose name begins with 'KEEP' is monitored and ignored. All other CPF7306 errors invoke the default exception/error handler.

Monitoring for Expected Exceptions

Exceptions often can be anticipated. Typically, different approaches are taken for handling expected and unexpected exceptions. Expected exceptions are usually handled with command level MONMSG commands.

Consider an interactive application that uses a temporary data area named APPDATA in the QTEMP library. Before the application menu is displayed, the data area must be created. The CL program XMPL702 in Figure 7.3 creates the data area and runs an application menu using the GO command.

```
 1.00 /******************************************************/
 2.00 /* Program Name: XMPL702 - Setup an application w/ temp DA   */
 3.00 /******************************************************/
 4.00
 5.00 PGM
 6.00
 7.00    CRTDTAARA   QTEMP/APPDATA   TYPE(*CHAR)   LEN(200)
 8.00
 9.00    GO          APPMENU
10.00
11.00 ENDPGM
```

Figure 7.3: Using a temporary object.

The first time it runs, the CL program (shown in Figure 7.3) works absolutely fine. However, if this program has already run before in the same job, the CRTDTAARA command attempts to create an object that already exists.

Expecting that this situation is likely to occur, the CL program can be modified to perform exception handling. The CHKOBJ (Check Object) command tests for (among other things) the existence of an object. The revised version of XMPL702 (shown in Figure 7.4) allows the CRTDTAARA command to run only if the data area doesn't already exist.

```
 1.00 /**************************************************************/
 2.00 /* Program Name: XMPL702 - Setup an application w/ temp DA    */
 3.00 /**************************************************************/
 4.00
 5.00 PGM
 6.00
 6.01    CHKOBJ     QTEMP/APPDATA  OBJTYPE(*DTAARA)
 6.02    MONMSG     MSGID(CPF9801) EXEC(DO)
 7.00               CRTDTAARA  QTEMP/APPDATA  TYPE(*CHAR)  LEN(200)
 8.00               ENDDO
 9.00
10.00    GO         APPMENU
11.00
12.00 ENDPGM:  ENDPGM
```

Figure 7.4: Using a temporary object with CHKOBJ.

Because the APPDATA data area doesn't exist the first time the CL program runs, running CHKOBJ generates exception message CPF9801 (Object &1 in library &2 not found) The MONMSG at line 6.02 monitors for MSGID CPF9801 and consequently runs the CRTDTAARA command specified on the EXEC parameter. Clearly, the non-existence of the APPDATA data area is not an error condition; it is simply a condition of which the CL program must be aware in order to function properly in all cases.

The version of XMPL702 shown in Figure 7.5 is an alternative and more economical way to code this example. Instead of monitoring for the exception that the data area doesn't exist the first time the CL program runs, it always runs the CRTDTAARA command and ignores the exception that it already exists.

```
 1.00 /*************************************************************/
 2.00 /* Program Name: XMPL702 - Setup an application w/ temp DA   */
 3.00 /*************************************************************/
 4.00
 5.00 PGM
 6.00
 7.00   CRTDTAARA  QTEMP/APPDATA  TYPE(*CHAR)  LEN(200)
 7.01     MONMSG   MSGID(CPF1023)
 8.00
 9.00   GO         APPMENU
10.00
11.00 ENDPGM
```

Figure 7.5: Using a temporary object with a local MONMSG.

The CRTDTAARA command is followed by a command level MONMSG for CPF1023 (Data area &1 exists in &2). Because the EXEC parameter is left blank, if the data area already exists, the CL program simply ignores the exception and continues with the next statement. The advantage of this approach is simplicity.

Monitoring for Unexpected Exceptions

Programmers write code to handle expected exceptions, and their programs won't run without it. It is the generic code for the unanticipated exception that often is omitted. Unfortunately, the absence of this code can be very costly. There is a lesson to be learned from a safety program at a steel mill.

During my college years, I worked summers in a "hot roll" mill. Being a particularly hazardous place to work, the company was very safety conscious. Regular safety meetings were held at which "hazard awareness" talks were delivered to employees. One frequently iterated cautionary phrase that has always stuck with me is to "expect the unexpected." I've found that advice especially appropriate as a programmer and application designer. It is wise to presume that, given the right combination of circumstances, every program is capable of failing. People make mistakes!

The IBM OS/400 developers followed this dictum when they developed OS/400 and the language compilers. OS/400 internal code is very carefully written to include its own exception handling logic, and "default exception handlers" have been provided to generically handle user-generated exceptions. A default exception handler is a set of code that runs whenever user-written code results in an otherwise unresolvable conflict.

For example, if the original version of CL program XMPL702 runs, it attempts to create the APPDATA data area without any error handling. If the object already exists, what is the program to do? If OS/400 didn't expect the unexpected by providing some exception handling logic, the CL program would hang. If you use a personal computer, you undoubtedly have experienced this phenomena.

When a low-level component sends an unmonitored escape message to the calling program's message queue, the OS/400 default exception handler provides the safety valve. It responds by sending an inquiry message about the problem to the job's external message queue and offering a choice of several alternative courses of action. For interactive jobs, as long as the default value of *RQD (Required) is accepted for the INQMSGRPY (Inquiry Message Reply) job attribute, the workstation operator is the final recipient of the message.

> **NOTE:** If INQMSGRPY(*DFT) or INQMSGRPY(*SYSRPYL) has been specified on the job description or on a CHGJOB command, a response to the inquiry message may be taken automatically by the system. (I don't recommend this approach for end-user jobs.)

Having a built-in safety valve is far better than letting the program hang! But using the default exception handler is a simplistic solution and, for interactive jobs, the user interface is far from friendly. The exception is described on the Program Messages display in language that even skilled programmers might find difficult to comprehend. And even if it *were* understandable to users, it is not the users' problem. Users are seldom qualified to decide which of the alternative options (C, D, I, or R) to select.

An additional problem for programmers is that many have learned to associate the cryptic Program Messages display with a program "blowing up". A typical user's perception of this experience includes feelings of being interrupted, frustrated, and confused. When unexpected program problems do occur, to protect an Information Services Department's image from damage, it is worthwhile to ensure the user is notified in a pleasant and understandable way that their work is being temporarily interrupted.

The real solution is to write programs that include code designed to expect the unexpected. An approach is required that, like the default exception handler, is generic and easy to implement but, unlike the default exception handler, yields control over the user interface.

In a CL program, you can avoid the OS/400 default exception handler by coding a global, generic MONMSG that causes a branch to an error-handling routine. What that routine should do depends on several factors, such as whether the job is interactive or batch and whether it is an application program or a utility program.

Another major consideration is personal preference; there are nearly as many implementations of CL error handling as there are programmers who have implemented it. No one implementation is necessarily better than any other. Nevertheless, in developing a scheme, you should try to identify some general objectives for a customized exception handler in various environments.

For batch application CL programs, the default exception handler is probably adequate because the recipient of the problematic inquiry messages for batch jobs is the QSYSOPR message queue. In most AS/400 installations, a technical staff person is available who is equipped to handle runtime errors in batch jobs. It is often possible to correct a problem and take the option to retry as long as the exception hasn't been monitored.

The requirements for generic error handling in interactive application CL programs are quite different. If the default exception handler is circumvented, it must be replaced with something else having a friendlier user interface. This chapter doesn't address the specifics of that interface. Rather, it focuses on how to write CL programs that handle exceptions without turning control over to OS/400.

A reasonable and simple approach is to make user menus responsible for the error handling user interface. If menus are implemented as display files in conjunction with CL programs, it is easy to add a generic error-handling routine that implements a sophisticated user interface. That routine could include a call to a special CL program that notifies the operator in a pleasant way that the user's work is being interrupted. The same CL program could log the errors to a database file; that would allow the errors to be easily summarized and analyzed.

If menus are not implemented as CL programs, there is still a convenient, though less sophisticated, interface available with the use of *message subfiles*. A message subfile can be an adequate interface if the message the user sees contains information that is non-threatening and non-incriminating. Message subfiles are convenient to use because all system menus and native-user menus use them to communicate with the user. Even if you write your own CL menus, you can still use message subfiles. Using message subfiles in CL is covered in detail in chapter 9.

If the user interface responsibility is assigned to menus, the requirements for an exception handler in an interactive application are fairly simple. The main requirements are to terminate the CL program and to communicate to its caller that it has aborted. It should also notify the Information Systems Department of the problem, including why the program aborted. One further requirement should be that these tasks are performed by an off-the-shelf program that can be called wherever it is needed. Such a modular approach is much easier to implement and greatly simplifies maintenance.

A GENERIC ERROR-HANDLER

Figure 7.6 illustrates a CL program, ERRORMGR, that is designed to be called from the error-handling routine of any CL application program. You should examine this program carefully.

```
 1.00 /**************************************************************/
 2.00 /* Program Name: ERRORMGR  - Generic Error Handler          */
 3.00 /**************************************************************/
 4.00 PGM
 5.00 DCL     &MSG            *CHAR       512
 6.00 DCL     &MSGID          *CHAR         7
```

Figure 7.6: Source for ERRORMGR program (part 1 of 2) .

```
 7.00 DCL      &MSGKEY        *CHAR      4
 8.00 DCL      &SENDER        *CHAR      720
 9.00 DCL      &PGMNAME       *CHAR      10
10.00 DCL      &USER          *CHAR      10
11.00 DCL      &WRKSTN        *CHAR      10
12.00
13.00 /*==============================================================*/
14.00 GETNAME:      /* Find out what program got the error (my caller) */
15.00   SNDPGMMSG  MSG('Get program name') KEYVAR(&MSGKEY)
16.00   RCVMSG     PGMQ(*PRV) MSGKEY(&MSGKEY) SENDER(&SENDER)
17.00
18.00   CHGVAR     &PGMNAME   VALUE(%SST(&SENDER 56  10))
19.00 /*==============================================================*/
20.00 RCV_ERR:      /* Receive the offending error message */
21.00   RCVMSG     PGMQ(*PRV) MSGTYPE(*EXCP) RMV(*NO) +
22.00                KEYVAR(&MSGKEY) MSG(&MSG) MSGID(&MSGID)
23.00   IF         (&MSGID = CPF9999) GOTO RCV_ERR
24.00
25.00 /*==============================================================*/
26.00 TIME1TEST:    /* Check if Original error or just percolating  */
27.00   IF         (&MSGID = CPF9897 +
28.00   *AND        %SST(&MSG 1 18) = 'We have discovered') +
29.00              GOTO POLITE_MSG
30.00
31.00 /*==============================================================*/
32.00 NOTIFY:       /* Original error, Notify IS & other 1-time actions */
33.00   CHGJOB     LOGCLPGM(*YES) LOG(4 00 *SECLVL)
34.00   RTVJOBA    USER(&USER) JOB(&WRKSTN)
35.00   SNDPGMMSG  MSG('An error occurred in' *BCAT &PGMNAME +
36.00                *BCAT 'for user' *BCAT &USER *BCAT 'at' +
37.00                *BCAT &WRKSTN *CAT '.  The error was:' +
38.00                *BCAT &MSG) TOUSR(QSYSOPR) MSGTYPE(*DIAG)
39.00
40.00   SNDBRKMSG  MSG('An error occurred in' *BCAT &PGMNAME +
41.00                *BCAT 'for user' *BCAT &USER *BCAT 'at' +
42.00                *BCAT &WRKSTN *CAT '.  The error was:' +
43.00                *BCAT &MSG) TOMSGQ(DSP01 HELPDESK)
44.00     MONMSG CPF0000
45.00
46.00 /*==============================================================*/
47.00 POLITE_MSG: /* Percolate a polite error message up the call stack */
48.00   SNDPGMMSG  MSGID(CPF9897) MSGF(QSYS/QCPFMSG) MSGDTA('We +
49.00                have discovered a problem in your +
50.00                application. MIS will contact you.') +
51.00                TOPGMQ(*PRV &PGMNAME) MSGTYPE(*ESCAPE)
52.00     MONMSG CPF0000
53.00
54.00 /*==============================================================*/
55.00 ERROR:
56.00   SNDPGMMSG  MSGID(CPF9897) MSGF(QCPFMSG) MSGDTA('Please +
57.00                notify I.S. immediately! Thank you.') +
58.00                TOPGMQ(*EXT) MSGTYPE(*INFO)
59.00     MONMSG CPF0000
60.00 ENDPGM
```

Figure 7.6: Source for ERRORMGR program (part 2 of 2).

First, notice that there are no global MONMSG commands following the DCL statements. The internal error handling for a generic error-handler requires special consideration. If the CL program could possibly call itself directly, or cause itself to be called indirectly, there would be a high likelihood of an infinite loop that could use an inordinate amount of system resources. This program represents a last-ditch effort to handle an error condition and, consequently, must be thoroughly tested; it must run without fail.

This approach isn't really abandoning the philosophy of "expect the unexpected." It's just that if ERRORMGR does fail, it's time to rely on OS/400's default error-handler. Although it's preferable to avoid the Program Messages display, it is always there when you need it. Once ERRORMGR is tested and debugged, however, it is very unlikely that it will fail.

ERRORMGR employs some interesting and useful techniques. ERRORMGR needs to know the name of the calling program so that later it can send a message to its caller's caller. Statements 14.00 through 18.00 form a routine that determines the name of ERRORMGR's caller by using the *sender data*. Sender data is information about the sender of a message that can be returned to a CL variable using the SENDER parameter of RCVMSG. You can learn more about sender information in chapter 12.

Statements 20.00 to 23.00 receive the exception message that caused the calling program to abort. Return variable parameters are used to receive the values for the message, the message key, and the message identifier. If the message identifier is CPF9999, it represents a function-check message that was caused by the actual error message not being monitored. Consequently, the previous exception message is received. The previous message must be the exception message that caused the function check. Because of the way this scheme gets implemented in the application CL programs, ERRORMGR always receives a CPF9999 message first (before receiving the actual error message). The role of the function-check message is further discussed later in this chapter.

Before examining the code from line 26.00 to line 44.00, it is important to understand the ultimate function of ERRORMGR. At line 48.00, ERRORMGR sends a "polite" escape message to its caller's caller—that is, to the caller of the program that failed. If that program is a CL menu, the error must be handled by the menu's error-handling routine. If it is a native user menu, the message will appear in the message subfile. If it is another application CL program, the message is percolated up the call stack and will eventually be sent to a menu or command-line program. If it is another HLL application program, the HLL program is responsible for handling the exception. To be consistent with the approach recommended here, all HLL application programs also should percolate the message up the call stack. Actually, other HLL programs could call ERRORMGR to perform that function.

There are two very important points to remember here. First, when an escape message is sent to a call message queue, the call stack below the target program is collapsed. In other words, all programs on the stack below the program to which the escape message is sent are immediately terminated. Therefore, ERRORMGR and the program that called it terminate when the escape message is sent. Therefore, it's not necessary to code a RETURN command at this point. And, control never returns to the calling program—it passes to the caller of the calling program.

Second, when the escape message arrives on the message queue of the target program (the failing program's caller), it causes an exception. If the target program is another CL program and the applications are consistently coded, the error handling routine in that CL program is invoked, and ERRORMGR is called again. Therefore, if CL programs are nested and the program at the lowest invocation fails, all programs in the stack fail one at a time until a menu finally traps the error and handles it.

ERRORMGR actually will be called by each of the failing CL programs. The Information Systems Department, however, needs to be notified of the error only once. Consequently, ERRORMGR must be able to distinguish between the original error and an error that has been percolated up the call stack. The easiest way to make that distinction is to determine the content of the message. The original error message is always sent by an IBM program or a user program. The subsequent escape messages percolated up the stack by ERRORMGR have a message identifier of CPF9897 and message text of "We have discovered a problem in your application. MIS will contact you." Understanding this concept is crucial to the discussion of this section of code.

At lines 26.00 to 29.00, ERRORMGR examines the message identifier and message text of the exception message to determine if it is the original error message or the more "polite" escape message sent by ERRORMGR. If it is the polite escape message, ERRORMGR has been called before by a CL program that had been lower on the stack. In this case, the GOTO at line 29.00 branches around the one-time "NOTIFY" code and the exception message is simply percolated or re-sent up the stack.

If it isn't the polite escape message, this invocation of ERRORMGR has received the exception message that caused the original failure. Therefore, statements 32.00 through 44.00 are performed. The CHGJOB at statement 33.00 facilitates problem diagnosis by maximizing the logging that is done.

The RTVJOBA (Retrieve Job Attributes) command is used to retrieve attributes of the current job into CL variables. After retrieving the current user profile and workstation name, messages are sent to non-program message queues that include that information as well as the text of the error message. For this example, ERRORMGR is coded to send break messages to workstations DSP01 and HELPDESK, and to send a diagnostic message to QSYSOPR. To implement this CL program, you will need to determine the best message queues to which to send these notifications.

Finally, at line 48.00, the polite escape message that eventually gets forwarded to a menu and appears in the message subfile is sent to the calling program's caller. As you will recall, the call stack below the target program of the escape message is collapsed, control is passed to the caller of the failing CL program, and the error-handling routine in that CL program is invoked. It is a good idea to customize the exact wording of the polite escape message.

The Standard Error Routine

To see how this scheme is implemented in each application CL program, refer to CL program XMPL703 (shown in Figure 7.7), a modified version of XMPL702.

In CL program XMPL703, a global MONMSG for CPF9999 causes an immediate branch to the error routine on any unmonitored exception. Note that the command-level MONMSG is kept after the CRTDTAARA command. Bear in mind that the global MONMSG handles unexpected errors. This command-level MONMSG allows the CL program to ignore the expected exception that would occur if the data area has already been created.

```
 1.00 /***********************************************************/
 2.00 /* Program Name: XMPL703 - Setup an application w/ temp DA   */
 3.00 /***********************************************************/
 4.00
 5.00 PGM
 5.01    MONMSG      CPF9999  EXEC(GOTO ERR_RTN)
 6.00
 7.00    CRTDTAARA   QTEMP/APPDATA   TYPE(*CHAR)   LEN(200)
 7.01       MONMSG   MSGID(CPF1023)
 8.00
 9.00    GO          APPMENU /* Display the menu */
 9.01    RETURN
 9.02 /*=======================================================*/
 9.03 ERR_RTN:
 9.04    DMPCLPGM
 9.05    CALL        ERRORMGR
 9.06    MONMSG      MSGID(CPF0001)  /* <- Very IMPORTANT!! */
10.00
11.00 ENDPGM
```

Figure 7.7: Using a standard error routine.

The RETURN command prevents control from falling through to the error routine at the end of normal processing. The error routine itself is simply a DMPCLPGM (Dump CL Program) command followed by a call to ERRORMGR.

The use of the DMPCLPGM in the error routine is optional but may provide valuable diagnostic information. DMPCLPGM causes a CL program dump listing to be produced that lists all messages in the call message queue and the values of all CL variables at the time of the dump. A more sophisticated implementation could allow the dump only in the CL program in which the original error occurred.

The command-level MONMSG command, following the call to ERRORMGR, is very important because the global MONMSG at line 5.01 will branch to ERR_RTN when an error occurs. If, for any reason, the CALL to ERRORMGR fails, the command-level MONMSG at line 9.06 overrides the global MONMSG. If this statement is omitted, and an error occurs, the program will loop indefinitely.

> **The Role of the Function Check:** Many programmers are accustomed to using CPF0000 on a global monitor. You could monitor for the generic CPF0000, but there are advantages to using CPF9999. If an exception message arrives on the call message queue and is not monitored, the function check message, CPF9999, is sent. This message contains the statement number of the failing statement, which is very useful information to have when diagnosing a problem. More important, there are error messages other than CPFxxxx messages that can cause a CL program to terminate (MCHxxxx, CEExxxx, etc.). By allowing the function check to occur, the problematic code is easier to locate, and you never have to worry about additional error message groups.

ERROR HANDLING IN UTILITY CL PROGRAMS

The requirements for generic error handling in interactive utility CL programs are quite different than those for application CL programs. Although it is still beneficial to circumvent the default exception handler for utility CL programs, an extremely friendly interface isn't really necessary. After all, if the utility is called directly from a command line or command entry screen, it can be presumed that the caller of the CL program is a technical user.

On the other hand, if the utility is invoked by an application CL program, it is only necessary that the application be informed that the utility failed by way of an escape message. The standard application error-handler, ERRORMGR, can deal with that exception in the same manner as an error generated by a system function.

What is really needed for utility CL programs is a standard routine for forwarding important messages to the program's caller, which could be either a command-entry interface or another program. While exactly what messages are deemed "important" is a matter of personal opinion, the importance of exception messages that cause a CL program to terminate is probably not open to debate. As for other types of messages, however, a reasonable approach might be to consider the last completion or informational message in the call message queue to be important.

Like an application error-handling function, a generic utility message-forwarding function should be implemented as an off-the-shelf, modular CL program that can be called wherever it is needed. In the event of an exception, it should terminate the failing CL program and communicate to its caller that it has aborted by forwarding a duplicate of the crucial error message. Otherwise, it should forward a duplicate of the last completion or informational message.

A Generic Message-Forwarder

As shown in Figure 7.8, FWDMSG is just such a CL program. In many respects, FWDMSG is similar to ERRORMGR. For instance, the code to determine the calling program's name is identical and the code to receive the last exception message (lines 49.00 – 5300) is very similar.

```
 1.00 /**********************************************************************/
 2.00 /* Program Name: FWDMSG  - Generic Message Forwarder                 */
 2.10 /**********************************************************************/
 3.00 PGM          PARM(&EXCEPTION)
 4.00 DCL          &EXCEPTION   *LGL
 5.00 DCL          &MSG         *CHAR   512
 6.00 DCL          &MSGID       *CHAR     7
 7.00 DCL          &MSGDTA      *CHAR   128
 8.00 DCL          &MSGF        *CHAR    10
 9.00 DCL          &MSGFLIB     *CHAR    10
10.00 DCL          &MSGKEY      *CHAR     4
11.00 DCL          &RTNTYPE     *CHAR     2
12.00 DCL          &COMP        *CHAR     2    VALUE('01')
13.00 DCL          &INFO        *CHAR     2    VALUE('04')
14.00 DCL          &MSGTYPE     *CHAR     5
15.00 DCL          &PGMNAME     *CHAR    10
16.00 DCL          &SENDER      *CHAR    80
17.00 MONMSG       MSGID(CPF0000)
18.00 /*========================================================*/
20.00 GETNAME:
21.00   SNDPGMMSG  MSG('Get program name') KEYVAR(&MSGKEY)
22.00   RCVMSG     PGMQ(*PRV) MSGKEY(&MSGKEY) SENDER(&SENDER)
23.00   CHGVAR     VAR(&PGMNAME) VALUE(%SST(&SENDER 56 10))
23.10 /*========================================================*/
25.00 FORWARD:
```

Figure 7.8: General-purpose, message-forwarding program (part 1 of 2).

```
26.00    IF        &EXCEPTION GOTO FWD_EXCP
26.10 /*======================================================================*/
28.00 RCVLAST:     /* Not an exception - Forward the last completion */
29.00    RCVMSG    PGMQ(*PRV) MSGTYPE(*LAST) RMV(*NO) +
30.00                KEYVAR(&MSGKEY) MSGDTA(&MSGDTA) +
31.00                MSGID(&MSGID) RTNTYPE(&RTNTYPE) +
32.00                MSGF(&MSGF) SNDMSGFLIB(&MSGFLIB)
33.00
34.00 IF           (&RTNTYPE = &COMP *OR &RTNTYPE = &INFO) DO
35.00              /* Forward the comp or info message */
36.00       IF     (&RTNTYPE = &COMP)    CHGVAR &MSGTYPE '*COMP'
37.00       ELSE   CHGVAR &MSGTYPE '*INFO'
39.00       IF     (&MSGID = ' ') +
40.00              SNDPGMMSG  MSG(&MSG) MSGTYPE(&MSGTYPE) +
41.00                TOPGMQ(*PRV &PGMNAME)
42.00       ELSE   SNDPGMMSG  MSGID(&MSGID) +
43.00                MSGF(&MSGFLIB/&MSGF) MSGDTA(&MSGDTA) +
44.00                MSGTYPE(&MSGTYPE) TOPGMQ(*PRV &PGMNAME)
45.00       ENDDO     /* Fwd the comp or info message */
46.00
47.00 RETURN
48.00
48.10/*======================================================================*/
49.00 FWD_EXCP:
50.00    RCVMSG    PGMQ(*PRV) MSGTYPE(*EXCP) RMV(*NO) +
51.00                KEYVAR(&MSGKEY) MSGDTA(&MSGDTA) +
52.00                MSGID(&MSGID) MSGF(&MSGF) SNDMSGFLIB(&MSGFLIB)
53.00    IF        (&MSGID = CPF9999) GOTO FWD_EXCP
54.00
55.00    SNDPGMMSG  MSGID(&MSGID) MSGF(&MSGFLIB/&MSGF) +
56.00                MSGDTA(&MSGDTA) TOPGMQ(*PRV &PGMNAME) MSGTYPE(*EXCAPE)
57.00 ENDPGM
```

Figure 7.8: General-purpose, message-forwarding program (part 2 of 2).

There are, however, some significant differences. FWDMSG receives a single, logical parameter, &EXCEPTION, the value of which determines whether FWDMSG forwards an escape message or the last completion or informational message to its caller's caller.

If the value of &EXCEPTION is true (line 26.00), the program branches to a routine to forward an exception message. Unlike ERRORMGR, FWDMSG uses the return variables on the RCVMSG command to send an escape message up the stack that is virtually identical to the message that caused the error.

If &EXCEPTION is false, the last message on the caller's call message queue is received (lines 28.00 – 32.00). If it is either a completion or an informational message, the return variables on the RCVMSG command are used to send an identical message up the call stack.

If the message being forwarded were originally sent by a system program, it would always be a predefined message. If it were sent by a user-written utility, it could be either a predefined or an immediate message. The code at statements 39.00 to 45.00 determines whether the message is predefined or immediate by interrogating the &MSGID variable and forwards the message appropriately. As shown in Figure 7.9, the CL program named CLROQ illustrates how FWDMSG is implemented.

```
 1.00 /****************************************************************/
 2.00 /* Program Name: CLROQ    - Submit a CLROUTQ to batch        */
 3.00 /****************************************************************/
 4.00 PGM   PARM(&OUTQ)
 5.00   DCL       VAR(&OUTQ) TYPE(*CHAR) LEN(10)
 6.00   MONMSG     CPF9999 EXEC(GOTO ERR_RTN)
 7.00
 8.00   IF        (&OUTQ *EQ '/') RTVJOBA OUTQ(&OUTQ)
 9.00   CHKOBJ    OBJ(&OUTQ) OBJTYPE(*OUTQ) AUT(*DLT)
10.00
11.00   SBMJOB    CMD(CLROUTQ OUTQ(&OUTQ)) +
12.00               JOB('CLR' *CAT %SST(&OUTQ 1 7) JOBD(PGMR)
13.00
14.00   CALL      PGM(FWDMSG) PARM('0')
14.00   RETURN
15.00
16.00 /******************************************/
17.00 ERR_RTN:
18.00   CALL      PGM(FWDMSG) PARM('1')
19.00     MONMSG MSGID(CPF0000)
20.00 ENDPGM
```

Figure 7.9: Using a message forwarding routine.

The CL program CLROQ receives one parameter, &OUTQ, and submits a batch job that clears the output queue specified as the parameter. Validation of the output queue to clear is accomplished with the CHKOBJ command. A function check for any unmonitored exception is trapped by the global MONMSG and causes a branch to the error routine.

The error routine simply calls FWDMSG passing a literal '1' (or true). The true flag indicates to FWDMSG that this CL program is failing and, therefore, to forward an exception message. If CLROQ runs successfully after submitting the batch job, it calls FWDMSG, passing a literal '0' (or false). The false flag indicates to FWDMSG that the last completion or informational message should be forwarded. The completion message generated by the SBMJOB command is forwarded to CLROQ's caller.

Figure 7.10 illustrates how the messages forwarded by FWDMSG are displayed. The CL program CLROQ is called, and the completion, diagnostic and exception messages for the program are displayed on the Command Entry display. The program CLROQ has been called twice—once with an invalid output queue and again after having been corrected. You can see that one of the benefits of a generic message-forwarding module is that it allows the message handling of utility CL programs to emulate that of system commands.

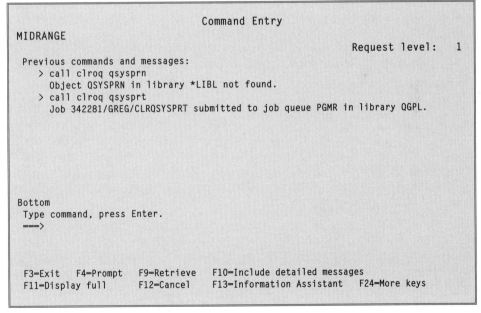

```
                            Command Entry
MIDRANGE
                                              Request level:    1
   Previous commands and messages:
     > call clroq qysprn
       Object QSYSPRN in library *LIBL not found.
     > call clroq qysprt
       Job 342281/GREG/CLRQSYSPRT submitted to job queue PGMR in library QGPL.




 Bottom
 Type command, press Enter.
 ===>



 F3=Exit  F4=Prompt   F9=Retrieve   F10=Include detailed messages
 F11=Display full     F12=Cancel    F13=Information Assistant   F24=More keys
```

Figure 7.10: Messages forwarded by FWDMSG.

The FWDMSG CL program is just one arbitrarily designed implementation of a generic message-forwarding module. Although it is important that you understand the principles that are applied here, you might reasonably employ a different philosophy for forwarding non-exception messages. For instance, you might want to pass additional parameters to your version of this program so that it can work in any of several different ways. With creative use of parameters, it is even possible to combine ERRORMGR and FWDMSG into a single, multi-purpose message-forwarding module.

REVIEW QUESTIONS

1. *There are two reasons for including error-handling logic in CL programs: to handle _____ exceptions, and to handle _____ or errors.*

2. *_____ MONMSGS best handle unexpected errors. _____ _____ MONMSGS best handle expected exceptions.*

3. *In a CL program, the OS/400 _____ _____ _____ can be avoided by coding a global, generic MONMSG that causes a branch to an error-handling routine.*

4. *A _____ _____-_____ allows the message handling of utility CL programs to emulate that of system commands.*

8

SUPPORTING
USER APPLICATIONS

CL programs that support applications vary from simple batch-job streams to complex programs that modify a job's work environment, create temporary objects, override files, and perform advanced message-handling functions. This chapter provides many examples of CL programs that support both batch and interactive applications.

BATCH APPLICATION CL SUPPORT

A compiled CL program offers flexibility, function, and good performance for controlling the steps of a batch job. The typical function of a batch CL program is to sequentially call HLL programs that update database files or run reports.

In an effort to be relevant to the "real world" of application programming, components of a hypothetical A/R (Accounts Receivable) application are used as examples of the functions performed by batch CL programs. As shown in Figure 8.1, ARJ801CL is an example of a simple CL program used as a batch-job stream that runs three HLL programs in sequence.

```
 1.00  /*********************************************************/
 2.00  /* ARJ801CL: Batch job stream for A/R Aging & Statements    */
 3.00  /*********************************************************/
 4.00
 5.00  PGM
 6.00
 7.00     CALL      ARU811RG  /* Apply cash         */
 8.00
 9.00     CALL      ARR812RG  /* A/R Aging Report */
10.00
11.00     CALL      ARR813RG  /* A/R Statements    */
12.00
13.00  ENDPGM
```

Figure 8.1: Batch job stream.

In Figure 8.1, the programs called by ARJ801CL apply cash receipts to an open A/R file and produce an aging report and statements. Often, among the calls to other programs, CL commands are included that directly manipulate the database. For instance, files may be copied, sorted, or cleared using CL commands. As shown in Figure 8.2, CL program ARJ802CL is a more realistic facsimile of an actual production job stream.

```
   1.00  /*********************************************************/
   2.00  /* ARJ802CL: Batch job stream for A/R Aging & Statements    */
   3.00  /*********************************************************/
   4.00
   5.00  PGM
   6.00
>  6.01     CLRPFM    ARAGIN00
>  6.02     CPYF      AROPEN00  TOFILE(ARBACK00)  MBROPT(*REPLACE)
   6.03
   7.00     CALL      ARU811RG  /* Apply cash         */
   8.00
   9.00     CALL      ARR812RG  /* A/R Aging Report */
  10.00
>10.01     FMTDTA    INFILE(AROPEN00)  OUTFILE(ARWORK00) +
  10.02                 SRCFILE(QFMTSRC) SRCMBR(ARSTMTS1) OPTION(*NOPRT)
  11.00     CALL      ARR813RG  /* A/R Statements    */
  12.00
  13.00  ENDPGM
```

Figure 8.2: Batch job stream with CPYF and FMTDTA.

The CLRPFM (Clear Physical File Member) command at line 6.01 removes all re-cords from the first member of the physical file ARAGIN00. CLRPFM has only two parameters, FILE and MBR (Member). When the file has only one member, it is normal to omit the MBR parameter and, thereby, accept the default of *FIRST. The file is cleared at the beginning of the CL program so that all new data can be written to it by the program ARU811RG.

When possible, housekeeping for work files should be done at the beginning of the CL program. If work files are not cleared at the beginning of a job stream and an unexpected problem causes the job to terminate early, confusion could be cre-ated by the existing data in the work files.

Copying Files

The CPYF (Copy File) command at line 6.02 copies all records from the first member of the file AROPEN00 to the first member in the file ARBACK00. The CPYF command has a number of parameters that control how data is copied. The most commonly used parameters are FROMFILE, TOFILE, FROMMBR (From Member), TOMBR (To Member), and MBROPT (Member Option: Replace or Add Records). The FROMMBR and TOMBR parameters both default to *FIRST, which suggests that AROPEN00 and ARBACK00 are single member files.

When the TOFILE parameter contains the name of a database physical file, the MBROPT parameter must be specified as either *ADD or *REPLACE. The MBROPT(*ADD) parameter causes the copied records to be added to the existing records in the to-file member. The MBROPT(*REPLACE) parameter clears the to-file member before copying the records. In the example, the CPYF command is used to backup the AROPEN00 file before the file is updated in the HLL applica-tion programs. For more information about the CPYF command, see the subhead-ing More about Copy File.

Sorting Files

The HLL program ARR813RG that produces the A/R statements in the example must process the records in the AROPEN00 file in a sequence in which they are not normally stored. The FMTDTA (Format Data) command at line 10.01 (Figure 8.2) sorts the records in the AROPEN00 file (INFILE parameter) and places the resulting records in the ARWORK00 file (OUTFILE parameter) for use by ARR813RG.

"Sort/Reformat specification" statements, which are stored in source members and processed by the FMTDTA command, determine the sequence of the sorted records and other characteristics of the sort process. The source physical file and source member containing the specifications for the sort are specified on the SRCFILE (Source File) and SRCMBR (Source Member) parameters, respectively. The *NOPRT option indicates that a report of the specification statements and resulting messages is not to be produced.

The FMTDTA command is not used often in modern AS/400 applications. Alternatives such as logical files and the OPNQRYF (Open Query File) command have replaced most sorts. FMTDTA seems to appear most often in applications that have been migrated from systems that don't support the AS/400 alternatives.

This is not to say, however, that there is anything intrinsically wrong with sorting. There are many cases in which the most efficient solution includes sorting records using the FMTDTA command. Sorting might be indicated when:

- The files to be re-ordered are very large (over 25,000 records).
- Re-ordered records are used only in batch programs.
- Several programs will process the re-ordered records.
- The records are processed in consecutive, physical order.

The choice of any method of ordering records should be validated with benchmarks.

File Overrides

Override-file commands are used to override the name or the attributes of a file referenced in a program. The override-file commands are:

- OVRDBF (Override with Database File).
- OVRDKTF (Override with Diskette File).
- OVRDSPF (Override with Display File).
- OVRICFF (Override ICF File).

- OVRPRTF (Override with Printer File).
- OVRTAPF (Override with Tape File).
- OVRSAVF (Override with Save File).
- OVRMSGF (Override with Message File).

The override applies to files that are opened after the Override-File command is issued. In the OPM environment, the override remains in effect until the:

1. Override is changed with another override command.
2. Override is deleted with a DLTOVR (Delete Override) command.
3. Program that issued the override ends.

An exception to the third item is when OVRSCOPE(*JOB) is specified. In this case, the override remains in effect for the duration of the job. The effect of overrides in ILE is discussed in chapter 13.

Batch CL programs commonly override printer files to alter such attributes as the number of copies or the form type, or to redirect the output to a specific printer. In Figure 8.3, the CL program ARJ803CL uses the OVRPRTF command.

```
   1.00  /****************************************************************/
   2.00  /* ARJ803CL: Batch job stream for A/R Aging & Statements    */
   3.00  /****************************************************************/
   4.00
   5.00  PGM
   6.00
 > 6.01    OVRPRTF    FILE(*PRTF)    USRDTA('Mnthly A/R')
 > 6.02    OVRPRTF    FILE(ARR812PR) COPIES(3)
   6.03    CLRPFM     ARAGIN00
   6.04    CPYF       AROPEN00  ARBACK00  MBROPT(*REPLACE)
   6.05
   7.00    CALL       ARU811RG /* Apply cash       */
   8.00
   9.00    CALL       ARR812RG /* A/R Aging Report */
  10.00
  10.01    FMTDTA     INFILE(AROPEN00)  OUTFILE(ARWORK00) +
  10.02               SRCMBR(ARSTMTS1)  OPTION(*NOPRT)
  11.00    CALL       ARR813RG /* A/R Statements   */
  12.00
  13.00  ENDPGM
```

Figure 8.3: Batch job stream with print file overrides.

```
 1.00 /*************************************************************/
 2.00 /* ARJ804CL: Batch job stream for A/R Aging & Statements    */
 3.00 /*************************************************************/
 4.00
 5.00 PGM
 6.00
 6.01    OVRPRTF    FILE(*PRTF)    USRDTA('Mnthly A/R')
 6.02    OVRPRTF    FILE(ARR812PR)  COPIES(3)
> 6.03   OVRDBF     ARWORK00  MBR(STATEMENTS)
> 6.04   ADDPFM     ARWORK00  MBR(STATEMENTS)
 6.05    CLRPFM     ARAGIN00
 6.06    CPYF       AROPEN00  ARBACK00  MBROPT(*REPLACE)
 6.07
 7.00    CALL       ARU811RG  /* Apply cash       */
 8.00
 9.00    CALL       ARR812RG  /* A/R Aging Report */
10.00
10.01    FMTDTA     INFILE(AROPEN00)  OUTFILE(ARWORK00) +
10.02               SRCMBR(ARSTMTS1)  OPTION(*NOPRT)
11.00    CALL       ARR813RG  /* A/R Statements   */
12.00
>12.01   RMVM       ARWORK00  MBR(STATEMENTS)
13.00 ENDPGM
```

Figure 8.4: Batch job stream with database file overrides.

In Figure 8.3, the OVRPRTF command at line 6.01 is used to place identifying text in the *user data field* of the overridden file. (User data is up to 10 characters of user-specified text that identifies the report on the output queue.) Specifying *PRTF for the FILE parameter indicates that the override applies to all printer files.

The OVRPRTF at line 6.02 (Figure 8.3) alters the number-of-copies attribute of ARR812PR, the aging report. The aged trial balance program, ARR812RG, can be called by other CL job-stream programs, and the number of copies required can be different depending on which job stream is run.

Both batch and interactive-application support CL programs may be used to override database files so that files other than those described in the program can be opened. As shown in Figure 8.4, the CL program ARJ804CL uses the OVRDBF command.

The OVRDBF command at line 6.03 (Figure 8.4) overrides the MBR (Member) parameter of the file ARWORK00 and causes subsequent references to ARWORK00 to open the data member named STATEMENTS. The override affects references to the file in all application programs and on some system commands. Table 8.1 lists the commands that ignore overrides.

Table 8.1: Commands That Ignore Overrides.

Command Name	Command Name
ADDLFM Add Logical File Member	DLTAUTLR Delete Authority Holder
ADDPFM Add Physical File Member	DSPDBR Display Database Relations
ALCOBJ AllocateObject	DSPFD Display File Description
APYJRNCHG Apply Journal Change	DSPFFD Display File Field Descriptions
CHGOBJOWN Change Object Owner	EDTDOCAUT Edit DLO Authority
CHGPTR Change Pointer	DSPJRN Display Journal
CHGSBSD Change Subsystem Description	EDTOBJAUT Edit Object Authority
CHGDDMF Change DDM File	ENDJRNPF End Journaling Physical File
CHGDKTF Change DisketteFile	GRTOBJAUT Grant Object Authority
CHGDSPF Change Display File	INZPFM Initialize Physical File Member
CHGICFF Change ICF File	MOVOBJ Move Object
CHGLF Change Logical File	RGZPFM Reorganize Physical File Member
CHGPF Change Physical File	RMVJRNCHG Remove Journal Changes
CHGPRTF Change Printer File	RMVM Remove Member
CHGSAVF Change Save File	RNMOBJ Rename Object
CHGSRCPF Change Source Physical File	RSTUSRPRF Restore User Profile
CHGTAPF Change Tape File	RVKOBJAUT Revoke Object Authority
CLRPFM Clear Physical File Member	SAVCHGOBJ Save Changed Object
CLRSAVF Clear Save File	SAVLIB Save Library
CPYIGCTBL Copy DBCS Font Table	SAVOBJ Save Object
CRTDKTF Create Diskette File	SAVPGMPRD Save Program Product
CRTDUPOBJ Create Duplicate Object	SAVSAVFDTA Save Savefile Data
CRTAUTLR Create Authority Holder	SAVSYS Save System
CRTSBSD Create Subsystem Description	SBMDBJOB Submit Database Jobs
CRTTAPF Create Tape File	SIGNOFF Sign Off
DLCOBJ De-allocate Object	STRDBRDR Start Database Reader
DLTF Delete File	STRJRNPF Start Journaling Physical File

All CRTxxxxxx commands that support SRCFILE and SRCMBR parameters apply overrides to those two parameters only.

The OPNQRYF (Open Query File) command allows overrides to the TOFILE, MBR, SEQONLY, LVLCHK, and INHWRT parameters only.

The FMTDTA command is affected by the file override and so is the program ARR813RG. Because ARWORK00 is named as the output file for the sort, the sorted records are placed in a member of ARWORK00 named STATEMENTS. The same member is opened later by ARR813RG.

In Figure 8.4, neither the ADDPFM (Add Physical File Member) command at line 6.04 nor the RMVM (Remove Member) command at line 12.01 is affected by the file override. The ADDPFM parameter is used to add a data member to a physical file. In the hypothetical application, the ARWORK00 file has several members, each of which is a sorted version of AROPEN00. RMVM removes a data member from a file.

In program ARJ804CL, a member named STATEMENTS is added; it is used as the output file for a sort, used as an input file to the statements program, ARR813RG, and then it is removed. It is best to locate ADDPFM commands near the beginning of the CL program with other housekeeping functions. Contemplating the possible effects of an unexpected problem serves to point out the value of this placement of the ADDPFM command.

If ARJ804CL were to terminate abnormally due to a power failure or other unforeseen event, the STATEMENTS member of ARWORK00 would not be removed. If the CL program were subsequently rerun without anyone being aware that it had not completed successfully, the ADDPFM would generate the error that the member already exists, alerting an operations department to the problem. Allowing the default exception handler to notify the system operator of the error and offer options to cancel the job, ignore the error, or retry the failing command is usually adequate. This type of exception is typically not anticipated, and it is likely that the assistance of technical staff would be required to resolve the problem.

If non-technical users must be informed of the problem and be relied upon to resolve it, more sophisticated error-handling techniques should be implemented in the CL program ARJ804CL. In either case, if the ADDPFM command is situated at the beginning of the CL program, the problem can be addressed before application programs have the opportunity to update files.

More about Copy File

The CPYF command is a very powerful and flexible command used to copy all or part of a file to another file. The file being copied can be a database physical or logical file, a Distributed Data Management (DDM) file, an in-line file, or a diskette or tape-device file. The target of the copy can be a database physical file, or a diskette, tape, printer, or DDM file.

CPYF can copy a single member, several members with a common generic name, or all members of a database file. CPYF can add records to or completely replace an existing data member. A new file can be created with the same format as the from-file by specifying *YES for the CRTFILE (Create File) parameter when the to-file doesn't already exist.

The CPYF command supports several methods of copying a subset of the file's records. The RCDFMT (Record Format) parameter allows a single record format of a multi-format logical file to be copied. A range of records can be copied in physical order using the FROMRCD (From Record) and TORCD (To Record) parameters. The NBRRCDS (Number of Records) parameter can be used to specify a maximum number of records to copy. The FROMKEY (From Key) and TOKEY (To Key) parameters can be used to copy records within a range of key values.

Using the INCCHAR (Include Characters) parameter, the CPYF command can copy records based on a comparison of a specified *string* to a specific position in a record or field, or a string contained anywhere in the record. The INCREL (Include Relationships) parameter can specify a logical expression used to select records based on the contents of specified fields.

Using the FMTOPT (Format Option) parameter, the CPYF command can be used to map like-named fields when the field attributes or relative locations in the record are different. The FMTOPT parameter also can be used to drop fields that exist in the from-file, but not in the to-file. These capabilities can be very useful for mapping data into a new version of a file in which one or more fields have been moved or eliminated or field sizes have been changed. Also, the FMTOPT parameter of the CPYF command can be used to convert standard database physical files to source physical files and source files to data files. The SRCOPT (Source

Option) parameter can specify that new sequence numbers and zero dates be inserted into copied source-file records.

Important Points to Remember When Copying Files

- Keyed files are copied in key order unless FROMRCD or TORCD is specified.

- Logical files don't actually contain data. When copying from a logical file, the data is copied from the based-on physical file member(s). Only fields selected in the logical file record format are copied.

- Copying a range of records by key (FROMKEY/TOKEY) can be significantly faster than copying the same set of records using INCCHAR or INCREL to do the record selection.

- When selecting a range of keys (FROMKEY/TOKEY) where one or more keyfields are numeric, specify *BLDKEY (Build the Key) for the "Number of key fields" element of the FROMKEY and TOKEY parameters. The number of keys is calculated automatically from the number of compare values specified. Also, the compare values are converted to the data type defined in the file.

To illustrate the last point, consider a file named BIRTHDAY that contains employee records keyed by century, year, month, and day of birth. Each of the four keyfields is defined with length 2,0. The following CPYF command prints a list of all employees who were born in the 1940s:

```
CPYF  FROMFILE(BIRTHDAY) TOFILE(*PRINT) +
        FROMKEY(*BLDKEY (19 40)) TOKEY(*BLDKEY (19 49))
```

The special value *BLDKEY is specified instead of the number of keyfields. Because two key values are specified in the list, only the first two key fields in the file, century and year, are used to determine the key range.

INTERACTIVE APPLICATION CL SUPPORT

A compiled program offers a high degree of flexibility and function for supporting interactive applications. Unlike CL programs that are submitted to batch subsystems, interactive CL programs seldom call other application programs in a specific sequence. More often, interactive CL programs prepare the work environment for a HLL application program or programs.

Pre-Opening Database Files

A common function of interactive application support CL programs is to pre-open database files so that the performance impact of HLL file opens is reduced. Pre-opening files is recommended in applications that are modular. Modular applications are broken down into many small programs (modules), each performing a single task. Repeatedly opening the same files in different modules creates substantial overhead. The drain on system resources caused by file opens can be reduced by opening commonly used files in a CL program prior to running specific application programs. As shown in Figure 8.5, CL program ARI851CL pre-opens the major A/R files and runs the A/R menu.

```
 1.00 /*********************************************************/
 2.00 /* ARI851CL:                                           */
 3.00 /*********************************************************/
 4.00
 5.00 PGM
 6.00
 7.00    OVRDBF    ARINVC00   SHARE(*YES)
 8.00    OVRDBF    ARSHIP00   SHARE(*YES)
 9.00    OVRDBF    ARCUST00   SHARE(*YES)
10.00
11.00    OPNDBF    ARINVC00   OPTION(*ALL)
12.00    OPNDBF    ARSHIP00   OPTION(*ALL)
13.00    OPNDBF    ARCUST00   OPTION(*ALL)
14.00
15.00    GO        ARMENU
16.00
17.00 ENDPGM
```

Figure 8.5: Pre-opening files.

The SHARE(*YES) option on the OVRDBF commands in the previous example (Figure 8.5) guarantees that the opened member uses a shared open-data path. The OPNDBF command opens a member of the file named on the FILE parameter (specified positionally in the example). The file specified must be a physical or logical database file or a Distributed Data Management (DDM) file. The specified number may be a join logical-file member.

The OPTION parameter specifies for which file I/O operations the specified file is opened: input, output, update, delete, or all (*INP, *OUT, *UPD, *DLT, *ALL). You can enter multiple values for this parameter. The specified option(s) must include all ways that the file can be opened in subsequent application programs. If no value is specified, the default is *INP. The OPNDBF command is discussed in more detail in chapter 11.

More about the OVRDBF Command

The OVRDBF command is an extremely powerful command that overrides the file or attributes of a file named in a HLL program. It applies to physical files, logical files, and DDM files and is used extensively in CL programming.

If the TOFILE (Overriding to Database File) parameter is used, it specifies the name of the database file that is used instead of the file specified on the FILE parameter.

If the file being overridden is a multiple member file, the MBR parameter allows a specific member of a file to be opened. In addition to a specific member name, the MBR parameter can be specified as:

- *FIRST (the first member of a database file is used).
- *LAST (the last member of a database file is used).
- *ALL (all members in the file are processed in order).

Parameters that are overridden by the OVRDBF command can be those specified in the file description, as well as others that control how the file is opened by an HLL.

Overriding File Description Parameters

The file description parameters that can be overridden are LVLCHK, WAITFILE, WAITRCD, FMTSLR, FRCRATIO, and SHARE.

The LVLCHK (Record Format Level Check) parameter allows normal record-format level checking to be ignored. When a file is opened, the system compares the record-format identifiers of each record format used by the program with the corresponding identifiers in the database member. The LVLCHK parameter specifies whether the level identifiers for the record formats of the database file are checked when the file is opened by the program. Although a file that was created with LVLCHK(*YES) can be overridden to LVLCHK(*NO), a file that was created with LVLCHK(*NO) cannot be overridden to LVLCHK(*YES).

The WAITFILE (Maximum File Wait Time) parameter specifies the number of seconds that the program waits for the allocation of the file resources when the file is opened. The WAITRCD (Maximum Record Wait Time) parameter specifies the number of seconds that the program waits for a record lock to be released when a file opened for update is read. If the record lock is not released before the wait expires, the program receives an exception. A record lock is needed to prevent another program from updating the record at the same time.

The FMTSLR (Record Format Selector Program) parameter specifies the name of a record format selection program that is called when a logical file member contains more than one logical record format. The user-written selection program is called when a record is inserted into the database file and a record format name is not included in the high-level language program.

The FRCRATIO (Number of Records to Force a Write) specifies the number of inserted or updated records that occur before those records are forced to auxiliary (disk) storage.

The SHARE (Share Open Data Path) parameter specifies whether the *open data path* (ODP) for the database file member is shared with other open operations of the same member in the same job. When an ODP is shared, the programs accessing the same file member share such things as the position being accessed, the file status, and the buffer.

If SHARE(*YES) is specified and the member is opened more than once, the same open data path (ODP) is shared with each program in the job that also specifies SHARE(*YES) when the member is opened. This includes several open operations in the same program. If SHARE(*NO) is specified, the ODP created for this member open is not shared. Every time a program opens the file member, a new ODP to the member is created. For an example of a CL program that includes an override to SHARE(*YES), see Figure 8.5, ARI851CL.

Overriding Program Parameters:

Parameters specified in an HLL program that can be overridden by the OVRDBF command are POSITION, SEQONLY, NBRRCDS, EOFDLY, EXPCHK, INHWRT, RCDFMTLCK, and DSTDTA.

The POSITION (Starting Position in File) parameter specifies the starting position for reading records from the database file. For more information about the POSITION parameter, see chapter 10.

The SEQONLY (Limit to Sequential Only) parameter is used to improve the performance of programs that process database files sequentially. It specifies, for database files whose records are processed in sequential order only, whether sequential-only processing is used on the file. If SEQONLY(*YES) is specified, a blocking factor—that is, the number of records transferred as a group to or from the database— also can be specified. The blocking factor can be from 1 through 32,767. If a number is not specified, a default number is calculated by the operating system.

The NBRRCDS (Records Retrieved at Once) parameter specifies the number of records copied from auxiliary storage to main storage when a file is read. It applies to files that use either sequential or random processing, but is specified only when the data records are physically located in the sequence in which they are processed. The specified value can be from 1 through 32,767.

The EOFDLY (End-of-File Retry Delay in Seconds) parameter specifies the number of seconds of delay before trying to read additional records after end-of-file has been reached. This delay is used to allow other jobs to add records to the file and have the new records processed without having to run the program again. When the delay time ends, the job is made active, and the system determines whether any new records were added. If no new records were added, the job waits for another time delay without informing the application program. When the EOFDLY parameter is specified, no end-of-file occurs in the HLL program.

The EXPCHK (Check Expiration Date) parameter specifies whether the expiration date of the member is checked. This check is valid only for physical file members. If EXPCHK is specified as *YES, the expiration date of the physical file member is checked. If the current date is later than the expiration date, an exception is sent to the program opening the file.

The INHWRT (Inhibit Write) parameter allows you to run a program without the processed records being written, deleted, or updated in the database file. If *YES is specified, processed records are prevented from being written into the database.

The RCDFMTLCK (Record Format Lock) parameter specifies the lock state to be enforced for one or more named record formats. This can be used to supersede the object lock state with a more restrictive lock state.

The DSTDTA (Distributed Data) parameter specifies the data retrieval method used for a distributed file. It can be used in a multisystem environment to override the distributed file data-retrieval method selected by the system.

Scoping Parameters

Parameters that scope or effect the override are OVRSCOPE, OPNSCOPE, and SECURE. The OVRSCOPE (Override Scope) parameter specifies the extent of influence of the override. The default value, OVRSCOPE(*ACTGRPDFN), indicates that the scope is determined by the activation group of the program running the OVRDBF command. This can sound confusing if you're not familiar with ILE concepts. Because OPM programs always run in the default activation group, the default scope is the program issuing the override and all programs beneath it in the call stack (called programs). The override remains in effect until the program that issued the override ends. This is the same as it always was prior to the introduction of ILE. When OVRSCOPE(*JOB) is specified, however, the override remains in effect for the duration of the job. The effect of OVRSCOPE in ILE is discussed in chapter 13.

The OPNSCOPE (Open Scope) parameter specifies the extent of influence of a subsequent open operation. The default value, OPNSCOPE(*ACTGRPDFN), indicates that the scope of a subsequent file open is determined by the activation group of the program running the OVRDBF command. Thus, for an OPM program, the default scope is the job issuing the override. The effect of OPNSCOPE in ILE is discussed in chapter 13.

The SECURE (Secure from Other Overrides) parameter specifies whether this file is safe from the effects of previous file overrides. The default is that the file is not protected from prior file overrides. You can protect the override from the effects of previous override commands by specifying SECURE(*YES).

REVIEW QUESTIONS

1. CL programs that support applications can be simple batch ___ _____ or complex CL programs that modify a job's ____ _____.

2. The typical function of a batch CL program is to sequentially call HLL programs that _____ and/or _____.

3. Housekeeping for work files should be done at the _____ of the CL program.

4. Override-file commands include _____, _____, _____, _____, _____, and _____ and are used to override the name and/or the attributes of a file referenced in a program.

5. In a typical OPM environment, a file override applies to files that are opened after the Override-File command is issued and remains in effect until _____, _____, or _____.

6. A common function of interactive application support CL programs is to _____ database files.

9

DISPLAY FILE PROCESSING

The capability to process a file in a control language is unique to AS/400 CL; neither OCL nor JCL supports the function. Despite some limitations, the file-handling capabilities of CL help make it a powerful programming language. A single database or display file can be defined in a CL program. Neither database nor display files are fully supported in a CL program. CL doesn't include either subfile or variable line-number support for display files. For a more detailed discussion of database file support in CL, see chapter 10.

A file used in a CL program must be declared at the beginning of the program using the DCLF (Declare File) command. DCLF has two parameters: FILE and RCDFMT (Record Format). The FILE parameter is required and, of course, specifies the file being declared. The RCDFMT parameter permits the specification of one or more formats to be used by the CL program. It is common to accept the default of *ALL for the RCDFMT parameter. However, a CL program that uses only a few formats of a multi-format file can be made smaller by using the RCDFMT parameter to include only the necessary format names.

The CL compiler uses the DCLF command to reference the external description of the file and defines a CL variable for each field of the specified record formats.

Consequently, files used in CL must be externally defined and must exist at the time the CL program is compiled.

The CL variables generated by the compiler have the same name as the fields in the file and are preceded by an ampersand. Indicators in a display file are declared as logical variables named &IN*nn* where *nn* is the indicator. For example, if a display file declared in a CL program includes a numeric input field named OPTION and uses indicator 03, the compiler declares a decimal CL variable named &OPTION and a logical variable named &IN03.

INTERACTIVE PROCESSING WITH CL

CL file processing is performed using three commands:

- SNDF (Send File).
- RCVF (Receive File).
- SNDRCVF (Send-Receive File).

The SNDF, RCVF, and SNDRCVF commands are the CL-equivalents of the RPG operation codes WRITE, READ, and EXFMT, respectively. SNDF writes a single record format of a display file to a screen. RCVF reads a single record format. SNDRCVF writes a record format to the screen and then reads it.

Simple display file handling is done very much the same in CL as in other HLLs such as RPG. Because display-file indicators map into logical variables, there are no problems interpreting or setting indicators.

Programs that use a display file to interact with a workstation operator are referred to as *interactive* programs. In most cases, interactive programs include a loop routine similar to the flowchart shown in Figure 9.1.

Depending on the function of the program, either the "Prepare output data" section or the "Process input data" section may be omitted. Some of the output fields, constants, or display attributes used in the display file may be conditional. In other words, the field, constant, or attribute is conditioned in the DDS (Data Definition Specifications) by one or more indicators. Indicators that condition output are called *output indicators* because their status (on or off) is set by the program and passed to the display with any other output data when the display file record is written.

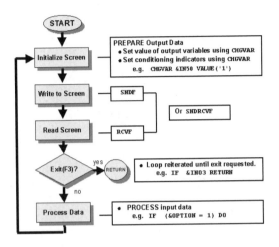

Figure 9.1: Interactive processing loop.

Setting the status of output indicators is performed as part of the "Prepare Output Data" step in the flowchart (Figure 9.1). In a CL program, the status of an output indicator is changed using the CHGVAR command. For example, indicator 50 can be set on with the following command:

```
CHGVAR  &IN50  VALUE('1')
```

The loop is reiterated (repeated) until *exit* is requested. Function key F3 is ordinarily used to request exit or to quit the application. An indicator is also assigned to the function key in the DDS. Indicators assigned to function keys are called *input indicators* because their status is returned to the program when the display file record is read.

In a CL program, the status of an indicator is tested with an IF command. For example, in the following command, if indicator 03 is on, the RETURN command will be run:

```
IF    &IN03  RETURN
```

Figure 9.2 is a facsimile of a display panel used by a utility application that uses an interactive CL program. RCDCNT is a user-defined command to display the number of records in a database file member. The command processing CL program, RCDCNTCL, uses a simple display file with one input indicator and one output indicator. If the member contains no records, the number-of-records field is displayed in reverse-image. Each time the Enter key is pressed, the number-of-records field is refreshed; F3 is the exit key.

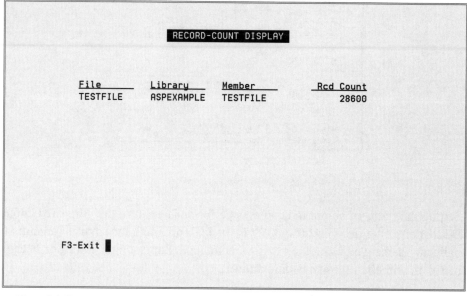

Figure 9.2: Record-count display panel.

The CL program accepts two parameters: the qualified file and the name of the data member. The command default for the file qualifier (that is, the library) is the predefined value *LIBL. If the default is accepted, the first occurrence of the file in the job's library list is used. The command default for the member parameter is the predefined value *FIRST. If the default for MBR is accepted, the first member in the file is used. In all cases, however, the actual library and member name are displayed. Validation of the parameter data is handled by a generic error-handling routine.

Figure 9.3 contains the DDS source for the display file RCDCNTDF. Notice that F3 is defined as the exit key; pressing F3 turns on indicator 03 (line 5.00), and indicator 50 conditions the reverse-image attribute on the RCDS field (line 26.00).

```
 1.00        ********************************************************
 2.00        *FILE: RCDCNTDF                                        *
 3.00        ********************************************************
 4.00
 5.00    A                                         CA03(03 'Exit')
 6.00    A                                         PRINT
 7.00      *
 8.00    A           R RCDCNT                      KEEP
 9.00                                              PUTOVR OVRDTA OVRATR
10.00    A                                      3 28' RECORD-COUNT +
11.00                                              DISPLAY '
12.00                                              DSPATR(RI)
13.00    A                                      7 12'File        '
14.00                                              DSPATR(UL HI)
15.00    A                                      7 25'Library     '
16.00                                              DSPATR(UL HI)
17.00    A                                      7 38'Member      '
18.00                                              DSPATR(UL HI)
19.00    A                                      7 54' Rcd Count'
20.00                                              DSPATR(UL HI)
21.00      *
22.00    A           FILE        10A  0   8 12
23.00    A           LIB         10A  0   8 25
24.00    A           MBR         10A  0   8 38
25.00    A           RCDS        10Y 00   8 54EDTCDE(3)
26.00      50                                      DSPATR(RI)
27.00      *
28.00    A                                     20 34'F3-Exit'
29.00      *
30.00      *
31.00      * * * * * * * *  E N D   O F   S O U R C E  * * * * * * *
```

Figure 9.3: DDS Source for record-count application.

Figure 9.4 contains the command definition source specifications for RCDCNT. Notice that the FILE parameter is required, (MIN(1) is specified on the PARM statement), the default for the file qualifier is *LIBL, and the default for MBR is *FIRST. For more detail on command definition, see chapter 14, Creating User-Written Commands.

```
 1.00 /******************************************************************/
 2.00 /* CMD: RCDCNT - Get Record-count of Physical File Member      */
 3.00 /*              PGM(RCDCNTCL)                                    */
 3.00 /******************************************************************/
 4.00
 5.00    CMD         PROMPT('Display Record-count')
 6.00
 7.00    PARM        KWD(FILE) TYPE(FILE) +
 8.00                   PROMPT('Physical file name') MIN(1)
 9.00 FILE: +
10.00    QUAL        TYPE(*NAME) LEN(10) EXPR(*YES)
11.00    QUAL        TYPE(*NAME) LEN(10) DFT(*LIBL) +
12.00                   SPCVAL((*LIBL)) EXPR(*YES) PROMPT('Library')
13.00
14.00    PARM        KWD(MBR) TYPE(*NAME) LEN(10) DFT(*FIRST) +
15.00                   SPCVAL((*FIRST)) EXPR(*YES) +
16.00                   PROMPT('Member name')
30.00
31.00 /* * * * * *  END OF CMD SOURCE * * * * * * * */
```

Figure 9.4: Command source for record-count application.

Figure 9.5 contains the CL source for RCDCNTCL, the CL program that is the command- processing program for the command RCDCNT. Two parameters, &FILELIB (the qualified file) and &MBR, are received by RCDCNTCL. The &FILELIB parameter is split into &FILE and &LIB at statements 15.00 and 16.00.

The declaration of &MBR seems rational, but is actually redundant and unnecessary. Remember that all fields defined in a declared file, such as RCDCNTDF, are automatically declared to the CL program. In this case, the redundant declare is allowed to remain because it more clearly communicates the parameter requirements to the reader of the source code. Note, however, that there are no DCL commands for either the display file fields FILE, LIB, and RCDS or the indicators 03 and 50.

The RTVMBRD (Retrieve Member Description) command (line 21.00) is used to retrieve the number of records in the member. RTVMBRD accepts parameters for the qualified file name (FILE) and the member name (MBR). The file can be qualified to the predefined value *LIBL and the MBR parameter defaults to *FIRST.

RTVMBRD supports several return variable parameters that can be used to return various attributes of the member into CL variables. The return variable parameters used in RCDCNTCL are RTNLIB (actual library in which file is found), RTNMBR (actual member name), and NBRCURRCD (Number of Records Currently in Member). RTNLIB and RTNMBR are useful when the defaults for the library and member are accepted.

```
 1.00 /*********************************************************/
 2.00 /* PGM: RCDCNTCL Get Record-count of Physical File Member */
 3.00 /*********************************************************/
 4.00
 5.00 PGM          PARM(&FILELIB &MBR)
 6.00
 8.00   DCL        &FILELIB  *CHAR  20
 9.00   DCL        &MBR      *CHAR  10
10.00
11.00   DCLF       RCDCNTDF
12.00
13.00   MONMSG     CPF9999  EXEC(GOTO ERR_RTN)
14.00 /*********************************************************/
15.00   CHGVAR     &FILE   VALUE(%SST(&FILELIB  1 10))
16.00   CHGVAR     &LIB    VALUE(%SST(&FILELIB 11 10))
17.00
18.00 /*****************************/
19.00
20.00 LOOP:
21.00   RTVMBRD    FILE(&LIB/&FILE) MBR(&MBR) +
22.00               RTNLIB(&LIB) RTNMBR(&MBR) NBRCURRCD(&RCDS)
23.00
24.00   IF         (&RCDS = 0)  CHGVAR &IN50 VALUE('1')
25.00   ELSE       CHGVAR &IN50 VALUE('0')
26.00
27.00   SNDRCVF
28.00   IF         (*NOT &IN03)  GOTO LOOP
29.00
30.00   RETURN
31.00 /*********Error handling******************/
32.00 ERR_RTN:
33.00   CALL       FWDMSG PARM('1')
34.00     MONMSG   CPF0000
35.00 ENDPGM
```

Figure 9.5: CL Source for record-count application.

RCDCNTCL employs the generic error-handling scheme for utility CL programs introduced in chapter 7. The global, generic monitor message provides validation of the passed parameters by trapping the potential exception messages generated by the RTVMBRD command. Additionally, any unanticipated errors are trapped as well.

A program loop begins with the RTVMBRD command that retrieves the number of records in the data member. Before displaying the record count, indicator 50 is set to appropriately condition the reverse-image display attribute. Then, the display file record is written and a read is issued. Once input is received, indicator 03 is tested to determine whether to repeat the loop or fall through to the RETURN command.

If you have created this example, you can easily test it by creating a primitive file with a 1-byte record length. Use the following command:

```
CRTPF  TESTFILE  RCDLEN(1)
```

Run the RCDCNT command:

```
RCDCNT  TESTFILE
```

The number of records should be 0 and the Record Count field should be displayed in reverse-image.

From another workstation or a secondary job, write a short RPG, COBOL, or other HLL program to add 100,000 records to TESTFILE in a loop. Next, submit a batch job to call the HLL program. Returning to the primary job, press the Enter key. If the batch job has begun, the record count changes and the display attribute changes from reverse-image to normal. Each time you press the Enter key, the number of records increases. After the test, don't forget to end the batch job and clear the file!

WAIT FOR INVITED DEVICES

By changing the requirements for this application slightly, you can create an opportunity to experiment with an interesting technique using CL and a display file. Instead of having to press the Enter key to see the updated record count, you can cause the displayed value to change automatically as the actual record count changes. You can accomplish this by imitating a technique used by *multiple requesting terminal* (MRT) programs.

MRT (pronounced "murt") programs invite multiple devices to respond to a read (RCVF) request and to process whichever device responds first. When a MRT issues a read to invited devices, it has the capability of regaining control if no device responds within a specified time limit. By taking advantage of this characteristic in the record-count utility, you can periodically re-retrieve the record-count and redisplay the screen.

Incorporating the MRT technique requires surprisingly few modifications to the existing code. Figure 9.6 contains the modified display file DDS source and

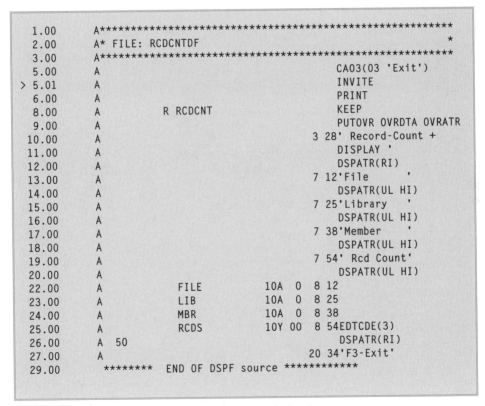

```
   1.00     A*********************************************************
   2.00     A* FILE: RCDCNTDF                                        *
   3.00     A*********************************************************
   5.00     A                                        CA03(03 'Exit')
>  5.01     A                                        INVITE
   6.00     A                                        PRINT
   8.00     A        R RCDCNT                         KEEP
   9.00     A                                        PUTOVR OVRDTA OVRATR
  10.00     A                                     3 28' Record-Count +
  11.00     A                                        DISPLAY '
  12.00     A                                        DSPATR(RI)
  13.00     A                                     7 12'File        '
  14.00     A                                        DSPATR(UL HI)
  15.00     A                                     7 25'Library     '
  16.00     A                                        DSPATR(UL HI)
  17.00     A                                     7 38'Member      '
  18.00     A                                        DSPATR(UL HI)
  19.00     A                                     7 54' Rcd Count'
  20.00     A                                        DSPATR(UL HI)
  22.00     A          FILE          10A  0  8 12
  23.00     A          LIB           10A  0  8 25
  24.00     A          MBR           10A  0  8 38
  25.00     A          RCDS          10Y 00  8 54EDTCDE(3)
  26.00     A  50                                    DSPATR(RI)
  27.00     A                                    20 34'F3-Exit'
  29.00     ********  END OF DSPF source ************
```

Figure 9.6: DDS changes for record-count with auto-write function.

Figure 9.7 contains the modified CL program source. The only change to RCDCNTDF is the addition of the file-level INVITE keyword at line 5.01. The inclusion of the INVITE keyword makes the display file a "multiple device file," a device file that allows more than one device to be acquired by a program.

```
     1.00 /********************************************************/
     2.00 /* PGM: RCDCNTCL Get Record-count of Physical File Member */
     3.00 /********************************************************/
     4.00
     5.00 PGM          PARM(&FILELIB &MBR)
     6.00
     8.00    DCL       &FILELIB  *CHAR  20
     9.00    DCL       &MBR      *CHAR  10
    10.00
    11.00    DCLF      RCDCNTDF
    12.00
    13.00    MONMSG     CPF9999  EXEC(GOTO ERR_RTN)
    14.00 /********************************************************/
    15.00    CHGVAR    &FILE  VALUE(%SST(&FILELIB  1 10))
    16.00    CHGVAR    &LIB   VALUE(%SST(&FILELIB 11 10))
 >  16.01    OVRDSPF   RCDCNTDF  WAITRCD(3)
    17.00
    18.00 /******************************/
    19.00
    20.00 LOOP:
    21.00    RTVMBRD   FILE(&LIB/&FILE) MBR(&MBR) +
    22.00                RTNLIB(&LIB) RTNMBR(&MBR) NBRCURRCD(&RCDS)
    23.00
    24.00    IF        (&RCDS = 0)  CHGVAR &IN50 VALUE('1')
    25.00    ELSE      CHGVAR &IN50 VALUE('0')
    26.00
 >  27.00    SNDRCVF   WAIT(*NO)
 >  27.01    WAIT
 >  27.02    MONMSG     CPF0889  EXEC(RCVMSG MSGTYPE(*EXCP) RMV(*YES))
    28.00    IF        (*NOT &IN03)  GOTO LOOP
    29.00
    30.00    RETURN
    31.00 /**********Error handling******************/
    32.00 ERR_RTN:
    33.00    CALL      FWDMSG PARM('1')
    34.00    MONMSG    CPF0000
    35.00 ENDPGM
```

Figure 9.7: CL changes for record-count application with auto-write function.

An output to a multiple device file invites the device to respond. That, in turn, allows the next read from the device to be issued as a read-from-invited-devices. A read-from-invited-devices is an input operation that waits for input from any of the invited program devices for a user-specified time.

Modifications required to the CL source are almost as simple as those for the DDS. The first change is to the SNDRCVF file statement at line 27.00. In order to "invite" the device, the WAIT parameter of SNDRCVF must be specified as *NO. This causes the CL program to not wait for input data; instead, commands continue to be processed until a WAIT command is reached later in the CL program. The best way to explain the significance of WAIT(*NO) is to compare it to leaving a voice-mail message for a friend saying "give me a ring sometime," and then leaving your phone off the hook; you're not taking any calls!

The second change to the CL source is the WAIT command that has been inserted following the SNDRCVF command. The WAIT command accepts input from a device that has been invited by a RCVF or a SNDRCVF command with WAIT(*NO) specified. Running the WAIT command is like hanging up the phone; you are now taking calls!

The advantage of this technique is that you can specify how long to wait before returning control to the CL program. The WAITRCD (Maximum Record Wait Time) attribute of a display file determines the number of seconds that the CL program waits for the completion of a read-from-invited-devices operation.

To guarantee that RCDCNTCL takes advantage of the time-out capability, an override to the WAITRCD attribute of RCDCNTDF has been added at line 16.01. Specifying WAITRCD(3) allows the display to be refreshed approximately every 3 seconds. Specifying WAITRCD(*IMMED) would provide a very impressive, continuously refreshed display, but it would use an excessive amount of machine resource. The override could be omitted entirely by specifying the WAITRCD value on the CRTDSPF (Create Display File) or CHGDSPF (Change Display File) commands for RCDCNTDF.

The last addition to RCDCNTCL is a MONMSG following the WAIT command. If a record is not returned within the time specified on the WAITRCD attribute, an escape message, CPF0889 (No data available for input request within specified time), is sent to the call message queue. If WAITRCD equals 3, an escape message is sent to the CL program approximately every 3 seconds. To prevent the job log from containing a large number of CPF0889 messages, the RCVMSG command specified on the EXEC parameter of the command level MONMSG receives and removes each exception message.

With these simple changes, the RCDCNT command becomes a very useful tool for monitoring the size of a rapidly growing file.

USING MESSAGE SUBFILES

There is one exception to the earlier statement that subfile support is omitted from display files processed in CL programs. A "single-output" message subfile is a special type of subfile that is supported extremely well in CL. As its name implies, this type of subfile may be filled with zero to many messages through a single output operation to the subfile control record.

Most AS/400 programmers are probably accustomed to seeing message subfiles. The message areas at the bottom of the PDM panels, the Programmer's Menu, menus created with Screen Design Aid, and all other input capable system screens are message subfiles. It makes a great deal of sense to implement them in your own interactive applications.

By taking a different approach to the record-count application, you can have a perfect example of a CL program that effectively uses a message subfile. Instead of a CL program that accepts parameters for the qualified file and member, consider using a CL program in conjunction with a display file that prompts for those values.

Figure 9.8 illustrates the revised record-count display panel. There are input capable fields for file, library and member. If the library or the member are input as blank, *LIBL or *FIRST are assumed. In all cases, however, the actual library and member name are displayed. The number of records in the selected file is displayed through a message in a message subfile at the bottom of the screen. Each press of the Enter key refreshes the message with the number of records, and F3 ends the program. At any time, any of the input fields can be changed or cleared before pressing Enter.

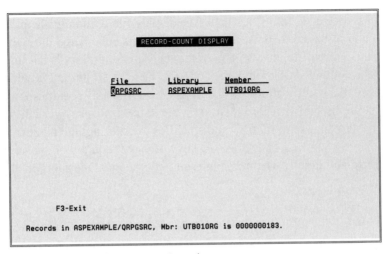

Figure 9.8: Record-count prompt panel.

Instead of causing the CL program to terminate, exception messages generated by the RTVMBRD command, as well as any other unanticipated errors, are displayed in the message subfile. Figure 9.9 illustrates the results of entering the name of a file that doesn't exist in the library list.

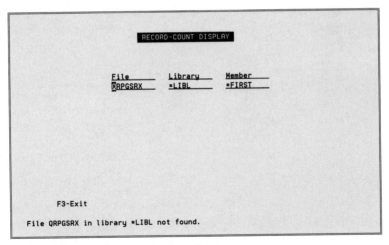

Figure 9.9: Record-count prompt panel with error message.

The DDS source code for RCDCNT2DF, the display file used in this application, can be found in Figure 9.10. Because the parameters are entered through input fields in the display file, this version of the record-count utility is not implemented as a command. Although the code for the RCDCNT format is self-explanatory, the specifications for the message subfile may require some interpretation. On the subfile record (MSGSFL), the SFLMSGRCD keyword designates the subfile as a "message subfile" and specifies the starting line number for the subfile. The SFLMSGKEY and SFLPGMQ keywords are required on the subfile record, but are not directly used for single-output type message subfiles.

```
 1.00        ****************************************************
 2.00        *FILE: RCDCNT2DF                                  *
 3.00        ****************************************************
 5.00     A                                    CA03(03 'Exit')
 6.00     A                                    PRINT
 8.00     A           R RCDCNT                 OVRDTA
 9.00     A                                    PUTOVR KEEP
10.00     A                               3 28' RECORD-COUNT +
11.00     A                                    DISPLAY '
12.00     A                                    DSPATR(RI)
13.00     A                               7 22'File      '
14.00     A                                    DSPATR(UL HI)
15.00     A                               7 35'Library    '
16.00     A                                    DSPATR(UL HI)
17.00     A                               7 48'Member     '
18.00     A                                    DSPATR(UL HI)
20.00     A           FILE      10A  B  8 22
21.00     A           LIB       10A  B  8 35
22.00     A           MBR       10A  B  8 48
24.00     A                              20 34'F3-Exit'
25.00     A****************************************************
26.00     A           R MSGSFL                 SFL
27.00     A                                    SFLMSGRCD(22)
28.00     A           MSGKEY                   SFLMSGKEY
29.00     A           PGMQ                     SFLPGMQ
30.00     A*
31.00     A           R MSGCTL                 SFLCTL(MSGSFL)
32.00     A                                    SFLINZ
33.00     A                                    OVERLAY
34.00     A                                    SFLDSP    SFLDSPCTL
35.00     A N40                                SFLEND
36.00     A                                    SFLSIZ(6) SFLPAG(3)
37.00     A           PGMQ                     SFLPGMQ
40.00     A* * * * * * E N D   O F   S O U R C E * * * * * * * *
```

Figure 9.10: DDS source for record-count application with message subfile.

On the control record (MSGCTL), the SFLINZ keyword earmarks the subfile as a single-output type message subfile. The SFLPGMQ keyword, although seemingly redundant with its counterpart on the subfile record, serves an important function for single-output message subfiles. SFLPGMQ specifies the name of a field—in this example, PGMQ—that must contain the name of a program whose call message queue contains messages to be loaded into the subfile. The program is responsible for initializing the designated field with the name of the call message queue.

Because the SFLINZ keyword is specified, a write to the control record initializes the subfile with all of the messages associated with the current request. Specifically, if there are request messages on the call message queue of the indicated program, a write to the control record causes the subfile to be initialized with all of the messages that have arrived on the queue after the last request message was received. A received request message on the call message queue constitutes a *request boundary*. Thus, a write to the control record causes the subfile to be initialized with all of the messages after the last request boundary. If there are no received request messages, the subfile is initialized with all of the messages on the call message queue.

The CL source code for the CL program RCDCNT2CL is shown in Figure 9.11. Both a numeric and a character version of the record-count field are declared. The decimal variable, &RCDS, is used to return the current number of records on the RTVMBRD command, and the character variable, &COUNT, is concatenated into a character-string message.

```
0.10 /****************************************************************/
0.20 /* Program Name: RCDCNT2CL - Get Record Count of Phy File Member    */
0.30 /****************************************************************/
1.00 PGM
2.00    DCL       &RCDS      *DEC   10
3.00    DCL       &COUNT     *CHAR  10
4.00    DCL       &MSGKEY    *CHAR   4
5.00    DCL       &ERRORS    *LGL
6.00    DCLF      RCDCNT2DF
7.00    MONMSG     CPF0000  EXEC(GOTO ERR_RTN)
12.00 /****************************************************************/
13.00    CHGVAR     &PGMQ  VALUE(RCDCNT2CL)
14.00    CHGVAR     &LIB   VALUE('*LIBL')
```

Figure 9.11: CL source for record-count application with message subfile (part 1 of 2).

167

```
15.00   CHGVAR    &MBR  VALUE('*FIRST')
19.00 LOOP:
20.00   SNDF      RCDFMT(RCDCNT)
21.00   SNDF      RCDFMT(MSGCTL)
22.00   RCVF      RCDFMT(RCDCNT)
23.00   CHGVAR    &ERRORS  '0'
25.00   IF        (&IN03)  RETURN
27.00   IF        (&LIB = ' ') CHGVAR &LIB '*LIBL'
28.00   IF        (&MBR = ' ') CHGVAR &MBR '*FIRST'
30.00 /* ——- Set request boundary ————-*/
31.00   SNDPGMMSG MSG('Get record-count for' *BCAT &FILE *TCAT +
32.00                 ', in' *BCAT &LIB *TCAT ', member is' +
33.00                   *BCAT &MBR *TCAT '.') TOPGMQ(*SAME) +
34.00                 MSGTYPE(*RQS) KEYVAR(&MSGKEY)
35.00   RCVMSG    MSGTYPE(*RQS) MSGKEY(&MSGKEY) RMV(*NO)
37.00 /* ——- Get rcd count ————————-*/
38.00   RTVMBRD   FILE(&LIB/&FILE) MBR(&MBR) +
39.00               RTNLIB(&LIB) RTNMBR(&MBR) NBRCURRCD(&RCDS)
41.00   CHGVAR    &COUNT &RCDS
42.00   SNDPGMMSG MSG('Records in' *BCAT &LIB *TCAT '/' *CAT +
43.00                 &FILE *TCAT ', Mbr:' *BCAT &MBR *BCAT 'is' +
44.00                   *BCAT &COUNT *TCAT '.') TOPGMQ(*SAME)
46.00   GOTO      LOOP
48.00 /******* Error handling ******************/
48.10 ERR_RTN:
49.00   IF        (&ERRORS)  DO
52.00             DMPCLPGM  /* Bail out */
53.00             CALL  FWDMSG PARM('1')
54.00              MONMSG  CPF0000
55.00             RETURN
56.00             ENDDO   /* Deep trouble, bail out */
58.00   CHGVAR    &ERRORS  '1'
59.00   GOTO      LOOP
60.00 ENDPGM
```

Figure 9.11: CL source for record-count application with message subfile (part 2 of 2).

At line 13.00, the &PGMQ CL variable is changed to the name of the CL program to satisfy the requirements for the SFLPGMQ keyword in the message subfile. The program loop begins (line 19.00) by writing both the RCDCNT record and the message subfile control record, MSGCTL, and then reading the RCDCNT record. The first time the MSGCTL record is written, there should be no messages in the subfile. Immediately after receiving input from the device, the &ERRORS switch is set to false. The &ERRORS switch plays a role in the error handling for this CL program.

After testing for the Exit key and values for library and member (lines 25.00 – 28.00), a request message is sent to, and subsequently received from, the call message queue. This serves two purposes. First, it makes an entry in the job log that indicates what values were entered for the inquiry request. In some applications, this would be an effective technique to log important information. Here, it is just an interesting feature.

Second, and more importantly, this technique plays a vital role in the circumvention of a problem inherent in the use of message subfiles. Recall that if there are no received request messages on the call message queue, a write to the control record of a single-output message subfile initializes the subfile with all of the messages on the call message queue. Consequently, if no request boundaries are set, the subfile could get larger and larger as more messages arrive on the queue. That is neither what you expect nor what you want to happen. You only want to see messages associated with the last information that was processed by the CL program.

There are two ways to solve this problem. One method is to remove all messages from the call message queue, or job log, after each display of the message subfile. The alternative, (and the method illustrated in CL program RCDCNT2CL) is to set a request boundary by sending and receiving a request message after each display of the subfile. As a result, a write to the subfile control record causes the subfile to be initialized with all of the messages on the call message queue for the current request (specifically, all messages that arrive on the queue after the received request message).

The correct strategy depends on the nature of the application, your willingness to obliterate part of the job log, and the value to you of a job log that indicates what was done rather than how it was done.

After retrieving the record-count through the RTVMBRD command, the &RCDS field is moved into its character counterpart so that it can be concatenated into an informational message sent to the call message queue. Like the request message, this message also serves two purposes. First, it is a permanent record in the job log of the result of the inquiry. Second, and also more importantly, because it is sent to the call message queue of RCDCNT2CL, it appears in the message subfile when it is displayed. This is the message that informs the application user of the number of records in the member.

The error handling requirements of this type of CL program are significantly different than the first example. Because CL program RCDCNT2CL uses a message subfile, all error messages are automatically displayed at the bottom of the screen, including unanticipated errors! There is, it would seem, no reason to cause the CL program to abort. Apparently, you could code the global MONMSG to branch to the top of the loop, allowing the message subfile to simply display the error.

However, error handling in a CL program that uses a message subfile to display errors must take into account that an error might occur on the SNDF command. An example of such an error is a level check on the display file. With standard error handling, the global MONMSG would cause a branch to the top of the loop, the CL program would attempt the SNDF command again, it would fail again, and the program would go into an infinite error loop.

The error handling logic in RCDCNT2CL is designed to avoid this situation. Upon entering the error routine for a typical error, such as that the requested file was not found, the &ERRORS switch is tested (line 50.00). Because it is, by default, false, control passes to the CHGVAR command at line 57.00, &ERRORS is set on, and the program branches to the top of the loop. Immediately after the display file I/O (input/output) operations are performed, the &ERRORS switch is set off again. Thus, ensuing errors are handled in identical fashion.

If, on the other hand, the error were generated due to a level-check on the display file, the logic flow would be different. The first time the level-check error occurs, the path through the error routine is identical to that of any other error. In other words, the DO group is bypassed, &ERRORS is turned on, and the program branches to the top of the loop. When the SNDF fails the second time, however, the branch to the error routine occurs prior to the CHGVAR command that sets the &ERRORS switch off!

The second time the error routine is entered, &ERRORS is still ON so the DO group at line 51.00 is performed. The CL program is dumped and the standard utility message-forwarding program is called, passing the exception flag, which causes the CL program to abort. The generic MONMSG and RETURN commands following the CALL to FWDMSG guarantee that even if the CALL itself fails, an infinite loop is avoided.

When testing this version of the record-count application, experiment with various combinations of invalid file, library, and member information. Also, display the number of records in various members of a source file, such as QRPGSRC.

REVIEW QUESTIONS

1. The compiler uses the DCLF command to reference the _____ _____ of the file and declares a CL variable for each field defined in the file.

2. CL file processing is performed using three commands: _____, _____, and _____.

3. Errors are displayed in the message subfile of CL programs that use them. CL supports a _____-_____ message subfile.

4. A write to the _____ record of a single-output message subfile initializes the subfile with all of the messages associated with the _____ _____.

5. Sending and receiving a request message in a CL program: (1) makes an entry in the ____ ____, and (2) sets a _____ _____.

10

DATABASE FILE PROCESSING

The capability to process a database file adds greatly to the usefulness of AS/400 Control Language. Despite some limitations, the database file-handling capabilities of CL help make it a powerful programming language. However, CL wasn't designed as a primary application language and, consequently, it lacks file support comparable to that in COBOL, RPG, and other high-level languages.

Of the limitations imposed on CL database file processing, the restriction that only one file may be defined in a CL program is not the most serious deficit. It does mean, however, that a database file cannot be used in the same CL program as a display file. Additional restrictions to database file usage in CL are that:

- Multi-format logical files are not permitted.
- Database records can be read but not written or updated.
- Records can only be processed sequentially.
- The file cursor cannot be reset. Once a record has been read, it cannot be read again.

Like display files, database files used in CL programs must be declared at the beginning of the program using the DCLF command. DCLF has two parameters: FILE and RCDFMT (Record Format). The FILE parameter is required and, of course, specifies the file being declared. Because only files with a single format are permitted, there is no need to specify the RCDFMT parameter for a database file.

The CL compiler uses the DCLF command to reference the external description of the file and declares a CL variable for each field defined in the file. The name used for a compiler-generated CL variable is the same as the field name in the file, preceded by an ampersand. For example, if a database file declared in a CL program includes a numeric field named EMPLNO, the compiler declares a decimal CL variable named &EMPLNO.

Unlike RPG and COBOL, which allow program defined files, all files used in CL must be externally defined and, therefore, must exist at the time the CL program is compiled.

SEQUENTIAL FILE PROCESSING

Of the three commands used by CL for file processing, SNDF, RCVF, and SNDRCVF, only RCVF can be used with database files. RCVF is the CL-equivalent of the READ, or FETCH, operation. It reads a record from the database file. If the file is keyed, the first record read is the first key in the file. Subsequent RCVF commands read records in key order. If the file is not keyed, records are read in physical, or arrival, sequence.

A file in a CL program is not opened until the first time a RCVF is issued. This allows OVRDBF commands in the same CL program to affect the file being processed. If a RCVF is issued to a file that has no records, or if it is issued after all records have already been read, an escape message is sent to the CL program. The CPF0864 message (End of file detected for file &1 in &2) can be treated as an end-of-file indicator. Typically, the CL program reads records in a loop and monitors for CPF0864 either globally or at a command level. At end-of-file, the program can be ended through the RETURN command or a GOTO command can be used to branch to a point beyond the loop. Figure 10.1 illustrates a typical read loop.

```
DCLF  FILE(ANYFILE)
READ:
  RCVF
    MONMSG  CPF0864  EXEC(GOTO EOF)
  .
  .
  .
  GOTO  READ
EOF:
```

Figure 10.1: Database file processing loop.

Figure 10.2 contains the source for a physical file, PGMLST00, and CL program
COMPILCL. PGMLST00 has a single field—PGMNAM. Each record in the file contains the name of an RPG/400 program to be compiled in a batch job.

```
 1.00  A*********************************************************
 2.00  A* Database physical file: PGMLST00                      *
 3.00  A*********************************************************
 4.00  A           R PGMLST
 5.00  A             PGMNAM        10
 6.00  A* * * * * *  E N D   O F   S O U R C E  * * * * * * * * *

 1.00  /************************************************************/
 2.00  /* Program Name: COMPILCL  Compile programs in a file      */
 3.00  /************************************************************/
 4.00
 5.00  PGM
 6.00
 7.00  DCLF      PGMLST00
 8.00     MONMSG    CPF9999 EXEC(GOTO ERR_RTN)
 9.00
10.00  READ:
11.00    RCVF
12.00      MONMSG    CPF0864  EXEC(RETURN)
13.00    CRTRPGPGM  PGM(OBJLIB/&PGMNAM) SRCFILE(SRCLIB/QRPGSRC) +
13.01              REPLACE(*YES)
14.00    MONMSG    CPF0000 EXEC(SNDPGMMSG MSG('Compile failed for program:' +
15.00              *BCAT &PGMNAM *TCAT '.') +
16.00              TOPGMQ(*PRV) MSGTYPE(*DIAG))
17.00    GOTO      READ
18.00  /*=====================================================*/
19.00  ERR_RTN:
20.00    CALL   FWDMSG   '1'
21.00      MONMSG MSGID(CPF0000)
22.00  ENDPGM
```

Figure 10.2: Reading a database file.

COMPILCL reads the PGMLST00 file and for each record runs the CRTRPGPGM (Create RPG Program) command. The CL variable &PGMNAM is specified for the PGM (Program Name to Create) parameter. The name of the program in each database record is automatically assigned to the CL variable &PGMNAM when the record is read.

When all records have been processed (the message CPF0864 is issued), the program ends. If a compile fails for any reason, a message is sent to the calling program.

RANDOM RECORD RETRIEVAL

As stated earlier, in a CL program database records can only be processed sequentially. There is no CL-equivalent of the RPG CHAIN operation code. However, if just one particular record must be read in a CL program, it is possible to open the file with the file cursor positioned at that record.

The key is to override the file using the POSITION (Starting Position in File) parameter of the OVRDBF command. The POSITION parameter can be used to specify:

- The starting position is the first record in the file (*START).

- The last record in the file (*END).

- A specific relative record number (*RRN followed by the record number).

- A record identified by a key operation (a key operation code, the number of key fields, the record format name, and the key value).

For example, to read the twenty-fifth record of a file named EXAMPL00, the following commands could be run in a CL program:

```
OVRDBF  FILE(EXAMPL00) POSITION(*RRN 25)
RCVF    RCDFMT(EXMPFMT)
```

The POSITION parameter of the OVRDBF command specifies that the file cursor is to be positioned at record number 25 when the file is opened. Consequently, the desired record is read with the first RCVF command.

Occasionally, the capability to open a keyed database file with the file cursor positioned at a record having a specific key is required in a CL program. For example, a CL program could be written to read a record from a file that is keyed by user profile and to place information about the user in the LDA for easy retrieval by all application programs. To avoid having to read through the records until the record with the required key is found, the POSITION parameter of the OVRDBF command can be used to specify the starting position in the file with a key operation code, the number of key fields, the record format name, and the key value. The key operation codes are as follows:

- *KEYB (Key Before): A record that precedes the record identified by the following search values is the first record read.

- *KEYBE (Key Before or Equal): The record identified by the following search values is the first record read. If no record matches those values, the record with the previous highest value is read.

- *KEY (Key Equal): The record identified by the following search values is the first record read.

- *KEYAE (Key After or Equal): The record identified by the following search values is the first record read. If no record matches those values, the record with the next highest value is read.

- *KEYA (Key After): A record that follows the record identified by the following search values is the first record read.

To read a record having a key of RACHELV from a file named XAUSER00 keyed by user profile, the following override command would be run prior to the first RCVF:

```
OVRDBF  XAUSER00  POSITION(*KEYAE 1 *N RACHELV)
```

Specifying *KEYAE for the key operation is the CL-equivalent of the RPG SETLL (Set Lower Limits) operation code. *KEYAE must be specified even when a record exactly matches the search values because an anomaly in CL prevents the *KEY operation from returning a record with an exact match.

The second value, 1 in this case, is the number of key fields to be used for the search. The number specified doesn't have to equal the actual number of key fields for the file. If 0 is specified, all key fields for the file are matched.

Specifying *N for the second value, record format name, indicates that all formats should be searched for a key match. The default value for any optional parameter or list element may be entered positionally by using the predefined value *N, allowing parameters that follow it to be entered in positional form. Because CL programs can only declare single-format files, *N may always be used for the record format name when the file is being processed in a CL program.

In the example, the key value RACHELV should match the key of a record in the file. If it doesn't, the record having the next higher key is read, and no warning or error message is generated. It is the programmer's responsibility to ensure that the key of the record that is read matches the search value. If the search value is higher than the highest key in the file, the exception CPF4137 (Position option for member &4 not valid) is sent to the CL program.

Figure 10.3 contains the source code for LODLDACL, a CL program that reads a record from a file that is keyed by user profile and places user information from the file in the LDA. The file XAUSER00 is declared. It contains information about each user on the system. Figure 10.4 shows the record format layout of the XAUSER00 file.

```
1.00   /********************************************************/
2.00   /* Program Name: LODLDACL- Load the LDA with user data    */
3.00   /********************************************************/
4.00
5.00 PGM
6.00   DCL        &USER    *CHAR 10
7.00   DCLF       XAUSER00
```

Figure 10.3: Random access by key (part 1 of 2).

```
 8.00    MONMSG      CPF9999 EXEC(GOTO ERR_RTN)
 9.00
10.00    RTVJOBA     USER(&USER)
11.00    OVRDBF      FILE(XAUSER00) POSITION(*KEYAE 1 *N &USER)
12.00    RCVF
13.00      MONMSG    CPF4137
14.00
15.00    IF          (&USER *NE &USUSR) DO
17.00                SNDPGMMSG MSGID(CPF9897) MSGF(QCPFMSG) +
18.00                   MSGDTA('Setup for' *BCAT &USER *BCAT +
19.00                   'failed.') TOPGMQ(*PRV) MSGTYPE(*ESCAPE)
20.00                ENDDO /* User not in user table */
21.00
22.00 LOAD:
23.00    CHGDTAARA   (*LDA ( 1 10)) VALUE(&USUSR)  /* User profile   */
24.00    CHGDTAARA   (*LDA (11 30)) VALUE(&USUSRN) /* User name      */
25.00    CHGDTAARA   (*LDA (41 20)) VALUE(&USNM20) /* User short name*/
26.00    CHGDTAARA   (*LDA (61 10)) VALUE(&USOUTQ) /* Normal OutQ    */
27.00    CHGDTAARA   (*LDA (71 10)) VALUE(&USOEOQ) /* Order OutQ     */
28.00    CHGDTAARA   (*LDA (81 10)) VALUE(&USPOOQ) /* Purch OutQ     */
29.00
30.00    SNDPGMMSG   MSG(&USER *BCAT 'Set up.') MSGTYPE(*COMP)
31.00
32.00    RETURN
33.00 /*══════════════════════════════════════════════════════════*/
34.00 ERR_RTN:
35.00    CALL        FWDMSG PARM('1')
36.00      MONMSG    MSGID(CPF0000)
36.00 ENDPGM
```

Figure 10.3: Random access by key (part 2 of 2).

```
File..: XAUSER00      Cross applic. user profile data
Format: USER00

Field Name Attributes Field Text

USUSR       A   10    User profile
USUSRN      A   30    User full name   (for reports)
USNM20      A   20    User short name  (for screens)
USOUTQ      A   10    Normal OutQ
USOEOQ      A   10    Order Entry Output Queue
USPOOQ      A   10    Purchase Order Output Queue
```

Figure 10.4: The XAUSER00 format.

The RTVJOBA (Retrieve Job Attributes) command can be used in a CL program to retrieve the values of one or more attributes of the job in which it is run and to assign the values to CL variables. At line 10.00, RTVJOBA is used to copy the name of the user profile associated with the job into the CL variable &USER. Then the OVRDBF command (line 11.00) positions the file cursor for XAUSER00 at the record having a key equal to the value of &USER. The MONMSG (line 13.00) following the RCVF command ignores the exception CPF4137.

At line 15.00, the search value (&USER) is compared to the key field in the received record (&USUSR). If they are different, the desired record does not exist in the file. Therefore, an escape message that the function failed for that user is sent to the calling program, and LODLDACL ends.

Beginning at line 23.00, the field values from the database record are placed in the LDA using the CHGDTAARA (Change Data Area) command.

Specifying *LDA for the DTAARA parameter causes the LDA to be changed. The CHGDTAARA command changes the value of the local data area associated with the job (*LDA), the group data area associated with a group job (*GDA), the program initialization parameter data area associated with a pre-start job (*PDA), or a specified data area stored in a library.

The DTAARA (Data Area Specification) parameter specifies the name and library of the data area whose value is being changed. It optionally specifies, for character data areas only, the substring (starting position and length) of the character string that is changed in the data area. This allows LODLDACL to place the various field values in discrete portions of the LDA.

The VALUE (New Value) parameter specifies the new value to be stored in the data area or in a substring of the data area. The new value must have the same type and a length less than or equal to the data area length or the specified substring length.

REVIEW QUESTIONS

1. Unlike RPG and COBOL, all files used in CL must be _____ _____ and, therefore, must exist at the time the CL program is compiled.

2. RCVF retrieves a record from a database file and is the CL equivalent of the _____, or _____ operation.

3. OVRDBF commands affect a file being processed in the same CL program because the file is not opened until _____.

4. The _____ message (End of file detected for file &1 in &2) can be treated as an end-of-file indicator.

5. It is possible to open a file with the file cursor positioned to a specific record by overriding the file using the _____ parameter of the OVRDBF command.

11

SUPPORTING
SYSTEM OPERATIONS

The arrival of interactive processing in the 1970s, and its entrenchment in
the '80s, radically changed the scope of the term *operations*. Traditional
"system operators" worked in data-processing departments, ran computers,
changed forms on printers, and distributed reports (after checking them, of
course). Today, many operations are performed by "workstation operators" who
run applications and print—and check—their own reports.

In conjunction with the change in the scope of operations, programs used for supporting operations handle a broader array of functions. Workstation operators, often
redundantly called "end-users," run their applications within a complex environment called a *job*. Typically, workstation operators are not technically trained and
are not responsible for the maintenance of that operating environment.

The tasks of establishing, monitoring, and modifying user operating environments can become overwhelming. On the AS/400, CL programs are often used to
modify a job's work environment—perhaps by changing the delivery mode of
the user's message queue or the job's runtime performance characteristics.

A GENERALIZED INITIAL PROGRAM

A common method of controlling the job environment is through the initial program associated with a user profile. An initial program is an excellent example of a type of CL program that supports operations because it is likely to contain many of the commands that are commonly used to control the work environment.

Although it is possible to have individualized initial programs for each user, a generalized CL program that performs all standard initialization functions is much easier to maintain. The generalized initial program can be specified on the INLPGM (Initial Program) parameter of either the CRTUSRPRF (Create User Profile) command or the CHGUSRPRF (Change User Profile) command. For example, the following command changes the user profile for AUSTINP to run INLPGMCL as its initial program:

```
CHGUSRPRF  AUSTINP INLPGM(INLPGMCL)
```

An example of a program that performs standard initialization routines for any user, Figure 11.1 contains the source for CL program INLPGMCL. INLPGMCL is not intended to be a program that is suitable for all installations. An initial program usually reflects operational strategies that have been selected and implemented by management. INLPGMCL is no exception. It is intended to be an example of an initial program that addresses many of the operational issues with which most installations must deal. You shouldn't presume that the strategies reflected by the example are necessarily the best strategies for any particular installation.

The display file INLPGMDF is declared at line 12.00. Often, signing on to the system can take a long time. The purpose of INLPGMDF is to display something on the screen during that wait. No DDS source is listed in this text for the INLPGMDF display file. One technique, however, is to display a daily quote, company news, or something of interest to the users.

```
 1.00 /*******************************************************/
 2.00 /* Program Name: INLPGMCL - Generalized Initial Program    */
 3.00 /*******************************************************/
 4.00
 5.00 PGM
 6.00    DCL        &WSID     *CHAR 10
 7.00    DCL        &USER     *CHAR 10
 8.00    DCL        &MENU     *CHAR 10
 9.00    DCL        &USRCLS   *CHAR 10
10.00    DCL        &MENURUN  *LGL
11.00    DCL        &ERROR    *LGL
12.00    DCLF       INLPGMDF
13.00    MONMSG      MSGID(CPF0000)
14.00    MONMSG      CPF9999 EXEC(GOTO ERROR_RTN)
15.00
16.00 CHKFOR_BYE:
17.00    RTVJOBA    JOB(&WSID) USER(&USER)
18.00    IF         (&USER - BYE) SIGNOFF *NOLIST
19.00
20.00 SETUP:
21.00    SNDF       RCDFMT(SIGNON )
22.00    RTVUSRPRF  USRCLS(&USRCLS) INLMNU(&MENU)
23.00    CHGLIBL    LIBL(QTEMP QGPL ASPUTIL &USER APLUS TEMP)
24.00    CHGJOB     OUTQ(&USER) PRTTXT('Print by:' *BCAT &USER)
25.00    IF         (%SST(&WSID 1 4) *EQ 'DIAL') +
26.00               RMVMSG  MSGQ(&WSID) CLEAR(*ALL)
27.00    CHGMSGQ    MSGQ(*WRKSTN) DLVRY(*BREAK)
28.00    OVRPRTF    FILE(*PRTF) OUTPTY(3) USRDTA('For' *BCAT %SST(&USER 1 6))
29.00    STRCMTCTL  LCKLVL(*CHG) NFYOBJ(ERRORSMQ *MSGQ)
30.00    CALL       PGM(LODLDACL)  /* load the LDA */
31.00
32.00 SPECIAL:      /* Call a pgm for special user setup */
33.00    CALL       PGM(USERPGMS/&USER)
34.00       MONMSG  MSGID(CPF0001)
35.00
36.00 OPENFILES:
37.00    IF         (&USRCLS *EQ '*USER') +
38.00               CALL    OPNFILCL
39.00
40.00 GO_MENU:
41.00    RCLRSC
42.00    CHGVAR     &MENURUN  '1'
43.00    IF         (&MENU *NE '*SIGNOFF')  GO &MENU
44.00    ELSE       IF   (&USRCLS *NE '*USER')  CALL QCMD
45.00    ELSE       CHGVAR &ERROR '1'
46.00
47.00 SIGNOFF:
48.00    SNDF       RCDFMT(SIGNOFF)
49.00    IF         (*NOT &ERROR)  SIGNOFF LOG(*LIST)
50.00 /*=====================================================*/
```

Figure 11.1: A generalized initial program (part 1 of 2).

```
51.00 ERROR_RTN:
52.00   IF         &ERROR  DO
53.00
54.00              SNDPGMMSG  MSGID(CPF9898) MSGF(QCPFMSG) MSGDTA(&USER +
55.00                *BCAT 'cannot sign on at device' *BCAT +
56.00                &WSID) TOMSGQ(QSYSOPR) MSGTYPE(*ESCAPE)
57.00              MONMSG  CPF0000
58.00              SNDPGMMSG  MSGID(CPC2402) MSGF(QCPFMSG) TOPGMQ(*PRV QCMD) +
59.00                MSGTYPE(*ESCAPE)
60.00              MONMSG  CPF0000
61.00              ENDDO /* in an error loop */
62.00 FIRST_ERR:
63.00   CHGVAR     &ERROR '1'
64.00   CHGJOB     LOG(4 00 *SECLVL)
65.00   IF         (&USRCLS *EQ '*USER') DO
66.00
67.00              IF     (*NOT &MENURUN)  GOTO SIGNOFF
68.00              ELSE    GOTO GO_MENU
69.00              ENDDO    /* end-user */
70.00   ELSE       DO    /* Technical user */
71.00              SNDPGMMSG MSG('ERROR: /* Errors in INLPGMCL! +
72.00                See previous messages in the job log.  */') +
73.00                TOPGMQ(*EXT) MSGTYPE(*RQS)
74.00              CALL QCMD
75.00              ENDDO /* Technical user */
76.00 ENDPGM
```

Figure 11.1: A generalized initial program (part 2 of 2).

Early Exit

At line 17.00, the RTVJOBA command is used to place the current workstation device name and user profile name into CL variables. Because this program is generalized for all users, it is especially critical that the current user profile be available in a CL variable for use by commands that perform user-specific functions. Both CL variables are used at various points throughout the CL program.

At line 18.00, a single-statement routine that provides a quick return from the secondary job sign-on screen refers to &USER for the first time. Occasionally, system request option 1 is inadvertently invoked, causing the TFRSECJOB (Transfer to Secondary Job) command to run. If there is no secondary job, the sign-on screen is presented. When this happens, the only way to return to the initial session is to sign on to the secondary session and then transfer back to the first session or sign off again.

The logic in the INLPGMCL program is dependent on the user signing on to the secondary job with the user profile BYE. If the current user is BYE, the SIGNOFF command is run immediately. The *NOLIST option prevents a job log from being produced. For this technique to be useful, the password would have to be known and easily remembered by all users. An obvious choice for a password would be BYE.

SETTING UP THE JOB ENVIRONMENT

Statements 22.00 – 30.00 perform general setup of the job environment. The RTVUSRPRF (Retrieve User Profile) command is used to get the current user's user class and initial menu. RTVUSRPRF places one or more of the values that are stored and associated with a user into CL variables. If the USRPRF (User Profile) parameter is omitted, the default of *CURRENT is used. *CURRENT specifies that values for the user of the current job are returned.

In INLPGMCL, the CL variables &USRCLS and &INLMNU are specified for the USRCLS (User Class) and INLMNU (Initial Menu) parameters, respectively. The &USRCLS variable will contain the user class for the current user and will be one of the special values:

- *USER.
- *SYSOPR (System Operator).
- *PGMR (Programmer).
- *SECADM (Security Administrator).
- *SECOFR (Security Officer).

The &INLMNU variable will contain the name of the initial menu that is to be run when the current user signs on to the system. Both CL variables are used in relational expressions later in the CL program.

An interactive job's initial library list comes either from the system value QUSRLIBL or from the INLLIBL (Initial Library List) attribute of the job description used to initialize the job. The CHGLIBL (Change Library List) command may then be used as applications requiring a specific library list are selected and run.

The CHGLIBL command is used to establish a library list that includes a library with the same name as the user profile. This is accomplished by using the CL variable &USER, which contains the current user profile, as one of the libraries in the list.

The CHGJOB (Change Job) command is used to change two of the current job's attributes: OUTQ (the default Output Queue) and PRTTXT (the default Print Text). Both of these job-level defaults affect printer file output produced by the job. The OUTQ attribute channels spooled output to the specified output queue for printer files having an attribute of OUTQ(*JOB). INLPGMCL specifies the CL variable &USER for the OUTQ parameter and assumes that an output queue exists for each user having the same name as the user profile. The PRTTXT attribute causes the specified text string to be printed at the bottom of every page of printed output for printer files having an attribute of PRTTXT(*JOB). Again, the CL variable &USER is used—this time, in a character string expression used for the print text value.

The workstation message queue is cleared for jobs where the first four characters of the workstation name is the string 'DIAL'. This code assumes a specific naming convention for dial-up devices and addresses a problem related to a dial-up network.

Many physical devices at various locations may share device descriptions in a dial-up environment. Consequently, a user signing on to a dial-up device could see workstation messages intended for the prior user of that device description. To avoid confusion, each time a user signs on, the workstation messages are cleared. The problem also can be minimized by using user profile message queues whenever possible.

The workstation message queue is placed in break-delivery mode. The delivery mode for the user profile message queue can be specified on the DLVRY attribute of the user profile. The delivery mode for a workstation message queue, however, is always changed to *NOTIFY by the system at sign-on. If you wish to automatically place the workstation message queue in break mode, the initial program is a good candidate for assigning that responsibility.

The CHGMSGQ (Change Message Queue) command changes the attributes of the specified message queue. The delivery mode specifies how the messages that are sent to this message queue are delivered. The method of delivery is in effect until it is changed by another CHGMSGQ command in the same job or until the job ends. If the delivery mode is being changed to *BREAK or *NOTIFY and if the message queue is not already in *BREAK or *NOTIFY mode or specifically allocated to another job, it is implicitly allocated by this command.

If the delivery mode is changed to *HOLD, the messages are held in the message queue until they are requested by the user or program. If the delivery mode is *BREAK, when a message arrives at the message queue, the job to which the message queue is allocated is interrupted, and the DSPMSG command is run.

A delivery mode of *NOTIFY specifies that when a message arrives at the message queue, an interactive job to which the message queue is allocated is notified by the message light turning on and the alarm sounding. If the delivery mode is *DFT, messages requiring replies are answered with their default reply and no messages are added to the message queue.

The OVRPRTF command is used to override the OUTPTY (Output Priority) and USRDTA (User Data) parameters for all printer files. The output priority is the priority used for scheduling output on the output queue and is normally 5. The override to a value of 3 causes spooled files created in interactive jobs to be scheduled ahead of those created by batch jobs. The user data can be used to help identify spooled files.

The STRCMTCTL (Start Commitment Control) command is used to start the commitment control environment. Commitment control is a strategy and implementation for committing updates to the database at a transaction, rather than a file/record, level. The LCKLVL (Lock Level) parameter specifies the level of record locking that occurs under the commitment-control environment. The NFYOBJ (Notify Object) parameter specifies the name and type of the object where notification text is sent if a system or routing step failure occurs or a routing step ends with uncommitted changes. A full discussion of commitment control is beyond the scope of this text but, if it is implemented, the initial program is a good place to start it.

At line 30.00, a CL program named LODLDACL is called. If the LDA is used to store standardized information across all applications, the initial program is a reasonable vehicle for copying that data to the LDA. In INLPGMCL, a modular approach is used for that function. See chapter 10 for additional information on the CL program LODLDACL.

Performing User-Specific Functions

In Figure 11.1, the program call at line 33.00 is one of the keys to successfully generalizing an initial program. There might be special functions that are to be performed for a specific user during the initial program. The scheme employed by INLPGMCL asserts that functions specific to a user should be incorporated into a separate CL program having the same name as the user profile and residing in a library named USERPGMS. For example, the user with the profile WENDYFV is one of only two users who need the payroll library in their library list. As shown in Figure 11.2, CL program WENDYFV will be called by INLPGMCL each time user WENDYFV signs on.

```
 1.00 /*****************************************************************/
 2.00 /* Program Name: WENDYFV - Initial user code module            */
 3.00 /*****************************************************************/
 4.00
 5.00 PGM
 6.00    MONMSG     CPF9999 EXEC(GOTO ERROR_RTN)
 7.00
 8.00    ADDLIBLE   PAYROLLIB
 9.00
10.00    RETURN
11.00 /*=============================================*/
12.00 ERROR_RTN:
13.00    DMPCLPGM
14.00    CALL       ERRORMGR
15.00     MONMSG    MSGID(CPF0000)
16.00 ENDPGM
```

Figure 11.2: An initial user code module.

In Figure 11.2, the ADDLIBLE command is used to add the library PAYROLLIB to the library list. The alternative methods of customizing a library list for a user is to use a separate initial program or a separate job description that specifies the correct library list.

In Figure 11.1, the MONMSG command at line 34.00 of INLPGMCL allows it to ignore the error message generated if a program with the name of the current user doesn't exist.

Pre-Open Database Files

If the current job's user is an "end-user" (specifically, if the value retrieved into &USRCLS at line 27.00 is '*USER'), a CL program named OPNFILCL is called (see lines 37.00 – 38.00 in Figure 11.1). Chapter 8 describes a CL program that pre-opens database files to reduce the performance impact of HLL file opens. If files that are used in several applications need to be pre-opened, that function can be performed by an initial program. INLPGMCL uses a modular approach for the file-open function. As shown in Figure 11.3, the CL program OPNFILCL pre-opens several database files.

```
 1.00  /*****************************************************/
 2.00  /* Program name: OPNFILCL - Pre-open application files     */
 3.00  /*****************************************************/
 4.00
 5.00  PGM
 6.00
 7.00     OPNDBF     ARINVCOO   OPTION(*ALL) COMMIT(*YES) TYPE(*PERM)
 8.00     OPNDBF     ARSHIPOO   OPTION(*ALL) COMMIT(*YES) TYPE(*PERM)
 9.00     OPNDBF     ARCUSTOO   OPTION(*ALL) COMMIT(*YES) TYPE(*PERM)
10.00
11.00  ENDPGM
```

Figure 11.3: Pre-opening application files.

There are several significant differences between OPNFILCL and the example provided in chapter 8. The first difference is that the earlier example included an OVRDBF command for each file to override the SHARE (Share Open Data Path) attribute to *YES. The override applies to files that are opened after the override-file command is issued. Because the application menu in the earlier example is invoked by the program that issues the overrides and opens the files, the overrides remain in effect for subsequent opens in application programs.

Conversely, OPNFILCL returns to INLPGMCL after the files are opened. Because overrides are implicitly deleted when the OPM program that issued the override ends, the strategy for pre-open files must be modified. There would be nothing at all wrong with including the overrides in the example, described in chapter 8, specifying OVRSCOPE(*JOB). However, the OPNFILCL example presumes that the specified files were created with, or changed to, SHARE(*YES). This prerequisite makes the overrides unnecessary.

The second difference is the use of the TYPE parameter of the OPNDBF command. The TYPE parameter specifies the recursion level at which the reclaim resources function is effective. (The RCLRSC command is discussed in this chapter under the subheading Error-Handling Routine and in chapter 13.) The default, TYPE(*NORMAL), allows the reclaim resources function to close the file if the program exits without doing a close operation. The CL program OPNFILCL specifies TYPE(*PERM), meaning that the file remains open until a close operation is done using the CLOF (Close File) command, or until the routing step ends. This approach prevents the original shared open data path from being closed by the command in a subsequently called program.

The third difference is the use of the COMMIT (Commitment Control Active) parameter that specifies this file is placed under commitment control. This example presumes the adoption of commitment control as a strategy for committing updates to the database at a transaction boundary.

OPNDBF has several additional parameters that aren't used in the example. The MBR (Member) parameter can be used to open a member other than the first. However, even if a specific member is pre-opened, HLL programs will subsequently open the first member unless the file is overridden to the specific member using the OVRDBF command.

OPNID (Open File Identifier) can be used to specify an identifier that could later be referred to on either the CLOF (Close File) or POSDBF (Position Database File) command. The possible values are *FILE, meaning the name of the file specified on the FILE parameter is used for the open identifier, or a specific name that you want to associate with this open file.

SEQONLY (Limit to Sequential Only) specifies whether sequential-only processing is used for the file, and specifies the number of records processed as a group when read or write operations are performed to the open query file.

DUPKEYCHK (Duplicate Key Check) specifies whether duplicate key checking should be done on input and output operations for the file opened by this command. If *YES is specified, duplicate key feedback is provided on input and output commands.

The ACCPTH (Access Path) parameter can be specified as *ARRIVAL if you want a HLL program to ignore the file's keyed access path for input or output operations.

Invoking the Appropriate Menu

The label GO_MENU begins the section of code responsible for invoking the proper menu. It is also the target of a GOTO command that can be run within the error handling routine. The RCLRSC and CHGVAR commands also are used in the error-handling scheme. The menu strategy that has been implemented in the example varies slightly from other common approaches.

There are two typical techniques for invoking user menus. The first approach takes full advantage of the initial program and initial menu attributes of a user profile. Typically, QCMD is the program called for a routing step. If specified on the user profile for the user, QCMD calls the initial program. If an initial menu is specified for the user, it is invoked by QCMD when the initial program ends. Allowing QCMD to invoke both the initial program and the initial menu is straightforward and simple, but has one drawback; the initial menu must be a native menu object, and not all menus are native menu objects.

The second approach is popular in AS/400 installations that use either a third-party or home-grown "soft" menuing system as well as installations that migrated from a System/38 environment. The System/38 doesn't support a menu object; user-written System/38 menus are implemented with display files and CL programs. Consequently, a System/38 user profile does not have an initial menu attribute. This approach requires the initial program to directly call the appropriate menu program. If the initial program is generalized for all users, the name of the program to call is determined by a table lookup or other method of associating a particular program with a user profile.

The strategy used in this example is a hybrid of these two approaches. Like the first approach, a generalized initial program and an initial menu is specified for all operators and most technical users. Some technical users may have *SIGNOFF specified for the initial menu attribute of their user profile. Like the second approach, the menu is invoked directly by the initial program, allowing overrides to remain in effect. The menu to run is the value retrieved into &MENU at line 22.00 (see Figure 11.1).

Statements 40.00 – 45.00 in Figure 11.1 invoke an appropriate menu or program. Because some technical users can have a value of *SIGNOFF for their initial menu, the GO command is run only if &MENU doesn't have a value of '*SIGNOFF'. If &MENU is equal to '*SIGNOFF' and the user class is not *USER, QCMD is called. Thus, technical users who have no initial menu are presented with the command entry display. If an operator has no initial menu specified, an error flag is set on before control drops down to the sign-off routine.

Signing Off

As shown in Figure 11.1, statements 47.00 – 49.00 control how the program ends. First, the SIGNOFF format of INLPGMDF is displayed. Then, if the error flag (&ERROR) has not been set on, the SIGNOFF command is run. If the error flag has been set on, control passes to the error-handling routine

Error-Handling Routine

The error-handling strategy in a generalized initial program must necessarily be specialized. Because the initial program is run for users and technical staff alike, consideration must be given to the user class. Also, there is little choice if an initial program is unable to run. The job must end.

The function check generated by any unmonitored escape message is monitored by the global MONMSG, causing control to branch to the error-handling routine beginning at line 51.00. If the error flag has been set on, the job is aborted. First, a message is sent to inform the system operator that the sign-on attempt has failed. Then, the escape message CPC2402 (Job canceled. Cancel message received at command processor.) is sent to the caller of QCMD (the job's external message queue).

TOPGMQ(*EXT) cannot be specified because escape messages cannot be sent to the external message queue directly. CPC2402 has a severity of 50 and causes the job to end abnormally. Both commands are followed by command-level MONMSG commands because, otherwise, any errors would be trapped by the global MONMSG—causing an infinite program loop.

If the error flag is not already on, control drops to line 62.00. The error flag is set on and the job's logging level is maximized. At this point, the logic diverges, depending on the class of user. For users, the action taken further depends on whether the menu has been invoked or the failure occurred earlier in the CL program.

At line 42.00, just before the menu is invoked, the logical variable &MENURUN is set on. Therefore, if &MENURUN is not on when control passes to the error-handling routine, the failure must have occurred before the menu was invoked. In that case, control branches to the SIGNOFF routine. At this point, because the error flag has been set on, the job aborts.

If &MENURUN is on, control branches to GO_MENU so that a second attempt can be made to run the menu with logging maximized. The RCLRSC (Reclaim Resources) command at line 41.00 is used to free the static storage and close any files that were left open by other programs in the application that are no longer active. The files that were pre-opened in OPNFILCL remain open, however, because they were opened permanently. See the example CL program OPNFILCL (Figures 11.1 and 11.2).

The RCLRSC command is normally used in the controlling program of an application. When one of the programs in the application (other than the controlling program) ends abnormally, RCLRSC closes files left open by the program and frees static storage used by the program. The storage and other resources may then be used by other programs running in the system.

The course of action is quite different when INLPGMCL fails and the user is technical (lines 71.00 –74.00). A request message is sent to the external job message queue informing the technical user that errors have occurred in INLPGMCL. Next, QCMD is called, presenting the command entry display. QCMD receives the request message, as though it were a command to run, and attempts to run it. Because the message is a valid command label and a comment, it is processed uneventfully by QCMD. The technical user looking at the command entry display, however, is aware that there has been a problem in INLPGMCL.

Bear in mind that INLPGMCL is a complex CL program that addresses many operational issues. Again, don't presume that the strategies reflected by the example are necessarily the best strategies for any particular installation.

CL MENUS FOR OPERATIONS CONTROL

In addition to the advent of interactive processing, the maturation of distributed processing has had a tremendous impact on how system operations are managed. Often, work is being done concurrently in another building, another city, or even on another continent. Although the data and programs may be centralized, the operators, workstations, and printers might be inaccessible to the information systems staff.

While programmatic control of the job environment is usually transparent to the user, some operations issues in a distributed environment require human interaction with the system. For instance, a printer is often shared by several users in a department or a remote location. Printers, and their associated writers, often need attention; they jam, they require forms changes, and they need to be started, stopped, or changed.

A Writer Control Menu

A menu with options for managing a printer writer is a good example of a CL program used for operations control. The requirements for this application are as follows:

- The CL program should receive three parameters: writer name, output-queue name, and printer-device name.

- The menu should include options to:
    1. Start the writer for the specified device and output queue, using the current user's message queue for writer messages.
    2. Work with the writer.
    3. End the writer, either immediately or controlled.
    4. Change the writer to use the specified output queue.
    5. Work with the specified output queue whether it is attached to the writer or not.

- Each menu option should allow full prompting of the underlying command for users with command line authority.

- The menu should support a command line and a message subfile.

- The job log should show commands run as menu options and resulting messages only.

The Menu Options

The function behind each of the five menu options is supported by a CL command.

Option 1. The STRPRTWTR (Start Printer Writer) command starts a spooling writer to the specified printer. For example, the following command starts a printer writer named MAIN that directs spooled output on the QPRINT output queue to the PRT01 printer device. Messages sent by the writer go to the DSP19 workstation message queue:

```
STRPRTWTR DEV(PRT01) OUTQ(QPRINT) MSGQ(DSP19) WTR(MAIN)
```

The DEV (Device) parameter specifies the name of the printer device used to print the spooled output. The OUTQ (Output Queue) parameter specifies the name of the output queue from which the writer processes spooled output files. The MSGQ (Message Queue for Writer Messages) parameter specifies the name of the message queue where this writer's messages will be sent. The WTR (Writer) parameter specifies the name of the spooling writer being started.

Option 2. The WRKWTR (Work with Writers) command gives the status of printers and writers. This can be the overall status of all writers, the overall status of all printers (along with writer information for these printers), or the detailed status of a specific writer. In this application, the WTR (Writer) parameter is used to specify the name of a specific spooling writer. For example, the following command gives the detailed status of the spooled writer named MAIN:

```
WRKWTR WTR(MAIN)
```

Option 3. The ENDWTR (End Writer) command ends the specified writer and makes its associated printer device available to the system. The OPTION (when to end writer) parameter specifies when the writer should stop processing. If OPTION (*CNTRLD) is specified, the writer stops processing at the end of the spooled file (or copy of a file) currently being written to a printer device. If OPTION(*IMMED) is specified, the writer stops processing immediately and the spooled file that is currently printing remains on the output queue. If OPTION(*PAGEEND) is specified, the writer is held at the end of a page. For example, the following command ends a printer writer named MAIN immediately:

```
ENDWTR WTR(MAIN) OPTION(*IMMED)
```

Option 4. The CHGWTR (Change Writer) command allows you to change various attributes of an active writer. The OUTQ (Output Queue) parameter specifies the name of the output queue this writer will use to process spooled output files. Thus, you can change and use another output queue for this printer without ending and starting the writer. For example, the following command changes a printer writer named MAIN to process spooled files from the QPRINTS output queue:

```
CHGWTR WTR(MAIN) OUTQ(QPRINTS)
```

Option 5. The WRKOUTQ (Work with Output Queue) command shows the overall status of all output queues or the detailed status of a specific output queue. The OUTQ (Output Queue) parameter is used to specify the name of the output queue whose detailed status information is to be displayed. For example, the following command shows the detailed status of all spooled files on the output queue named QPRINTS:

```
WRKOUTQ OUTQ(QPRINTS)
```

ADVANCED TECHNIQUES

An example CL program, WTRMNUCL, meets the requirements of this application and incorporates several advanced CL programming techniques. In some cases, a particular technique is included as much for its illustrative value as for its specific applicability to this function.

Calling QCMDCHK

One of the techniques introduced in WTRMNUCL involves calling the system-supplied program QCMDCHK to prompt a command without running it, followed by calling QCMDEXC to run the command using the parameter values specified on the prompt.

QCMDCHK is a system-supplied program that performs syntax-checking and optionally prompts a command but does not actually run the command. When the command to syntax-check is stored in a CL variable and prompting is requested, the completed command string is returned in the variable. The syntax for QCMDCHK is identical to that of QCMDEXC. They each require two parameters: the command string and the length of the string.

Both QCMDCHK and QCMDEXC can be called from a command line, from the Command Entry display, or within any CL or HLL program. For example, if the following command is run in an interactive CL program, the display job menu is presented:

```
CALL    QCMDEXC PARM('DSPJOB' 6)
```

QCMDEXC receives the command DSPJOB, syntax-checks it, and runs it. If the following command is run, however, nothing seems to happen at all:

```
CALL    QCMDCHK PARM('DSPJOB' 6)
```

QCMDCHK receives the command DSPJOB and syntax-checks it. Because there are no syntax errors and prompting is not requested, QCMDCHK ends uneventfully.

The syntax-checking function provided by QCMDCHK can be useful in user-written programs that must accept a command as input. QCMDEXC could be used to provide a similar function to the syntax-checking found when adding commands to menus in SDA, when editing user-defined options in PDM, or when editing a CL program source in SEU. Syntax-checking can be demonstrated by including the following command in a CL program:

```
CALL   QCMDCHK PARM('DSPJOB OPTION(SPLF)' 19)
```

Because SPLF is not a valid value for the OPTION parameter of the DSPJOB command, the call to QCMDCHK fails, generating the following error message:

```
'SPLF     ' not valid for parameter OPTION.
```

QCMDCHK is often used to prompt a command without running it. By preceding the command in the first parameter with a question mark (?), the command is prompted as in the following example:

```
CALL QCMDCHK PARM('?DSPJOB' 7)
```

When the command runs, the DSPJOB command is prompted as shown in Figure 11.4.

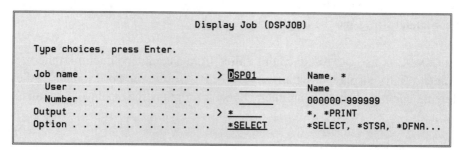

Figure 11.4: Prompt using CALL QCMDCHK PARM('?DSPJOB' 7).

The value of prompting a command without running it is only apparent when QCMDCHK is called in a program and the command to prompt is stored in a CL program variable. The completed command string is returned in the CL variable with the updated parameter values as entered on the prompt. For example, consider the following commands in a CL program:

```
DCL   &CMD   *CHAR 100 VALUE('?DSPJOB')
.

.
CALL  QCMDCHK PARM(&CMD 100)
```

Figure 11.5 shows the prompted DSPJOB command.

```
                        Display Job (DSPJOB)

Type choices, press Enter.

Job name . . . . . . . . . . . > DSP19        Name, *
  User . . . . . . . . . . . .                Name
  Number . . . . . . . . . . .                000000-999999
Output . . . . . . . . . . . . > *            *, *PRINT
Option . . . . . . . . . . . . > *SPLF        *SELECT, *STSA, *DFNA...
```

Figure 11.5: Prompt using CALL QCMDCHK PARM(&CMD 100).

The values for one or more parameters can be changed. For instance, *PRINT can be entered for OUTPUT and *PGMSTK can be entered for the OPTION parameter (see Figure 11.6).

```
                        Display Job (DSPJOB)

Type choices, press Enter.

Job name . . . . . . . . . . .   *            Name, *
  User . . . . . . . . . . . .                Name
  Number . . . . . . . . . . .                000000-999999
Output . . . . . . . . . . . .   *print       *, *PRINT
Option . . . . . . . . . . . .   *pgmstk      *SELECT, *STSA, *DFNA...
```

Figure 11.6: CALL QCMDCHK PARM(&CMD 100) with PARMS entered.

The value of the CL variable &CMD is changed to reflect the changed parameter values:

```
&CMD = 'DSPJOB OUTPUT(*PRINT) OPTION(*PGMSTK)'
```

The *RTVMSG* Command

Another technique used in WTRMNUCL introduces the RTVMSG (Retrieve Message) command as a tool for building a command string. The RTVMSG command is used by a CL program to retrieve a specified predefined message from a message file and copy it into CL variables in the program. The MSGID (Message Identifier) and MSGF (Message File) parameters specify the message identifier of the predefined message that is being retrieved and the message file that contains the predefined message.

If the predefined message contains substitution variables, the MSGDTA (Message Data Field Values) parameter can specify a character string for the substitution values that are used in the retrieved message. The MSGDTA parameter can be either a character string literal or a CL variable. The MSG (first-level message text) parameter specifies the name of the CL variable into which the first-level message text is retrieved. Additional parameters support retrieving the second-level text and the lengths of both the first and second-level text strings.

The example shown in Figure 11.7 demonstrates retrieving the first-level text of message CPF0001 in QCPFMSG (Error found on &1 command).

```
DCL      &MSG   *CHAR  512
  .
  .
RTVMSG   MSGID(CPF0001) MSGF(QCPFMSG) MSGDTA('BOGUS') MSG(&MSG)
```

Figure 11.7: Retrieving first-level text.

When the RTVMSG command runs, the following value is assigned to the CL variable &MSG:

```
'Error found on BOGUS command.'
```

Message identifier CPF0001 contains a single message field: &1. Note that &1 is replaced by the message data, 'BOGUS', in the string returned in the CL variable &MSG.

WTRMNUCL uses this technique in a somewhat unusual way. One of the requirements for the application is that the job log should show commands run as menu options and resulting messages only. This is accomplished by creating the CL program with the LOGCLPGM parameter specified as *NO and writing the commands run as options to the job log by sending them as request messages to the call message queue. Taking explicit control of writing the job log produces clear, concise job logs that indicate what the application does, rather than the CL commands that are run.

Because some of the command parameters are CL variables, creating a command string to send as a request message can involve complex character-string concatenation. The code can be made simpler and more compact by creating a message that contains the command string with message fields where variable parameters are to be substituted.

The RTVMSG command can then be used with variable message data to build the string. For example, this technique can be used with the STRPRTWTR command. The parameter values for the writer name, print device, output queue, and message queue are supplied as CL variables in the example.

The first step is to decide on a message file to contain the message for the command. A temporary message file, specific to this example, can be created in the QTEMP library as follows:

```
CRTMSGF    MSGF(QTEMP/MENUMSGF) TEXT('temporary messages')
```

Message descriptions can be added to MENUMSGF using the WRKMSGD command. However, it is more direct to use the ADDMSGD (Add Message Description) command as shown in Figure 11.8.

```
ADDMSGD    MSGID(OPTCODE) MSGF(QTEMP/MENUMSGF) +
           MSG('STRPRTWTR DEV(&3) OUTQ(&2) MSGQ(&4) WTR(&1)') +
           FMT((*CHAR 10)(*CHAR 10)(*CHAR 10)(*CHAR 10))
```

Figure 11.8: Using ADDMSGD to add a message description.

The ADDMSGD command describes a message and stores it in the specified message file for later use. The message description remains in the message file until the file is deleted or until the message is removed with the RMVMSGD (Remove Message Description) command.

The MSGID (Message Identifier) parameter specifies the message identifier under which the message is stored in the message file. Every message must have an identifier, and every identifier in the message file must be unique. The message identifier must be seven characters in length in the format *pppnnnn*, where *ppp* must be a code consisting of an alphabetic character followed by two alphameric characters, and *nnnn* may consist of numbers ranging from 0 through 9 and characters ranging from A through F. The message identifier OPTC0DE, used in the example, meets the requirements. Note that the character in the fifth position is the digit zero (0) and not the letter O.

The MSGF (Message File) parameter specifies the name of the message file where the message is to be stored.

The MSG (first-level message text) parameter specifies the first level message text of the message being defined. In the example, four message fields are specified in the text, &1, &2, &3, and &4, one for each of the variable parameters in the STRPRTWTR command.

The FMT (Message Fields Format) parameter specifies the formats of the message fields with a list of attributes: the type of data in the field, the total length of the field, and, optionally, the number of decimal digits to the right of the decimal point.

Once the message description has been added, it can be specified on the RTVMSG command. The commands shown in Figure 11.9 illustrate retrieving the OPTC0DE message in a CL program:

```
DCL        &CMD   *CHAR   512
  .
  .
RTVMSG     MSGID(OPTCODE) MSGF(QTEMP/MENUMSGF) MSG(&CMD) +
              MSGDTA('MAIN          QPRINT      PRTO1      DSP19        ')
CALL       QCMDEXC (&CMD 512)
```

Figure 11.9: Retrieving a message in a CL program.

When the RTVMSG command runs, the following value is assigned to the CL variable &CMD:

```
'STRPRTWTR DEV(PRTO1) OUTQ(QPRINT) MSGQ(DSP19) WTR(MAIN)'
```

Note that each of the four values in the message data must be blank-padded to be the exact length specified on the FMT parameter of the ADDMSGD command. However, trailing blanks for character message fields are truncated in the resulting message text. Also, note that the value for &1 must be the first value in the message data, even though it doesn't appear first in the resulting message text.

Selective Prompting

A third technique employed by WTRMNUCL is the use of *selective prompting*. Selective prompting allows you to control the parameters that are displayed when a command is prompted as well as how they are displayed. Selective prompting is specified by placing special prompting characters immediately before the keyword of parameters being selected for prompting.

When using SEU to enter source for a CL program, you can control the selection of parameters to be prompted when the CL program is run by prompting the command and entering the selective prompt characters in the first two positions of the entry field for the parameter. The selective prompt characters listed in Table 11.1 can be displayed by prompting a command, and then pressing F13 (How to use this display). F3 must be pressed to display the selective prompt characters.

Selective prompt characters can be used with commands run from any of the command entry points: from the Command Entry display, from a command line, or from within a CL program. They affect the way the command prompt is displayed and the way the completed command appears in the job log. For example, preceding a command in a

Table 11.1: Selective Prompt Characters.

Selective Prompt Characters	Description
?-	Parameter not displayed. Default used if value omitted.
??	Parameter displayed and input capable.
?<	Parameter displayed and input capable. (Use default value unless changed by user.)
?*	Parameter displayed. Not input capable.
?/	Parameter displayed. Not input capable. (Use default value no matter what value is specified.)

CL program with a question mark (?) causes the command to be prompted as though F4 were pressed:

```
1.00   ? DSPJOB
```

Running the preceding DSPJOB command in a CL program causes the prompt shown in Figure 11.10 to be displayed.

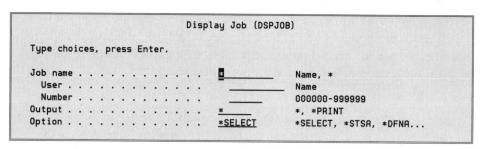

```
                        Display Job (DSPJOB)

 Type choices, press Enter.

 Job name . . . . . . . . . . .   *           Name, *
   User . . . . . . . . . . . .   _____    Name
   Number . . . . . . . . . . .   _____      000000-999999
 Output . . . . . . . . . . . .   *           *, *PRINT
 Option . . . . . . . . . . . .   *SELECT     *SELECT, *STSA, *DFNA...
```

Figure 11.10: The prompt resulting from the command 1.00 ? DSJOB.

A command also can be prompted by preceding each parameter with the selective prompt characters (??). If every parameter is selected for prompting with (??), the command is prompted as though F4 were pressed. Each of the parameters is displayed and is input-capable:

```
2.00   DSPJOB  ??JOB() ??OUTPUT() ??OPTION()
```

Running the preceding DSPJOB command in a CL program causes the prompt shown in Figure 11.11 to be displayed:

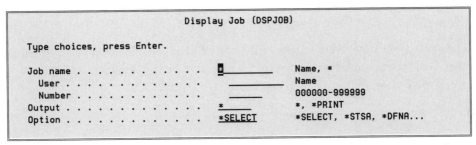

Figure 11.11: The prompt resulting from the command DSPJOB ??JOB() ??OUTPUT() ??OPTION().

If none of the parameter values is changed, the command is written to the job log without parameters, as shown in Figure 11.12.

```
*...+....1....+....2....+....3....+....4....+....5....+....6....+....7....+....8....+....9....+....0....+....1....+....2....+....3..
TIME    MSGID  SEV TYPE  MESSAGE TEXT                                              FROM PGM   INST TO PGM     INST
053020              CMD       200 - DSPJOB                                         QCADRV     0000 XMPL1101CL 0000
```

Figure 11.12: Job log entry produced by command shown in Figure 11.11.

There are important differences between prompting a command with a preceding (?) and prompting each parameter with (??). For instance, if values are specified for parameters on a command prompted with a preceding (?), they are displayed on the prompt but cannot be changed. Parameters that aren't specified are displayed and input-capable:

```
3.00   ?DSPJOB  JOB(DSP01) OPTION()
```

Running the preceding DSPJOB command in a CL program causes the prompt in Figure 11.13 to be displayed:

```
                       Display Job (DSPJOB)

  Type choices, press Enter.

  Job name . . . . . . . . . . . > DSP01        Name, *
    User . . . . . . . . . . . .                Name
    Number . . . . . . . . . . .                000000-999999
  Output . . . . . . . . . . . .  *             *, *PRINT
  Option . . . . . . . . . . . .  *SELECT       *SELECT, *STSA, *DFNA...
```

Figure 11.13:The prompt from the command ?DSPJOB JOB(DSP01) OPTION( ).

Only parameters that were not specified can be changed. However, if values are specified for parameters preceded by the selective prompt characters (??), they are displayed on the prompt and can be changed. For example:

```
4.00   DSPJOB  ??JOB(DSP01) ??OUTPUT(*) ??OPTION()
```

Running the preceding DSPJOB command in a CL program causes the prompt in Figure 11.14 to be displayed:

```
                       Display Job (DSPJOB)

  Type choices, press Enter.

  Job name . . . . . . . . . . . > DSP01         Name, *
    User . . . . . . . . . . . .                 Name
    Number . . . . . . . . . . .                 000000-999999
  Output . . . . . . . . . . . . > *             *, *PRINT
  Option . . . . . . . . . . . .   *SELECT       *SELECT, *STSA, *DFNA...
```

Figure 11.14: The prompt from the command DSPJOB ??JOB(DSP01) ??OUTPUT(*) ??OPTION( ).

All parameter values are input-capable and can be changed. For example, see Figure 11.15.

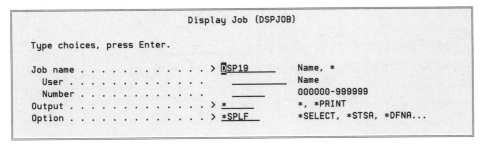

```
                            Display Job (DSPJOB)

     Type choices, press Enter.

     Job name . . . . . . . . . . . . > DSP19        Name, *
        User . . . . . . . . . . . . .               Name
        Number . . . . . . . . . . . .               000000-999999
     Output . . . . . . . . . . . . . > *            *, *PRINT
     Option . . . . . . . . . . . . . > *SPLF        *SELECT, *STSA, *DFNA...
```

Figure 11.15: The prompt from the command DSPJOB *??JOB(DSP01) ??OUTPUT(*) ??OPTION( ) with option parameter entered.*

In the preceding example, the values for Job name and Option were changed to DSP19 and *SPLF, respectively. The changes are reflected in the command written to the job log as shown in Figure 11.16.

```
*...+....1....+....2....+....3....+....4....+....5....+....6....+....7....+....8....+....9....+....0....+....1....+....2....+....3..
 TIME   MSGID  SEV TYPE  MESSAGE TEXT                                                          FROM PGM   INST TO PGM      INST
 053040        CMD       400 - DSPJOB  ??JOB(DSP19) ??OUTPUT(*) ??OPTION(*SPLF)                QCADRV     0000 XMPL1101CL 0000
```

Figure 11.16: Job log entry produced by command shown in Figure 11.15.

The command that is written to the job log always includes each parameter that has a value specified or that is changed, even if the specified value is the default value for the parameter.

If any parameters are preceded by the selective prompt characters (??), other parameters that are specified without selective prompt characters, or are omitted entirely, aren't displayed on the prompt (even if F4 is pressed):

```
5.00   DSPJOB   JOB(DSP01) ??OPTION(*PGMSTK)
```

Running the preceding DSPJOB command in a CL program causes the prompt in Figure 11.17 to be displayed:

```
                        Display Job (DSPJOB)

Type choices, press Enter.

Option . . . . . . . . . . . . . >  PGMSTK        *SELECT, *STSA, *DFNA...
```

*Figure 11.17: The prompt for the command DSPJOB JOB(DSP01) ??OPTION(*PGMSTK).*

Parameters preceded by the selective prompt characters (?-) are not displayed on the command prompt. The default value is used if the value is omitted. The ?- selective prompt characters are permitted only in commands preceded by a (?):

```
    6.00    ? DSPJOB   ?-JOB(DSP01) OPTION(*PGMSTK)
```

Running the preceding DSPJOB command in a CL program causes the prompt in Figure 11.18 to be displayed:

```
                        Display Job (DSPJOB)

Type choices, press Enter.

Output . . . . . . . . . . . . .  *            *, *PRINT
Option . . . . . . . . . . . . . >  *PGMSTK       *SELECT, *STSA, *DFNA...
```

*Figure 11.18: The prompt for the command ? DSPJOB ?-JOB(DSP01) OPTION(*PGMSTK).*

Parameters preceded by the selective prompt characters (?*) are displayed on the command prompt but are not input-capable:

```
    7.00    DSPJOB   ??OUTPUT( ) ?*OPTION(*JOBLCK)
```

Running the preceding DSPJOB command in a CL program causes the prompt shown in Figure 11.19 to be displayed.

```
                    Display Job (DSPJOB)

 Type choices, press Enter.

 Output . . . . . . . . . . . .   █           *, *PRINT
 Option . . . . . . . . . . . . > *JOBLCK      *SELECT, *STSA, *DFNA...
```

*Figure 11.19: The prompt for the command DSPJOB ??OUTPUT( ) ?*OPTION(*JOBLCK).*

Note in the preceding example that the value for the option parameter is not input-capable.

The selective prompt characters ?< and ?/ are seldom used and are presented here for theoretical value only. Parameters preceded by the selective prompt characters (?<) are displayed on the command prompt and are input-capable. However, if the displayed value is not changed by the user, the default value is used. For example:

```
8.00   DSPJOB   ?<OUTPUT( ) ?<OPTION(*PGMSTK)
```

Running the above DSPJOB command in a CL program causes the prompt in Figure 11.20 to be displayed:

```
                      Display Job (DSPJOB)

  Type choices, press Enter.

  Output . . . . . . . . . . . .   █           *, *PRINT
  Option . . . . . . . . . . . .   *PGMSTK      *SELECT, *STSA, *DFNA...
```

*Figure 11.20: The prompt for the command DSPJOB ?<OUTPUT( ) ?<OPTION(*PGMSTK).*

In the preceding example, if the user presses Enter without changing any parameter values, the default values are used for the command. Note that the value *PGMSTK for the option parameter is ignored. The command is written to the job log with no parameters specified, as shown in Figure 11.21.

```
*...+....1....+....2....+....3....+....4....+....5....+....6....+....7....+....8....+....9....+....0....+....1....+....2....+....3...
 TIME   MSGID  SEV TYPE  MESSAGE TEXT                                                              FROM PGM   INST TO PGM    INST
 053080            CMD       800 - DSPJOB                                                          QCADRV     0000 XMPL1101CL 0000
```

Figure 11.21: The job log entry produced when no parameters are changed.

Values that are changed by the user are accepted as changed (see Figure 11.22).

```
                            Display Job (DSPJOB)

    Type choices, press Enter.

    Output . . . . . . . . . . . . .   *           *, *PRINT
    Option . . . . . . . . . . . . > *SPLF         *SELECT, *STSA, *DFNA...
```

Figure 11.22: The prompt for the command DSPJOB ?<OUTPUT( ) ?<OPTION(*PGMSTK) with option parameter entered.

In the preceding example, the user changed the option parameter to *SPLF. The command is written to the job log as shown in Figure 11.23.

```
*...+....1....+....2....+....3....+....4....+....5....+....6....+....7....+....8....+....9....+....0....+....1....+....2....+....3...
 TIME   MSGID  SEV TYPE  MESSAGE TEXT                                                              FROM PGM   INST TO PGM    INST
 053085            CMD       800 - DSPJOB  *<OPTION(*SPLF)                                         QCADRV     0000 XMPL1101CL 0000
```

Figure 11.23: The job log entry produced by the command shown in Figure 11.22.

Parameters preceded by the selective prompt characters (?/) are displayed on the command prompt but are not input-capable. The default value is always used, no matter what value is specified:

```
    9.00   DSPJOB   ?/OUTPUT( ) ?/OPTION(*SPLF)
```

Running the preceding DSPJOB command in a CL program causes the prompt shown in Figure 11.24 to be displayed:

```
▮                          Display Job (DSPJOB)

   Type choices, press Enter.

   Output . . . . . . . . . . . . .   *              *, *PRINT
   Option . . . . . . . . . . . .   *SPLF          *SELECT, *STSA, *DFNA...
```

*Figure 11.24: The prompt for the command DSPJOB ?/OUTPUT( ) ?/OPTION(*SPLF).*

Note that in the preceding example, both parameters are displayed but are not input-capable. Note that the value *SPLF for the option parameter is ignored. The command is written to the job log as shown in Figure 11.25.

```
*...+....1....+....2....+....3....+....4....+....5....+....6....+....7....+....8....+....9....+....0....+....1....+....2....+....3..
TIME    MSGID  SEV TYPE  MESSAGE TEXT                                                           FROM PGM  INST TO PGM    INST
053090         CMD  900 - DSPJOB                                                                QCADRV    0000 XMPL1101CL 0000
```

Figure 11.25: Job log entry produced by command in Figure 11.24.

THE WRITER CONTROL MENU

Figure 11.26 contains the menu display of the printer control menu.

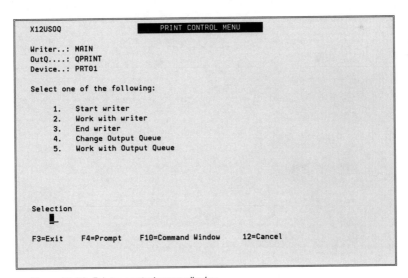

```
X12USOQ                    PRINT CONTROL MENU

   Writer..: MAIN
   OutQ....: QPRINT
   Device..: PRT01

   Select one of the following:

       1.    Start writer
       2.    Work with writer
       3.    End writer
       4.    Change Output Queue
       5.    Work with Output Queue




   Selection
   ▮_

   F3=Exit    F4=Prompt    F10=Command Window    12=Cancel
```

Figure 11.26: Printer control menu display.

Figure 11.27 contains the DDS for WTRMNUDF, the display file used with
WTRMNUCL. Several features incorporated in the DDS deserve attention.

```
 1.00   /****************************************************************/
 2.00   /* Dspfile Name: WTRMNUDF- Display writer control menu         */
 3.00   /****************************************************************/
 4.00
 5.00   A*  CRTDSPF PARMS: RSTDSP(*YES)
 6.00   A                                        CA03(03 'Exit')
 7.00   A N50                                    CF04(04 'Prompt')
 8.00   A                                        CF10(10 'Command Window')
 9.00   A                                        CA12(12 'Cancel')
10.00   A                                        HOME(25 'Home')
11.00   A                                        PRINT
12.00   A                                        HELP  ALTHELP(CA01)
13.00   A ***************************************************************
14.00   A            R MENU                      KEEP OVERLAY
15.00   A                               1  2'X12USOQ'
16.00   A                               1 26'    PRINT CONTROL MENU        '
17.00   A                                        DSPATR(RI)
18.00   A                               3  2'Writer..:'
19.00   A            WTR           10  0  3 12
20.00   A                               4  2'OutQ....:'
21.00   A            OUTQ          10  0  4 12
22.00   A                               5  2'Device..:'
23.00   A            DEV           10  0  5 12
24.00   A                               7  2'Select one of the following:'
25.00   A                               9  7'1.   Start writer'
26.00   A                              10  7'2.   Work with writer'
27.00   A                              11  7'3.   End writer'
28.00   A                              12  7'4.   Change Output Queue'
29.00   A                              13  7'5.   Work with Output Queue'
30.00   A                              19  2'Selection'
31.00   A            OPTION        2Y OI 20  6
32.00   A N50                          22  2'F3=Exit    F4=Prompt     -
33.00   A                                      F10=Command Window    12=Cancel'
34.00   A  50                          22  2'F3=Exit         -
35.00   A                                      F10=Command Window    12=Cancel'
36.00   A ***************************************************************
37.00   A            R MSGSFL                    SFL
38.00   A                                        SFLMSGRCD(23)
39.00   A               MSGKEY                   SFLMSGKEY
40.00   A               PGMQ                     SFLPGMQ
41.00   A  *
42.00   A            R MSGCTL                    SFLCTL(MSGSFL)
43.00   A                                        LOCK OVERLAY
44.00   A N40                                    SFLEND
45.00   A                                        SFLDSP    SFLDSPCTL
46.00   A                                        SFLINZ
47.00   A                                        SFLSIZ(9) SFLPAG(2)
48.00   A               PGMQ                     SFLPGMQ
49.00   A ***************************************************************
```

Figure 11.27: Display file for writer control menu.

One of the application requirements states that each menu option should allow full prompting of the underlying command for non-limited users. The CL program WTRMNUCL is responsible for determining users who are permitted to prompt commands; indicator 50 is set on if the user is limited. Consequently, in the display file, indicator N50 conditions the prompt key (F4) at line 7.00 and the function key text at the bottom of the display (lines 32.00 – 35.00). When the menu display is written with indicator 50 set on, there is no function key text displayed for the F4 key.

Another of the application requirements states that the menu should support a message subfile. The message subfile formats are coded on statements 37.00 – 48.00 in the DDS source for WTRMNUDF.

Conforming to the Consistent User Access (CUA) component of the standards set forth in the SAA (Systems Application Architecture), OS/400 allows F1 to be used as an alternate Help key. Although no help screens are defined for WTRMNUDF, the ALTHELP DDS keyword used in conjunction with the HELP keyword allows the F1 key to be used for requesting second-level message text for messages that appear in the message subfile.

Figure 11.28 contains the source for the CL program WTRMNUCL. To review CL menu-processing basics—including error handling and message subfile processing—see chapter 9.

```
  1.00    /*****************************************************************/
  2.00    /* Program Name: WTRMNUCL- Process writer control menu        */
  3.00    /*****************************************************************/
  4.00
  5.00 PGM (&WTR &OUTQ &DEV)
  6.00    DCL    &WTR        *CHAR  10
  7.00    DCL    &OUTQ       *CHAR  10
  8.00    DCL    &DEV        *CHAR  10
  9.00    DCL    &MSGQ       *CHAR  10
 10.00    DCL    &LMTCPB     *CHAR  10
 11.00    DCL    &CMD        *CHAR 512
 12.00    DCL    &MSGKEY     *CHAR   4
 13.00    DCL    &ERRORS     *LGL        VALUE('1')
 14.00    DCLF   WTRMNUDF
```

Figure 11.28: A CL program to process a writer-control menu (part 1 of 3).

```
15.00
16.00    MONMSG    CPF0000 EXEC(GOTO ERR_RTN)
17.00
18.00    CHGVAR    &PGMQ VALUE(WTRMNUCL)
19.00    RTVUSRPRF MSGQ(&MSGQ) LMTCPB(&LMTCPB)
20.00    IF        (&LMTCPB = '*YES') /* IN50 restricts prompt */ +
21.00              CHGVAR &IN50 '1'
22.00    CRTMSGF   MSGF(QTEMP/MENUMSGF) TEXT('temporary for menu options')
23.00      MONMSG  CPF2112 EXEC(RCVMSG MSGTYPE(*EXCP) RMV(*YES))
24.00
25.00    ADDMSGD   MSGID(OPTCODE) MSGF(QTEMP/MENUMSGF) MSG('&1,&2,&3,&4') +
26.00                FMT((*CHAR 10)(*CHAR 10)(*CHAR 10)(*CHAR 10))
27.00      MONMSG  CPF2412   EXEC(DO) /* Message exists, change it */
28.00              RCVMSG MSGTYPE(*EXCP) RMV(*YES)
29.00              CHGMSGD MSGID(OPTCODE) MSGF(QTEMP/MENUMSGF) +
30.00                FMT((*CHAR 10)(*CHAR 10)(*CHAR 10)(*CHAR 10))
31.00              ENDDO              /* Message exists, change it */
32.00
33.00    CHGMSGD   MSGID(OPTCODE) MSGF(QTEMP/MENUMSGF) +
34.00              MSG('WTRMNU started for writer &1, OUTQ &2.')
35.00    RTVMSG    MSGID(OPTCODE) MSGF(QTEMP/MENUMSGF) MSG(&CMD) +
36.00              MSGDTA(&WTR *CAT &OUTQ)
37.00    SNDPGMMSG MSG(&CMD) TOPGMQ(*SAME) MSGTYPE(*RQS) KEYVAR(&MSGKEY)
38.00    RCVMSG    MSGTYPE(*RQS) MSGKEY(&MSGKEY) RMV(*NO)
39.00
40.00 MENU:
41.00    SNDF      RCDFMT(MSGCTL)
42.00    SNDRCVF   RCDFMT(MENU)
43.00    CHGVAR    &ERRORS '0'
44.00
45.00    IF        (&IN03) RETURN
46.00    IF        (&IN12) RETURN
47.00
48.00    IF        (&IN10) DO /* Command Entry */
49.00              CALL QUSCMDLN
50.00              GOTO MENU
51.00              ENDDO      /* Command Entry */
52.00
53.00 OPTIONS:
54.00    IF        (&OPTION = 1) +
55.00              CHGMSGD MSGID(OPTCODE) MSGF(QTEMP/MENUMSGF) +
56.00              MSG('STRPRTWTR DEV(&3) +
57.00              OUTQ(&2) MSGQ(&4) WTR(&1)')
58.00    ELSE      IF  (&OPTION = 2) +
59.00              CHGMSGD MSGID(OPTCODE) MSGF(QTEMP/MENUMSGF) +
60.00                  MSG('WRKWTR WTR(&1)')
61.00    ELSE      IF  (&OPTION = 3) +
62.00              CHGMSGD MSGID(OPTCODE) MSGF(QTEMP/MENUMSGF) +
63.00                  MSG('ENDWTR ?*WTR(&1) ??OPTION()')
64.00    ELSE      IF  (&OPTION = 4) +
65.00              CHGMSGD MSGID(OPTCODE) MSGF(QTEMP/MENUMSGF) +
```

Figure 11.28: A CL program to process a writer-control menu (part 2 of 3).

```
 66.00                       MSG('CHGWTR WTR(&1) OUTQ(&2)')
 67.00    ELSE      IF   (&OPTION = 5) +
 68.00              CHGMSGD MSGID(OPTCODE) MSGF(QTEMP/MENUMSGF) +
 69.00                       MSG('WRKOUTQ OUTQ(&2)')
 70.00    ELSE      GOTO MENU
 71.00
 72.00 /* ———- Build command ———-*/
 73.00    RTVMSG    MSGID(OPTCODE) MSGF(QTEMP/MENUMSGF) MSG(&CMD) +
 74.00              MSGDTA(&WTR *CAT &OUTQ *CAT &DEV *CAT &MSGQ)
 75.00 /* ———- Set request boundary ———*/
 76.00   SNDPGMMSG MSG(&CMD) TOPGMQ(*SAME) MSGTYPE(*RQS) KEYVAR(&MSGKEY)
 77.00   RCVMSG    MSGTYPE(*RQS) MSGKEY(&MSGKEY) RMV(*NO)
 78.00
 79.00 PROMPT:
 80.00    IF        (&IN04 *OR &OPTION = 3) +
 81.00              DO /* Prompt requested */
 82.00              CHGVAR    &CMD VALUE('?' *BCAT &CMD)
 83.00              CALL      QCMDCHK (&CMD 512)
 84.00                MONMSG CPF0000 EXEC(GOTO MENU)
 85.00              RMVMSG    MSGKEY(&MSGKEY)
 86.00              SNDPGMMSG MSG(&CMD) TOPGMQ(*SAME) MSGTYPE(*RQS) +
 87.00                        KEYVAR(&MSGKEY)
 88.00              RCVMSG    MSGTYPE(*RQS) MSGKEY(&MSGKEY) RMV(*NO)
 89.00              ENDDO /* Prompt requested */
 90.00
 91.00 RUNOPTION:
 92.00    CALL      QCMDEXC (&CMD 512)
 93.00       MONMSG CPF0000
 94.00
 95.00    GOTO      MENU
 96.00 97.00 /* ———- Error handling ———-*/
 98.00 ERR_RTN:
 99.00    IF        (&ERRORS) +
100.00              DO      /* Deep trouble, bail out */
101.00              CALL     FWDMSG '1'
102.00                MONMSG CPF0000
103.00              RETURN
104.00              ENDDO    /* Deep trouble, bail out */
105.00
106.00    CHGVAR    &ERRORS '0'
107.00    GOTO      MENU
108.00
109.00 ENDPGM
```

Figure 11.28: A CL program to process a writer-control menu (part 3 of 3).

As demanded by the application requirements, CL program WTRMNUCL receives three parameters to work with:

- The writer.
- The output queue.
- The printer device.

At line 19.00, the RTVUSRPRF command is used to retrieve the name of the user profile message queue and the value of the limit capabilities attribute for the current user. The MSGQ (Message Queue) parameter of RTVUSRPRF specifies the name of a CL variable that is used to retrieve the name of the message queue associated with the specified user.

The LMTCPB (Limit Capabilities) parameter specifies the name of a CL variable that is used to retrieve the value for the limit capabilities attribute for the user profile of the current user. The LMTCPB attribute of a user profile specifies the limit to which the user can run the CHGPRF command, change values on the sign-on screen, and run commands from a command line. A user who has limited capabilities (LMTCPB(*YES)) cannot run most commands from a command line. There are a few commands, such as SIGNOFF and DSPMSG, that can be run by limited users. Such commands have an ALWLMTUSR (Allow Limited Users) attribute of (*YES). If the current user is limited, indicator 50 is set on to disallow prompting in the display file.

At statements 22.00 – 31.00, a temporary message file named MENUMSGF is created in the QTEMP library to support the RTVMSG technique for building command strings. The MONMSG command at line 23.00 removes the exception message generated if the message queue already exists.

After the message file is created, a generalized message with the message identifier of OPTCODE is added to MENUMSGF. The message contains formats for four message fields:

- Writer
- Output queue
- Device
- Message queue

The MONMSG command at line 27.00 executes a DO group that removes the exception message generated if the message identifier already exists and runs the CHGMSGD (Change Message Description) command to make sure the message description has the correct format required by the application.

The section of code from line 33.00 to 38.00 places a message on the job log that this program is starting and identifies the name of the writer and output queue received as parameters. The technique used to generate and log this message is the basis for all explicit logging done in the program. The message text for message identifier OPTC0DE in MENUMSGF is changed to the desired message, including message fields for the writer and output queue.

Next, the RTVMSG command retrieves the first level message text into the CL variable &CMD. The substitution data, &WTR concatenated to &OUTQ, is supplied through the MSGDTA parameter. Because &WTR and &OUTQ are each declared with the same length as their corresponding format in message OPTC0DE, *CAT is the correct character string operator. Concatenation with blank truncation would yield erroneous results. The CL variable &CMD is sent as a request message to the call message queue. The message reference key (MRK) is captured in the CL variable &MSGKEY. The MRK is subsequently supplied for the MSGKEY parameter of the subsequent RCVMSG command. Receiving the request message flags it as an old message and establishes a request boundary.

Menu processing begins at line 40.00. After the message subfile and menu formats are written and received, the values of function key input indicators are tested and appropriate action is taken. The F3 and F12 keys (&IN03 and &IN12) both cause WTRMNUCL to end.

The F10 key (&IN10) invokes a DO group that includes a call to the system-supplied program QUSCMDLN. QUSCMDLN, the display command line window API, displays a window with a command line. Figure 11.29 shows the menu display after F10 has been pressed. From the command line, the user can prompt, use help for, and run commands. The F9 key allows the user to retrieve commands that have been run using any of the command entry interfaces as well as commands run as menu options and written to the call message queue as request messages.

```
X12USOQ                        PRINT CONTROL MENU

Writer..: LASERPRT
OutQ....: LASERPRT
Device..: LASERPRT

Select one of the following:

     1.   Start writer
     2.   Work with writer
     3.   End writer
     4.   Change Output Queue
     5.   Work with Output Queue




    ...........................................................
    :                         Command                         :
    :                                                         :
    : ===> █                                                  :
    : F4=Prompt   F9=Retrieve   F12=Cancel                    :
    :                                                         :
    :.........................................................:
```

Figure 11.29: Printer control menu with command line window.

As long as end-users are limited users, it is safe to allow them access to the command line because a user who has limited capabilities can only run commands that have an ALWLMTUSR attribute of (*YES).

The five possible options are handled by statements 53.00 – 70.00. Each option runs the CHGMSGD command to change the first level message text of OPTC0DE in MENUMSGF to the appropriate command string with message fields for the variable data. Note that although the order of the message fields is arbitrary, they must be used consistently. In this example, &1 is always used for the WTR parameter, &2 is used for OUTQ, &3 is used for DEV, and &4 is used for &MSGQ.

The command string for the CHGWTR command specified as the message text for option 3 includes selective prompt characters for the WTR and OPTION parameters. Therefore, whenever option 3 is selected, the CHGWTR command is prompted. The WTR parameter is displayed with the value for &WTR received by WTRMNUCL, but it is not input-capable. The OPTION parameter is displayed with the default value and can be changed by the user.

At line 73.00, the RTVMSG command is used to build the command string. Note that this command is generalized for all options. The message data includes all four variables even though they are not used by all of the options. Message data that exceeds the requirements of the message fields is ignored.

The combination of the SNDPGMMSG and RCVMSG commands serves two important roles. First, it sets a request boundary. As discussed in chapter 9, sending and receiving a request message is crucial to the operation of the message subfile. Because the SFLINZ keyword is specified, a write to the control record initializes the subfile with all of the messages associated with the current request or with all of the messages after the last request boundary. Second, it satisfies the requirement for explicit job logging. The actual command to run for the option is written to the job log.

If F4 is pressed, signified by indicator 04 being on, prompting is requested for the option. If option 3 is selected or prompting is requested through F4, the command to run must be prompted. In the DO group from line 81.00 to 89.00, a (?) is inserted at the beginning of the command string, which is passed to QCMDCHK. The command string is returned in the CL variable &CMD with the updated parameter values as entered on the prompt. To update the job log with the modified command, the request message that had been sent is removed, and the modified request is sent and received—resetting the request boundary.

At line 92.00, the command is run by passing the command string to QCMDEXC. The GOTO command at line 95.00 branches back to the top of the loop, at which point the display file I/O is performed again. Any messages generated by the prior command appear in the message subfile.

REVIEW QUESTIONS

1. *A common method of controlling the job environment of an interactive job is with an _____ _____ associated with the user profile.*

2. The _____ command places one or more of the values that are stored and associated with a user into CL variables.

3. An interactive job's initial library list comes either from the system value _____ or from the _____ attribute of the job description used to initialize the job.

4. In a generalized initial program, special functions that are to be performed for a specific user can be incorporated in _____.

5. The error handling strategy in a generalized initial program necessarily must be specialized. Because the initial program is run for end-users and technical staff alike, consideration must be given to the user _____. Also, if an initial program is unable to run, the job must _____.

6. The RCLRSC command is normally used in the _____ program of an application. When one of the called programs in the application ends abnormally, RCLRSC _____ files that have closed abnormally and frees _____ _____.

7. The STRPRTWTR (Start Printer Writer) command starts a _____ _____ to the specified printer.

8. _____ is a system supplied program that performs syntax checking and optionally prompts a command.

9. When the command to be syntax-checked is stored in a CL variable and prompting is requested, the _____ _____ _____ is returned in the variable.

10. The RTVMSG command is used by a CL program to retrieve a _____ _____ _____ from a _____ _____ and copy it into _____ _____ in the program.

11. _____ _____ allows you to control which parameters are displayed when a command is prompted and how they are displayed. It is specified by placing special characters immediately before the _____ of parameters being selected for prompting.

12. _____, the display command line window API, displays a window containing a command line.

13. It is safe to allow "end users" access to the command line as long as they are _____ users, because a user who has _____ _____ can only run commands that have an _____ attribute of (*YES).

12

ADVANCED CL
PROGRAMMING FEATURES

This chapter includes several example CL programs that illustrate advanced message-handling techniques, outfile processing, and an advanced version of the initial program discussed in chapter 11. Topics presented include break-handling programs, interpreting sender data, interpreting message data, sending a command to a message queue, and using the SNDUSRMSG command.

BREAK-HANDLING PROGRAMS

The AS/400 supports several methods of temporarily interrupting a job to perform some other task. For an interactive job, the *system request key* provides this type of function by suspending the application while the system request menu is displayed. This menu can be used to run a number of tasks. When the system request task is completed, the previous display is restored and processing of the original application continues.

Another method of interrupting a job is to place a message queue in *BREAK mode for the job. For an interactive job, messages sent to the message queue in break mode interrupt the current application and display the message on the workstation. This is the most common use of *break messages*.

The system also provides a method for user applications to take control when a message queue receives a message while in break mode. This allows you to specify a user-written CL program to be called when a message arrives on the message queue that is in break mode.

The CHGMSGQ (Change Message Queue) command is used to control the message handling for a message queue. The PGM (Break-Message Handling Program) parameter is used to specify either the system default message handler or a user-written program name.

The system default handler is specified as PGM(*DSPMSG), which causes the DSPMSG (Display Message) command to be run when a message arrives on the queue. If a user-written program name is specified on the PGM parameter, the specified program, referred to as a *break-handling program*, is called when a message arrives on the queue. The break-handling program is responsible for handling the message that caused it to be invoked.

For example, the following command puts the message queue for the current user in break delivery mode and specifies that BRKPGM01 is the program to handle messages:

```
CHGMSGQ  MSGQ(*USRPRF) DLVRY(*BREAK) PGM(BRKPGM01)
```

A user-written break-handling program must receive the parameters listed in Table 12.1.

These values are passed to the break- handling program by OS/400 when a message is sent to the

Table 12.1: Required Parameters for a Break-Handling Program.

Parameter	Data Type and Size	Description
MSGQ	Char(10)	Name of the message queue where the message was sent.
MSGQLIB	Char(10)	Name of the message queue library
MSGKEY	Char(4)	The message reference key assigned to the message.

message queue. A user-written break-handling program normally uses the message queue, library, and MRK to receive the message. This causes the message's status to be changed to "old."

The CL program BRKPGM01 in Figure 12.1 is an example of a break-handling program that causes inquiry messages to be displayed while ignoring other types of messages:

```
 1.00 /**********************************************************/
 2.00 /* Program Name: BRKPGM01 - Ignore info messages          */
 3.00 /**********************************************************/
 4.00
 5.00 PGM          (&MSGQ &MSGQLIB &MSGKEY)
 6.00    DCL       &MSGQ    *CHAR   10
 7.00    DCL       &MSGQLIB *CHAR   10
 8.00    DCL       &MSGKEY  *CHAR    4
 9.00    DCL       &CMD     *CHAR  512
10.00    DCL       &RTNTYPE *CHAR    2
11.00
12.00    RCVMSG    MSGQ(&MSGQLIB/&MSGQ) MSGKEY(&MSGKEY) +
13.00                RMV(*NO) MSG(&CMD) RTNTYPE(&RTNTYPE)
14.00    /* Inquiry message? */
15.00    IF        (&RTNTYPE = '05')  +
16.00                DSPMSG MSGQ(&MSGQLIB/&MSGQ)
17.00
18.00 ENDPGM
```

Figure 12.1: A sample break-handling program.

BRKPGM01 receives the three parameters and receives the message that caused the CL program to be invoked. The RCVMSG command includes the RTNTYPE parameter so that the message type can be determined. If the message received is an inquiry message (&RTNTYPE = '05'), the DSPMSG command is used to display the messages in the message queue.

Table 12.2 lists the possible message-type return codes. These codes are received by the CL variable specified on the RTNTYPE parameter of the RCVMSG command. Another application for a break-handling program is illustrated by the CL program BRKPGM02 shown in Figure 12.2.

In Figure 12.2, the text of the message is received into the CL return variable &CMD. The variable &CMD is then passed to QCMDEXC to be run.

A job can place a message queue named RUNCMD in break mode with BRKPGM02 specified as the break-handling program, as follows:

```
CHGMSGQ  MSGQ(RUNCMD) DLVRY(*BREAK)
PGM(BRKPGM02)
```

Any message sent to RUNCMD that contains a valid command causes the job to be suspended while the command runs. For example, the following CL command could be used to run the DSPJOB command in the job that has message queue RUNCMD in break mode:

```
SNDMSG  ('DSPJOB') TOMSGQ(RUNCMD)
```

Table 12.2:
Message-Type Return Codes.

Code	Type of Message
01	Completion
02	Diagnostic
04	Information
05	Inquiry
08	Request
10	Request with prompting
14	Notify
15	Escape
21	Reply, not checked for validity
22	Reply, checked for validity
23	Reply, message default used
24	Reply, system default used
25	Reply, from system reply list

```
 1.00 /**************************************************************/
 2.00 /* Program Name: BRKPGM02 - Run a command                     */
 3.00 /**************************************************************/
 4.00
 5.00 PGM          (&MSGQ &MSGQLIB &MSGKEY)
 6.00   DCL        &MSGQ    *CHAR    10
 7.00   DCL        &MSGQLIB *CHAR    10
 8.00   DCL        &MSGKEY  *CHAR     4
 9.00   DCL        &CMD     *CHAR    512
10.00
11.00   RCVMSG     MSGQ(&MSGQLIB/&MSGQ) MSGKEY(&MSGKEY) +
12.00                RMV(*NO) MSG(&CMD)
13.00
14.00   CALL       QCMDEXC (&CMD 512)
15.00     MONMSG   CPF0000
16.00 ENDPGM
```

Figure 12.2: A sample break-handling program that runs a command.

The job that had placed RUNCMD in break mode is suspended while the DSPJOB command runs. If the job is an interactive session, the Display Job Menu is displayed. If it is a batch job, the job information is printed

Break-handling programs have operational characteristics that must be considered. When a message arrives at the message queue, the specified break-handling program is added to the end of the call stack. Job environment changes made by the break-handling program, such as changing the library list or the default output queue, remain in effect after the program ends.

File overrides issued by the break-handling program are no longer in effect after the program ends unless they specified OVRSCOPE(*JOB). Also, if the break-handling program runs the SETATNPGM (Set Attention Program) command, the attention-key-program reverts to its prior setting when the program ends. Finally, adopted authorities do not propagate to the break-handling program.

The possibilities for a CL program such as BRKPGM02 are endless. The capability to run any command within another job can be quite useful, but it also can be very risky. For example, if a prankster were to send the message 'SIGNOFF *NOLIST' to a message queue in break-handling mode with BRKPGM02, the job that had allocated the message queue would sign off the system. To harness the useful power of CL break-handling programs such as BRKPGM02, controlling measures should be implemented.

Certainly, far more security-related issues would have to be considered than are illustrated here. To protect against security problems, OS/400 security can be used to limit authority to the message queue. Also, the break-handling program could support only a subset of commands to be run.

INTERPRETING SENDER DATA

Another approach to protecting against abuse of a CL program such as BRKPGM02 is to include control measures in the program based on the sender data that is part of each message. Sender data is information about the sender of a message that can be copied into a CL return variable through the SENDER parameter of RCVMSG. The commands shown in Figure 12.3 can be used to retrieve the sender information of a message.

```
DCL      &SENDER      *CHAR  80
.
.
RCVMSG  MSGQ(DSP19)  SENDER(&SENDER)
```

Figure 12.3: An example of retrieving sender information.

As shown in Figure 12.3, the RCVMSG command receives sender information of the first message in the DSP19 workstation message queue. The information is returned in the &SENDER CL variable.

The sender data includes the identification of and information about the job and program from which the message was sent, the date and time the message was sent, and the message queue to which it was sent. Sender data comes in two formats— short and long. The value specified for the SENDERFMT parameter determines which format is returned. The default, SENDERFMT (*SHORT), returns 80 bytes of data and is most appropriate with OPM programs. For this discussion, the short format is used. For a discussion of the long format, see chapter 13. The short format of the sender data is listed in Table 12.3.

Table 12.3:
***SHORT Format of the Sender Data.**

From	To	Size	Description
1	10	10	Job name
11	20	10	Job user profile ID
21	26	6	Job number
27	38	12	Sender program name
39	42	4	Sender program line number
43	49	7	Date sent DatFmt(cyymmdd)
50	55	6	Time sent TimFmt(hhmmss)
56	65	10	Sent-To program name
66	69	4	Sent-To program line number
70	70	1	Sender Program Type 0 = OPM or SLIC <= 12 1 = ILE Proc <= 256 2 = ILE Proc > 256 3 = SLIC > 12
71	71	1	Sent-To Program Type 0 = OPM 1 = ILE Proc <= 256 2 = ILE Proc > 256
72	80	9	Reserved for Future Use

BRKPGM02 can be changed to take advantage of the sender data. This information can be used to implement controls as to who can run commands at other jobs. Figure 12.4 contains the CL source for the RUNMSGCMD CL break-handling program. It is somewhat more advanced than the previous break handlers; it runs only request messages sent by the current user or users with a user class or group profile of the security officer or system operator.

```
 1.00  /****************************************************************/
 2.00  /*   Program:  RUNMSGCMD — Break-Handling Program            */
 3.00  /****************************************************************/
 4.00
 5.00  PGM          PARM(&MSGQ &MSGQLIB &MSGKEY)
 6.00    DCL        &MSGQ      *CHAR   10  /* MSG queue name */
 7.00    DCL        &MSGQLIB   *CHAR   10  /* MSG queue library */
 8.00    DCL        &MSGKEY    *CHAR    4  /* Message ref key */
 9.00    DCL        &MSGCMD    *CHAR  512  /* Command to run */
10.00    DCL        &MSGLEN    *DEC     5  /* Length of message */
11.00    DCL        &LENGTH    *DEC (15 5) /* Length for QCMDEXC */
12.00    DCL        &RTNTYPE   *CHAR    2  /* Message type */
13.00    DCL        &SENDER    *CHAR   80  /* Sender data */
14.00    DCL        &GRPPRF    *CHAR   10  /* Group Profile */
15.00    DCL        &USRCLS    *CHAR   10  /* User class */
16.00    DCL        &CURUSER   *CHAR   10  /* Current user */
17.00    DCL        &MSGUSER   *CHAR   10  /* Message sender */
18.00    DCL        &RQS       *CHAR    2  VALUE('08')
19.00    MONMSG     MSGID(CPF0000) EXEC(GOTO ENDPGM)
20.00
21.00    RCVMSG     MSGQ(&MSGQLIB/&MSGQ) MSGKEY(&MSGKEY) +
22.00                 RMV(*NO) MSG(&MSGCMD) MSGLEN(&MSGLEN) +
23.00                 SENDER(&SENDER) RTNTYPE(&RTNTYPE)
24.00    CHGVAR     VAR(&MSGUSER) VALUE(%SST(&SENDER 11 10))
25.00    RTVUSRPRF  RTNUSRPRF(&CURUSER) GRPPRF(&GRPPRF)  +
26.00                 USRCLS(&USRCLS)
27.00    IF         (&RTNTYPE *EQ &RQS) DO
28.00               IF  (&MSGUSER *EQ &CURUSER  *OR +
29.00                    &USRCLS  *EQ '*SECOFR' *OR +
30.00                    &USRCLS  *EQ '*SYSOPR' *OR +
31.00                    &GRPPRF  *EQ 'QSECOFR' *OR +
32.00                    &GRPPRF  *EQ 'QSYSOPR' *OR +
33.00                    &MSGUSER *EQ 'QSECOFR' *OR +
34.00                    &MSGUSER *EQ 'QSYSOPR') DO
35.00                    /* Log the command to the job log  */
36.00                    SNDPGMMSG  MSG(%SST(&MSGCMD 01 &MSGLEN)) TOPGMQ(*SAME) +
37.00                               MSGTYPE(*RQS) KEYVAR(&MSGKEY)
38.00                    RCVMSG     MSGKEY(&MSGKEY) RMV(*NO)
39.00                    CHGVAR     VAR(&LENGTH) VALUE(&MSGLEN)
40.00                    CALL       QCMDEXC PARM(&MSGCMD &LENGTH)
41.00                    ENDDO
42.00               ENDDO
43.00  ENDPGM
```

Figure 12.4: CL Source for the RUNMSGCMD program.

Break-Handling Commands

In addition to the CL break-handling program shown in Figure 12.4, two other CL programs and two corresponding command definitions, shown in Figures 12.5 through 12.8, can be used for a more complete remote command-processing system through messages and break-handling programs. For more details on command definition, see chapter 14.

```
1.00   /*******************************************************/
2.00   /*  To compile the CMD, run the following command:    */
3.00   /*    CRTCMD CMD(STRMSGCMD)  PGM(STRMSGCMD)            */
4.00   /*******************************************************/
5.00   CMD        PROMPT('Start MSG Command processing')
6.00   PARM       KWD(MSGLIB) TYPE(*NAME) DFT(QUSRSYS) EXPR(*YES) +
7.00                  PROMPT('Library name for message queue')
8.00   /*********** End of CMD Source ***********/
```

Figure 12.5: Command definition source for STRMSGCMD.

```
1.00   /*******************************************************/
2.00   /*  To compile this CMD, run the following command:   */
3.00   /*    CRTCMD CMD(SNDMSGCMD)  PGM(SNDMSGCMD)            */
4.00   /*  Note:  Order of parameter on the prompter is       */
5.00   /*         control through "Order prompt is displayed" */
6.00   /*         element of the PROMPT parameter.            */
7.00   /*******************************************************/
8.00
9.00   CMD        PROMPT('Send message to run as command')
10.00
11.00  PARM       KWD(JOB) TYPE(*CHAR) LEN(6) DFT(*CURRENT) +
12.00                 SPCVAL((*CURRENT 000000)) FULL(*YES) +
13.00                 PROMPT('Run command at job number' 1)
14.00  PARM       KWD(MSGLIB) TYPE(*NAME) DFT(QUSRSYS) +
15.00                 PROMPT('Message queue library name' 3)
16.00  PARM       KWD(CMD) TYPE(*CMDSTR) LEN(512) +
17.00                 PROMPT('Command to run' 2)
18.00  /*********** End of CMD Source ***********/
```

Figure 12.6: Command definition source for SNDMSGCMD.

```
 1.00 /****************************************************************/
 2.00 /*  Program:  STRMSGCMD — Start running message as commands     */
 3.00 /****************************************************************/
 4.00
 5.00 PGM         PARM(&MSGLIB)
 6.00   DCL       &MSGLIB   *CHAR  10
 7.00   DCL       &JOBNBR   *CHAR   6 /* Job number */
 8.00   DCL       &PREFIX   *CHAR   3 VALUE('CMD')
 9.00   DCL       &DFTLIB   *CHAR  10 VALUE('QUSRSYS')
10.00   DCL       &BRKPGM   *CHAR  10 VALUE('RUNMSGCMD')
11.00   DCL       &BRKLIB   *CHAR  10 VALUE('*LIBL')
12.00   MONMSG    MSGID(CPF9999) EXEC(GOTO ERR_RTN)
13.00 /*============================================================*/
14.00   RTVJOBA   NBR(&JOBNBR)
15.00
16.00   IF        (&MSGLIB *EQ ' ') +
17.00               CHGVAR  VAR(&MSGLIB) VALUE(&DFTLIB)
18.00
19.00   CRTMSGQ   MSGQ(&MSGLIB/(&PREFIX *TCAT &JOBNBR)) +
20.00               TEXT('Used to set up job to run commands +
21.00               sent to a MSGQ')
22.00     MONMSG    MSGID(CPF2112) /* Ignore if already exists */
23.00
24.00   CHGMSGQ   MSGQ(&MSGLIB/(&PREFIX *TCAT &JOBNBR)) +
25.00               DLVRY(*BREAK) PGM(&BRKLIB/&BRKPGM)
26.00 /*============================================================*/
27.00 /*  Send this program's user a completion message             */
28.00
29.00   SNDPGMMSG MSG('Job' *BCAT &JOBNBR *BCAT 'ready to +
30.00               receive remote commands.') TOPGMQ(*PRV) +
31.00               MSGTYPE(*COMP)
32.00   RETURN
33.00
34.00 /*============================================================*/
35.00 ERR_RTN:
36.00   CALL      PGM(FWDMSG) PARM('1') /* Forward messages    */
37.00     MONMSG    MSGID(CPF0000)       /* <— Very Important! */
38.00 ENDPGM
```

Figure 12.7: CL source for the STRMSGCMD program.

```
 1.00 /****************************************************************/
 2.00 /*  CL Program:  SNDMSGCMD — Run a command at another job       */
 3.00 /****************************************************************/
 4.00 PGM         PARM(&JOBNBR &MSGLIB &CMD)
 5.00   DCL       &JOBNBR   *CHAR   6 /* Job name */
 6.00   DCL       &CMD      *CHAR 512 /* Command to run */
 7.00   DCL       &MSGLIB   *CHAR  10 /* Message queue library */
 8.00   DCL       &DFTLIB   *CHAR  10 VALUE('QUSRSYS')
 9.00   DCL       &PREFIX   *CHAR   3 VALUE('CMD')
10.00   MONMSG    MSGID(CPF0000) EXEC(GOTO ERR_RTN)
```

Figure 12.8: CL source for the SNDMSGCMD program (part 1 of 2).

```
11.00 /*===============================================================*/
12.00    IF        (&JOBNBR *EQ '000000') RTVJOBA NBR(&JOBNBR)
13.00
14.00    IF        (&CMD *EQ ' ') DO   /* No command?  */
15.00              SNDPGMMSG  MSG('No command specified.  No message sent +
16.00                            to job number' *BCAT &JOBNBR) +
17.00                         TOPGMQ(*PRV) MSGTYPE(*DIAG)
18.00              RETURN
19.00              ENDDO
20.00 /*===============================================================*/
21.00 /*         Syntax check the command before sending it.           */
22.00    CALL      PGM(QCMDCHK) PARM(&CMD 512)
23.00    IF        (&MSGLIB *EQ ' ')  CHGVAR  VAR(&MSGLIB) VALUE(&DFTLIB)
24.00
25.00    CHKOBJ    OBJ(&MSGLIB/(&PREFIX *TCAT &JOBNBR)) OBJTYPE(*MSGQ)
26.00      MONMSG  MSGID(CPF9801) EXEC(DO)
27.00              SNDPGMMSG  MSG('Job' *BCAT &JOBNBR *CAT 'not set up to +
28.00                            handle remote commands, or is not +
29.00                            active.') TOPGMQ(*PRV) MSGTYPE(*DIAG)
30.00              RETURN
31.00              ENDDO
32.00
33.00 /*===============================================================*/
34.00 /*  Send the command to the remote message queue                 */
35.00    SNDPGMMSG  MSG(&CMD) TOMSGQ(&MSGLIB/(&PREFIX *TCAT &JOBNBR)) +
36.00                 MSGTYPE(*RQS)
37.00
38.00 /*===============================================================*/
39.00 /*  Send this program's user a completion message                */
40.00    SNDPGMMSG  MSG('Command <' *BCAT &CMD *BCAT '> sent to job' +
41.00                 *BCAT &JOBNBR) TOPGMQ(*PRV) MSGTYPE(*COMP)
42.00    RETURN
43.00 /*===============================================================*/
44.00 ERR_RTN:
45.00    CALL      PGM(FWDMSG) PARM('1') /* Forward messages */
46.00      MONMSG  MSGID(CPF0000)  /* <- Very Important! */
47.00 ENDPGM
```

Figure 12.8: CL source for the SNDMSGCMD program (part 2 of 2).

Table 12.4 contains a chart of the five modules that make up a break-handling system. Although none of them are necessarily required, they do provide a convenient set of utilities. If these modules are used in day-to-day production, it is recommended that they be thoroughly tested before being implemented.

Table 12.4: Break-Handling Modules.

Source Member	Type	Purpose
STRMSGCMD	CMD	Can be used to set up the current job with RUNMSGCMD as its break-handling program. The MSGLIB parameter of this command allows the user to indicate a library name where the message queue is to be created.
STRMSGCMD	CLP	The command-processing program for the STRMSGCMD command.
SNDMSGCMD	CMD	The command used to send a command to be run at another job. The target job number is specified and a valid command is specified. Also, the target job must have been set up using the STRMSGCMD command to run commands sent to it.
SNDMSGCMD	CLP	The command-processing program for the SNDMSGCMD command.
RUNMSGCMD	CLP	The break-handling program. It is called whenever a message is sent to a job message queue that is in break mode, and has this program as its break handler.

INTERPRETING MESSAGE DATA

The message-data record that provides the substitution values used in the text of most predefined messages can be received by a CL variable. The message data is received as a single character string with a maximum length of 512 characters. The format of the string can be determined by displaying the description of the message identifier being received.

For example, message identifier CPC1221 is the completion message sent by the SBMJOB command. You can display the description for message identifier CPC1221 using the DSPMSGD (Display Message Description) command. The Formatted Message Text display shows the first level text of the message as follows:

```
Job &3/&2/&1 submitted to jobq &4 in &5.
```

The message text contains several *message fields*. Message fields are identified by an ampersand (&) followed by a number 1 to 99 and are used for runtime substitution when the message is sent. There are five message fields for the message CPC1221. To display the message description for CPC1221, run the following command:

```
DSPMSGD CPC1221
```

This Display Message Description command, as the name implies, displays the description of message CPC1221. The DSPMSGD command can be used to determine the quantity and type of message fields. There is, however, no descriptive text information provided on the message fields. Determining the meaning of a message field can be accomplished only by observing how it is used in the message. You can see the message text for message identifier CPC1221, complete with substitution data, by submitting a job to batch from the Command Entry display as follows:

```
===> sbmjob cmd(dlyjob 5) job(demojob) jobd(qbatch)
```

The message identifier CPC1221 is sent by the SBMJOB command and is displayed as shown below:

```
===> sbmjob cmd(dlyjob 5) job(demojob) jobd(qbatch)
      Job 014027/LINDAC/DEMOJOB submitted to jobq QBATCH in QGPL.
```

By comparing the final form message to the first level message text on the Formatted Message Text display, you can determine the format of the message data. The job name 'DEMOJOB' in this example, corresponds to message field &1 in the message description. As listed in Table 12.5, message field 1 has a length of 10, and the job name is in positions 1 to 10 of the message data.

The job user, 'LINDAC', corresponds to message field &2. Message field 2 also has a length of 10, and it is in position 11 to 20 of the message data.

By repeating this process for each one of the message fields, the format of the message data can be determined. Table 12.5 lists the format of the message data fields for message identifier CPC1221.

Positions		Data Type and Size	Message Field	Field Description
From	To			
1	10	Char(10)	&1	Job name
11	20	Char(10)	&2	Job user profile ID
21	26	Char(6)	&3	Job number
27	36	Char(10)	&4	Job queue name
37	46	Char(10)	&5	Job queue library name

Table 12.5: Message Data Fields for CPC1221.

Using this information, a CL program can interpret the message data included with the CPC1221 message. For example, after the SBMJOB command is run in a CL program, the last message in the call message queue is this completion message. Specifying MSGTYPE(*LAST) on the RCVMSG command guarantees that the correct message is received. The message data can be copied into a return variable as shown in Figure 12.9.

```
DCL    &MSGDTA   *CHAR  46
.
SBMJOB  CMD(DLYJOB 5) JOB(DEMOJOB) JOBD(QBATCH)
RCVMSG  MSGTYPE(*LAST) MSGDTA(&MSGDTA)
```

Figure 12.9: An example of copying message data into a return variable.

The &MSGDTA CL variable then contains the message-field substitution data that was sent with the CPC1221 message and appears similar to the following:

```
*...v....1....v....2....v....3....v....4....v.
Jobname+++Username++JobNbrJobQ++++++JobQLib+++
'DEMOJOB    LINDAC    014027QBATCH    QGPL        '
```

A CL program can use this information to isolate a particular piece of data about the submitted job. For example, the job number assigned to the batch job can be retrieved from positions 21 through 26 of the message data as in Figure 12.10:

```
    DCL   &MSGDTA  *CHAR  46
>   DCL   &JOBNBR  *CHAR   6
    .
    SBMJOB   CMD(DLYJOB 5) JOB(DEMOJOB) JOBD(QBATCH)
    RCVMSG   MSGTYPE(*LAST) MSGDTA(&MSGDTA)
>   CHGVAR   &JOBNBR  VALUE(%SST(&MSGDTA 21 6))
```

Figure 12.10: Extracting message data fields for CPC1221.

The RCVMSG command receives the completion message from the SBMJOB command and copies the message data to the CL variable &MSGDTA. The %SST (Substring) built-in function is used with the CHGVAR command to assign the 6 characters beginning in position 21 of &MSGDTA to the CL variable &JOBNBR.

THE SNDUSRMSG COMMAND

The SNDUSRMSG (Send-User Message) command, one of the most useful message-sending commands, is used to send an inquiry (requiring a reply) or information (no reply) message to a user message queue. The command includes the MSGRPY parameter. MSGRPY can be used to receive the user's reply to an inquiry message. Additionally, the syntax of the SNDUSRMSG command allows you to specify a list of valid replies. For example, the command shown in Figure 12.11 sends the message 'Go or Cancel?' to the system operator message queue.

```
    DCL   &RPY  TYPE(*CHAR)  LEN(1)
    SNDUSRMSG  MSG('Go or Cancel? (G C)') VALUES(G C) +
                 TOMSGQ(*SYSOPR) MSGRPY(&RPY)
```

Figure 12.11: Sending message text to system operator message queue.

Traditionally, messages that require a reply include text that describes the valid replies. The choice of valid replies assists the user in making a reply.

In the preceding example, only the values G and C are allowed as a reply. However, by default, lowercase responses are automatically translated to uppercase. The TRNTBL parameter of the SNDUSRMSG command allows you to specify a translation table object that translates the user's reply. Because TRNTBL is not specified in the example, the default translation table QSYSTRNTBL is used. QSYSTRNTBL converts lowercase characters to uppercase.

A CL program issuing the SNDUSRMSG command will wait for the user to reply if MSGTYPE(*INQ) is specified. The user's reply is returned in the CL variable specified for the MSGRPY parameter (&RPY in the example). The MSGRPY CL variable can be up to 132 characters, but typically 1 to 5 characters is adequate.

The powerful SNDUSRMSG command simplifies many message-sending tasks.

CL EXAMPLES USING OUTFILES

Although limited to read-only operations, the database file support in CL allows many useful functions to be performed by CL programs. The majority of CL programs that process database files are written to perform system functions and must process information generated by system commands. Many system-display (DSPxxx) commands provide an option to direct output to the display or the printer and, in many cases, to a database file. These database files are referred to as *output files* (or more commonly, *outfiles*).

For example, to display a list of all output queue names found on your library list, the DSPOBJD (Display Object Description) command, can be used, as follows:

```
DSPOBJD  OBJ(*ALL) OBJTYPE(*OUTQ)
```

The OUTPUT parameter (not shown above) defaults to OUTPUT(*). This causes the output from the command to be sent to the display for interactive jobs and to the printer for batch jobs. The OUTPUT parameter also supports the *OUTFILE option. This option allows the output from the DSPOBJD command to be sent to a database physical file. The following example illustrates the use of an outfile with the DSPOBJD command:

```
DSPOBJD  OBJ(*ALL) OBJTYPE(*OUTQ) +
            OUTPUT(*OUTFILE) OUTFILE(QTEMP/OUTQLIST)
```

The preceding command creates a database file named OUTQLIST in the QTEMP library that contains a record for each output queue (OUTQ). To display the contents of the OUTQFILE file, run the RUNQRY (Run Query) command as follows:

```
RUNQRY  QRYFILE(QTEMP/OUTQLIST)
```

If the DSPOBJD command is run again, the contents of the OUTQLIST file will be replaced. To avoid replacing the data, that is to add to the file, the *ADD option must be specified for the OUTMBR parameter. For example:

```
DSPOBJD  OBJ(QGPL/*ALL)  OBJTYPE(*OUTQ)  OUTPUT(*OUTFILE) +
           OUTFILE(QTEMP/OUTQLIST)  OUTMBR(*FIRST *ADD)
```

Each command that supports an outfile has one or more predefined formats. If the specified outfile does not exist when the command runs, it is created using a predefined format. If the file already exists, it must have the same format as the system-defined outfile.

To use outfile data in a CL program, the file must exist before the CL program can be compiled. Also, the names of the fields in the file must be known before they can be used in the program.

There is an easy way to determine this information. At least one format file exists in QSYS for each DSPxxx command that supports the OUTFILE parameter. The DSPFD (Display File Description) command, however, supports more than 20 format files. All system format files begin with the letters 'QA'. To display a list of available output files, run the following command:

```
WRKF  FILE(QSYS/QA*)  FILEATR(*PF)
```

The file's text description identifies which CL command uses the format file as the basis for its output files.

By declaring a file with the same name as the system format file in QSYS, the actual outfile used by the CL program at runtime doesn't need to exist at compile time. As an example, consider an application to automate the process of

optimizing all programs on the system. Programs can be optimized using the OP-
TIMIZE parameter of the CHGPGM (Change Program) command, as follows:

```
CHGPGM  PGM(PAYROLL/*ALL) OPTIMIZE(*YES)
```

The preceding CHGPGM command optimizes all programs in the PAYROLL library. To optimize all programs in all libraries, a CL program could be written
that processes a database file containing a list of all libraries. Using the outfile
support for the DSPOBJD command, a database file named OPTMIZE that contains
one record for each library on the system can be generated as follows:

```
DSPOBJD  OBJ(QSYS/*ALL) OBJTYPE(*LIB) +
            OUTPUT(*OUTFILE) OUTFILE(OPTMIZE)
```

Each record in the file will contain the name and description of an object that
meets the criteria of the DSPOBJD command. Specifically, the file will contain
one record for each object in QSYS with an object type of *LIB. Because every library on the system meets that criteria, the file will contain one record for each library. It would be a simple task to write a CL program that uses a standard loop
to read the records in the resulting file and, using the value of a database field for
the name of the object, run the CHGPGM command for each library on the system.

There are only two problems to overcome. The first problem is that the file declared in the CL program is QADSPOBJ in QSYS, and the file containing the data is
named OPTIMIZE. That can be resolved easily with an OVRDBF command such as
the following:

```
OVRDBF  QADSPOBJ TOFILE(OPTIMIZE)
```

The second problem is that the name of the CL variable to use for the library
name is not known. The name of the field in QADSPOBJ that contains the object
name can be determined by running the DSPFFD (Display File Field Description)
command, as follows:

```
DSPFFD  FILE(QADSPOBJ)
```

The DSPFFD command provides field-level information for one or more files. By examining the output from this command, the field ODOBNM is determined to contain the object name.

At this point, a CL program can be written and compiled. Figure 12.12 contains the CL source code for OPTMZ1CL, which declares the file QADSPOBJ. File OPTMIZ00 in QTEMP is specified as the outfile for the DSPOBJD command.

```
 1.00 /****************************************************************/
 2.00 /* Program Name: OPTMZ1CL- Optimize all programs on system   */
 3.00 /****************************************************************/
 4.00
 5.00 PGM
 6.00    DCLF       QADSPOBJ
 7.00    MONMSG      CPF9999    EXEC(GOTO ERROR_RTN)
 8.00 /****************************************************************/
 9.00
10.00    DSPOBJD    OBJ(QSYS/*ALL) OBJTYPE(*LIB) +
11.00                  OUTPUT(*OUTFILE) OUTFILE(QTEMP/OPTIMIZE)
12.00
13.00    OVRDBF     QADSPOBJ TOFILE(QTEMP/OPTIMIZE)
14.00
15.00 LOOP:
16.00    RCVF
17.00    MONMSG      CPF0864    EXEC(RETURN)
18.00
19.00    CHGPGM      PGM(&ODOBNM/*ALL) OPTIMIZE(*YES)
20.00    MONMSG      CPF0545
21.00    GOTO        LOOP
22.00
23.00 ERROR_RTN:
24.00    CALL        FWDMSG     PARM('1')
26.00    MONSMG      MSGID(CPF0000)
25.00 ENDPGM
```

Figure 12.12: Processing an OUTFILE.

It is good practice to create temporary work files in the QTEMP library to guarantee that there will be no conflict with other users. Even though the file used at runtime is not the same as the one declared in the CL program, no errors will occur. The OVRDBF command ensures that the file created in QTEMP is the one opened in the CL program.

Lines 15.00 through 21.00 constitute a standard sequential read loop within which the mission-crucial CHGPGM command is run. Consequently, CHGPGM will run once for each record in the file. Each time a record is read, the value of &ODOBNM will be the name of a different library. OPTMZ1CL will therefore optimize all programs in each library on the system.

The MONMSG for CPF0545 on line 20.00 allows the CL program to continue if the error message "No programs changed." is sent to OPTMZ1CL. This exception occurs if there are no programs in the specified library or if all programs in the library are already optimized.

The advantage to declaring the system format file is that the CL program processing the outfile can be compiled without requiring the file with the desired name to be created first. An alternative technique is to run the appropriate display command to create the necessary file. Then compile the CL program.

To create the OPTIMIZE file used by the OPTMZ1CL program, the DSPOBJD command can be run using any object that exists on the system. For example:

```
DSPOBJD  OBJ(QSYS/QCMD) OBJTYPE(*PGM) +
    OUTPUT(*OUTFILE) OUTFILE(MYLIB/OPTIMIZE)
```

If the program QCMD did not exist in QSYS, the outfile would not be created. The library for the outfile should be one that is always in the library list used for compiles.

Once OPTIMIZE is created, the CL program could be written to reference OPTIMIZE directly, instead of referencing QADSPOBJ. For example:

```
DCLF  FILE(MYLIB/OPTIMIZE)
.
.
.
RCVF
```

The file OPTIMIZE is declared on the DCLF command, but the record format name, QLIDOBJD, is not specified for the RCVF parameter. Because CL supports only single-format files the format name isn't necessary.

USING OPNQRYF IN CL PROGRAMS

Any database file can be dynamically manipulated using only CL commands. The OPNQRYF (Open Query File) command allows any database file to be queried. For example, using OPNQRYF, you can dynamically select specific records from one or more files. The OPNQRYF command opens the file but filters the database so that only selected records are presented to the HLL program.

This section presents an overview and illustrates some of the powerful capabilities of Open Query File. However, it isn't the intent of this section to cover all aspects of the OPNQRYF command,. That would take an entire volume in itself. More detailed information about Open Query File can be found in the AS/400e series, *DB2 for AS/400 Database Programming* manual or *Open Query File Magic!: A Complete Guide to Maximizing the Power of OPNQRYF—Second Edition* by Ted Holt, published by Midrange Computing.

Like OPNDBF, the OPNQRYF command pre-opens a file that will be used in a subsequently called HLL program. Once opened, the records in the file are accessed by HLL programs that share the ODP of the file. The ODP can later be closed using the CLOF (Close File) command. The OPTION, OPNID, SEQONLY, DUPKEYCHK, COMMIT, and TYPE parameters of OPNQRYF perform the same functions as on the OPNDBF command.

Unlike OPNDBF, however, OPNQRYF is used to define and open a *view* of the data. That is, OPNQRYF opens a file to a set of database records that satisfies a database-query request. The query request can perform any combination of the following database functions:

- Join records from more than one file, member, and record format. The join may be either equal or non-equal in nature.

- Calculate new field values using numeric and character operations on field values and constants.

- Group records by like values of one or more fields, and calculate aggregate functions, such as minimum field value and average field value, for each group.

- Select a subset of the available records, with selection both before and after grouping the records.

- Arrange result records by the value of one or more key fields.

The preceding list of functions suggests that there is some degree of redundancy and overlap among OS/400 database tools. To appreciate the role Open Query File plays in OS/400, it is helpful to understand that a single OS/400 component, the OS/400 Query Component, is used to process database query requests. The OS/400 Query Component is sometimes referred to as the "query engine," the "query compiler," or the "query optimizer." Actually, the optimizer is just one module of the Query Component.

Several OS/400 facilities—for example, SQL/400, Query/400, Query Management/400, Q&A Database, and Client Access File Transfer—provide a front-end to the Query Component. Also, several third-party products provide easy-to-use, SQL-like front-ends to the Query Component. The Reformat Utility (SORT) and Logical File compiler provide additional overlapping database functionality. The primary purpose of Open Query File is to provide an interface to the Query Component for use by your application. Your application must provide the front-end.

OPNQRYF Parameters

Many readers are familiar with the syntax and use of Structured Query Language (SQL). While progressing through the capabilities of Open Query File and the parameters of the OPNQRYF command, the following sections draw parallels to the analogous SQL clauses. If you are familiar with the syntax for Logical File DDS and/or QUERY/400, you might find it beneficial to relate the material presented here to a syntactical environment that you know well.

Database Query Parameters

FILE. The FILE parameter supplies the information that would be found on the SQL from clause. It specifies one or more files, members, and record formats to be queried.

```
OPNQRYF FILE((*LIBL/POMAST *FIRST *ONLY))
```

When more than one file is specified, the files are joined to create a single set of records. Join queries are discussed later in this section. If the file being queried doesn't have SHARE(*YES) specified, an OVRDBF command that overrides the SHARE attribute to *YES must be processed ahead of the OPNQRYF command.

```
OVRDBF      FILE(POMAST) SHARE(*YES)
OPNQRYF     FILE(POMAST)
```

FORMAT. The information that would be supplied on an SQL SELECT clause is provided to OPNQRYF indirectly by the FORMAT and MAPFLD parameters. The SQL SELECT clause specifies the file fields and defines derived fields used in the query. The OPNQRYF command uses a database file format, named on the FORMAT parameter, to define the fields used in the query. If a single file is queried and all fields in the file will exist in the query, the default of FORMAT(*FILE) can be used.

If a subset of the fields are used, a physical or logical file that has exactly the fields needed on the query, sometimes referred to as a *format file*, must exist. A format file is also required if fields in the query result are defined differently than in the file being queried. In this case, the database field values are mapped to and take on the attributes of the like-named fields in the format file.

The FORMAT parameter specifies the name of the format file and the record format used for records available through the open query file. If no record format name is specified, *ONLY is the default. If the file has more than one record format, a record format name must be specified. The attributes of the fields in the database files and the format file do not have to be the same. If they differ, the fields are mapped using the same rules as used by the CHGVAR command.

The FILE being overridden and the file declared in the HLL program must match the file named on the FORMAT parameter. The file being queried is specified on the TOFILE parameter of the OVRDBF command.

```
OVRDBF      FILE(POMASTQRY) TOFILE(POMAST) SHARE(*YES)
OPNQRYF     FILE(POMAST) FORMAT(POMASTQRY)
```

Usually, the format file is defined with DDS and created with the CRTPF command. It is no different than any other database file except that it typically contains no data and, consequently, need not contain any data members. The approach of using a format file to define the query fields allows the file to be externally defined in a HLL program.

MAPFLD. If derived fields are needed in the query, a format file that has the fields defined exactly as they are needed on the query must be created. The derived fields are defined to OPNQRYF on the MAPFLD parameter.

```
OVRDBF      FILE(POMASTQRY) TOFILE(POMAST) SHARE(*YES)
OPNQRYF     FILE(POMAST) FORMAT(POMASTQRY) +
              MAPFLD((DISCNT 'AMOUNT * PERCNT') +
              (ADDR3 'CITY *TCAT ", " *CAT STATE'))
```

In the preceding example, the format file POMASTQRY must include the fields DISCNT and ADDR3, as well as any other database fields needed for the query. The MAPFLD parameter is made up of six elements:

- Mapped-field name.
- Mapped-field definition.
- Field-type.
- Field-length.
- Field-decimals.
- CCSID (Coded Character Set Identifier).

The mapped-field name must be unique. Other parameters or mapped-field definitions may refer to this mapped field by name.

The mapped-field definition must be a quoted string containing an expression that defines the mapped field in terms of other fields that either exist in one of the queried files or are defined by some other mapped-field definition appearing earlier in the list. Depending on the data type of the fields used in the definition, either numeric operations or string operations are allowed. One of the strengths of OPNQRYF lies in its capability to define derived fields. More than 60 built-in string, arithmetic, trigonometric, and statistical functions are supported.

The values derived from expressions on the MAPFLD parameter are usually mapped to and take on the attributes of the fields with the same name in the format file. In the preceding example, the product of the database fields AMOUNT and PERCNT maps to and takes on the attributes of the field DISCNT in the format file. The field-type, field length, and field decimals need to be specified only when the mapped field does not appear in the format file. This is the case if the only purpose of the mapped field is for other parameters or mapped-field definitions to refer to it by name.

CCSID. The Coded Character Set Identifier is important only in a multi-lingual environment.

QRYSLT. The QRYSLT (Query Selection Expression) parameter is analogous to the SQL WHERE clause. It is used to specify the criteria that determines which records will be selected for the query. If the QRYSLT parameter is omitted, all records in the queried files are selected. The query-selection expression is specified as a quoted string that contains a logical expression made up of one or more relational expressions. The relational expressions compare database fields and constant values or functions of database fields and constant values.

```
OPNQRYF      FILE(POMAST) FORMAT(POMASTQRY) +
             QRYSLT('STATE *EQ "OH" *AND DISCNT *GE 100') +
             MAPFLD((DISCNT 'AMOUNT * PERCNT'))
```

In the preceding example, only POs with a state of Ohio and a calculated discount (Amount x Percent) of at least $100 are selected.

Note that character constant values are surrounded by double quotes to distinguish them from database field names. Numeric constant values are not quoted. For a more thorough discussion of the QRYSLT expression, see the subheading Using Variable Information in the Selection Criteria.

KEYFLD. The OPNQRYF equivalent of the SQL ORDER BY clause is the KEYFLD (Key Field Specifications) parameter. The KEYFLD parameter specifies the fields that are used to order the records in the query. KEYFLD is made up of three elements:

- The key field name.
- The key field order (*ASCEND or *DESCEND).
- Order by absolute value (*ABSVAL, if used, or left blank).

Specifying the single value KEYFLD(*FILE) causes the queried records to be processed in the same order as the access path of the first file specified on the FILE parameter.

If the order of the records is not important, the single value *NONE may be used. However, if a specific order different than the file's access path is desired, you can specify up to 50 key field names. Key fields can be either database fields or derived fields, but they must appear in the query record.

```
OPNQRYF    FILE(POMAST) FORMAT(POMASTQRY) +
             KEYFLD((STATE) (DISCNT *DESCEND)) +
             MAPFLD((DISCNT 'AMOUNT * PERCNT')
```

In the preceding example, the records are ordered by the calculated discount (Amount x Percent) in descending order within state.

The Grouping Function

GRPFLD. The GRPFLD (Grouping Field Names) parameter specifies the field names that are used to group query results. More specifically, the group is defined by the collection of records that has the same set of values for the fields specified on this parameter. Although neither Open Query File nor SQL will directly produce a report with subtotals, the Open Query File grouping function, like the SQL GROUP BY clause, allows you to summarize data from the queried files. The result can be a single record containing aggregate, or summary, fields for the entire file or a record for each group containing aggregate and common, or grouping, fields for the group.

A grouping query almost always requires a format file to accommodate the aggregate fields. Aggregate fields are defined on the MAPFLD parameter using special built-in aggregate functions. An aggregate field can be a total, a statistical average, a variance, or a standard deviation, the highest or lowest value, or a simple count of the records for the group. You may order the query by the values of aggregate fields by specifying them on the KEYFLD parameter. Every field specified also must exist in the format-file record.

```
OVRDBF      FILE(POMASTQRY) TOFILE(POMAST) SHARE(*YES)
OPNQRYF     FILE(POMAST) FORMAT(POMASTQRY) +
              GRPFLD((STATE)(TYPE)) +
              MAPFLD((NBRPOS '%COUNT') +
                    (AVGPCT '%AVG(PERCNT)'))
```

In the preceding example, one record is produced for each combination of state and type. The format file must include only the fields STATE, TYPE, NBRPOS, and AVGPCT.

GRPSLT. The GRPSLT (Group Selection Expression) parameter, like the SQL HAVING clause, can be used to specify a selection criteria expression used after grouping. Each query record that is created is either made available through the open query file or is discarded, depending on the selection values specified on this parameter. The syntax for GRPSLT is the same as for QRYSLT.

Typically, only aggregate fields are specified on the GRPSLT parameter. It is more efficient for Open Query File to discard unwanted records prior to performing the aggregate functions. Consequently, you should use the QRYSLT parameter to specify non-aggregate selection.

```
OVRDBF      FILE(POMASTQRY) TOFILE(POMAST) SHARE(*YES)
OPNQRYF     FILE(POMAST) FORMAT(POMASTQRY) +
              QRYSLT('STATE *EQ "OH" *OR STATE *EQ "IN"') +
              GRPFLD((STATE)(TYPE)) +
              GRPSLT(('AVGPCT *GE 2.5')) +
              MAPFLD((NBRPOS '%COUNT') +
                    (AVGPCT '%AVG(PERCNT)'))
```

In the preceding example, one record is produced for each combination of state and type where the state is Ohio or Indiana. Then, because of the GRPSLT parameter, all groups with a calculated average percent of less than 2.5 are discarded.

The Join Function

The Open Query File Join function allows you to dynamically join two or more files in a query. This function is similar to, but less restrictive than, join logical files. For instance, both selection and ordering can be performed over fields in more than one file. Using the join function impacts the use of several other parameters previously discussed.

The FILE parameter must be used to specify all files, members, and record formats processed by the join query. The first file specified on the FILE parameter is called the *join primary files*, and all other files are called *join secondary files*. A format file is required to specify the desired fields from each of the joined files. As is always the case when a format file is used, the FILE specified on the OVRDBF command and the file declared in the HLL program must match the file named on the FORMAT parameter. However, for a join query, the TOFILE parameter of the OVRDBF command must match the join primary file (the first file specified on the OPNQRYF FILE parameter).

If a field name is not unique across all files in a join query—that is, if the same field name appears in more than one file—the MAPFLD parameter must use qualified field names in the definition expressions. For example, if the field VNDNUM exists in the format file and appears in two or more files of a join Open Query File, it must be defined on the MAPFLD parameter using the syntax:

```
MAPFLD((simple-field-name 'qualified-field-name'))
```

The simple field name must match the field name in the format file. It usually, although not necessarily, also matches the database field name. There are two syntax forms for qualifying field names: *file/field* and *file-number/field*. Examples of both syntax forms follow:

```
OVRDBF     FILE(POMASTQRY) TOFILE(POMAST) SHARE(*YES)
OPNQRYF    FILE((POMAST)(VENDORS)) FORMAT(POMASTQRY) +
              MAPFLD(VNDNUM 'VENDORS/VNDNUM')
OPNQRYF    FILE((POMAST)(VENDORS)) FORMAT(POMASTQRY) +
              MAPFLD(VNDNUM '2/VNDNUM')
```

In the preceding example, you can presume that the field VNDNUM exists in both the POMAST and the VENDORS files. Consequently, it must be qualified to one or the other. In the second example, the number 2 refers to the second file specified on the FILE parameter. Other parameters that reference database field names (QRYSLT, KEYFLD, GRPFLD, and GRPSLT) also need to specify qualified field names if a field name is not unique across all files in a join query. Typically, however, if a field that is qualified on the MAPFLD parameter is used on other parameters, the mapped-field simple name is used on the other parameters.

JFLD. The JFLD (Join Field Specifications) parameter is comparable to the SQL JOIN BY or JOIN ON clause and specifies how to join field values from the files specified on the FILE parameter. JFLD specifies a list of relational expressions that compare two fields (one from each of two files being joined). The joined fields may be mapped fields but not aggregate functions.

The relational expression takes the unusual form (*field1 field2* [*join-operator*]). The join-operator specifies the type of join that is performed for the specified fields. The possible join operators are *EQ, *GT, *GE, *LT, *LE, and *NE. The default and, by far, the most commonly used join operator is *EQ. The type of join operation performed for this operator is called an *equal join* or "equi-join."

```
OVRDBF      FILE(POMASTQRY) TOFILE(POMAST) SHARE(*YES)
OPNQRYF     FILE((POMAST)(VENDORS)) FORMAT(POMASTQRY) +
              JFLD((1/VNDNUM 2/VNDNUM)) +
              MAPFLD(VNDNUM '2/VNDNUM')
```

In the preceding example, the PO master is joined to the vendor file on vendor number. Neither the mapped-field-simple name nor the optional join-operator were specified. The JFLD parameter also could have been specified as JFLD((1/VNDNUM VNDNUM *EQ)). Note that the MAPFLD parameter is required only if the VNDNUM field is defined in the format file.

The JFLD parameter is convenient but not really necessary. The join criteria also can be specified on the QRYSLT parameter; just as with SQL the JOIN BY criteria can be specified on the WHERE clause. The following OPNQRYF command using QRYSLT is functionally equivalent to the preceding example:

```
OPNQRYF      FILE((POMAST)(VENDORS)) FORMAT(POMASTQRY) +
             QRYSLT('1/VNDNUM *EQ 2/VNDNUM) +
             MAPFLD(VNDNUM '2/VNDNUM')
```

JDFTVAL. The JDFTVAL (Join with Default Values) parameter specifies whether the Open Query File performs an *inner join* or a *left-outer join*. The default JDFTVAL(*NO) produces an inner join. An inner join discards all records from both the primary and secondary join files that don't meet the join criteria. The join in the prior example is an inner join. It will return records only for POs that have a vendor number with a match in the Vendors file.

Specifying JDFTVAL(*YES) produces a left-outer join. A left-outer join keeps all records from the primary join file, but discards records from the secondary join file if they don't meet the join criteria.

```
OPNQRYF      FILE((POMAST)(VENDORS)) FORMAT(POMASTQRY) +
             JFLD((1/VNDNUM 2/VNDNUM)) +
             JDFTVAL(*YES) +
             MAPFLD(VNDNUM '2/VNDNUM')
```

The join in the preceding example is a left-outer join. It will return a record for every PO, but only records for vendors that are referred to on POs.

The derivation of this parameter's name, "Join with Default Values," stems from the way that Open Query File supplies values for non-matching secondary file fields. If there are no records in a secondary file that join with a primary file record and JDFTVAL is *YES, a query record is constructed using default values for all fields obtained from the join secondary. Usually, the default values are blanks and zeros for character and numeric fields respectively. If the DDS for the secondary file contains the 'DFT' DDS keyword, the specified default value is used.

If JDFT(*ONLYDFT) is specified, Open Query File discards all records except those produced by using default values in constructing the join. This option is often referred to as an *exception join*. If *ONLYDFT is specified, no join logical files may be specified on the FILE parameter.

```
OPNQRYF    FILE((POMAST)(VENDORS)) FORMAT(POMASTQRY) +
           JFLD((1/VNDNUM 2/VNDNUM)) +
           JDFTVAL(*ONLYDFT) +
           MAPFLD(VNDNUM '2/VNDNUM')
```

The join in the preceding example is an exception join and could be very useful for checking data integrity. It will return a record for every PO that doesn't have a valid vendor number. By reversing the primary and secondary files, the join would select inactive vendors. In other words, the join would return records only for vendors having no POs that refer to them.

JORDER. The JORDER (Join File Order) parameter allows you to determine whether the join order must match the order specified on the FILE parameter. If the join order is varied, the query records are generated in a different arrangement. (This parameter is ignored if *YES or *ONLYDFT is specified for JDFTVAL. Changing the join order can change which records are returned when join default-value processing is required, as in the preceding example.)

The default, *ANY, indicates that any order of files may be used by the system to create the query records. It is possible for a query to return result records in a different arrangement if the same query is run twice consecutively. If JORDER (*FILE) is specified, the order of the files specified on the FILE parameter are preserved in the join operation. JORDER is discussed further under the subheading KEYFLD, JORDER, and ALWCPYDTA Revisited.

Other OPNQRYF Parameters

ALWCPYDTA. The ALWCPYDTA (Allow Copy of Data) parameter specifies whether Open Query File can use a copy of the data, or more descriptively, a "snapshot" of the queried files. Note that even if the default, ALWCPYDTA(*YES), is specified, Open Query File will typically avoid using a copy of the data because the copy doesn't reflect changes made to the database after the information is copied. A copy of the data is used only when it is needed to perform the requested query functions.

Certain requests require that the data be copied in order to perform the specified query functions. If you specify ALWCPYDTA(*NO), and it is necessary to use a copy of the data to perform the requested query functions, the query file is not opened and an error message is sent to the application program.

A third option, ALWCPYDTA(*OPTIMIZE), is discussed under the subheading, OPNQRYF Performance Optimization.

IGNDECERR. The IGNDECERR (Ignore Decimal Data Errors) parameter specifies whether Open Query File ignores decimal data errors during query processing. If *YES is specified, Open Query File ignores decimal data errors. When errors in decimal data are encountered, the invalid values are replace with valid values.

UNIQUEKEY. The UNIQUEKEY (Unique Key Fields) parameter allows you to stipulate that only records with unique key values are returned by the Open Query File. You specify the number of key fields from 1 through the number of key fields specified on the KEYFLD parameter. Only the first record of several having the same value for the specified number of consecutive key fields is returned by the Open Query File.

You may specify *ALL, in which case only the first record of several having the same value for the all key fields is returned. The default, *NONE, indicates that all query records are returned by the Open Query File regardless of key value.

OPNQRYF Performance Optimization

It is beyond the scope of this text to fully explore all the design considerations that affect performance of Open Query File. This section is limited to a brief introduction to the OS/400 Query Optimizer and a discussion of the OPNQRYF parameters that directly affect performance. For a more thorough treatment of this topic, see Appendix D, *Query Performance: Design Guidelines and Monitoring* in the AS/400e series, *DB2 for AS/400 Database Programming* manual.

The optimizer is a major part of the OS/400 Query component. It is the module that makes the decisions regarding the most efficient methods to access the data required by any of several OS/400 facilities, including OPNQRYF. Depending on the goals of the query, the optimizer attempts to balance the time spent selecting a query implementation plan and the time spent processing the query. Another way to say the same thing is that the optimizer attempts to achieve the best balance between initial response time and total use of machine resources.

The primary factor that the optimizer analyzes and uses is existing indexes (access paths). The existence of certain indexes can greatly impact the performance of selection, ordering, and joining. Sometimes, the optimizer will even create a temporary index to improve overall performance of the query. In other instances, the optimizer might perform a sort operation to satisfy an ordering requirement if an appropriate index doesn't exist.

OPTIMIZE. The parameter having the most direct impact on OPNQRYF performance is OPTIMIZE (Performance Optimization). Use this parameter to stipulate the optimization goal that should be used by the optimizer in deciding how to perform the query.

The default is OPTIMIZE(*ALLIO), which satisfies the most common optimization goal. Typically, Open Query File is used for dynamic selection on batch reporting. (Interactive requirements are usually better served by the use of logical files.) For *ALLIO processing, the optimizer attempts to improve the total time to process the whole query, assuming that all query records are read from the file.

Specifying OPTIMIZE(*MINWAIT) will bias the optimizer toward front-end loading the query processing. The optimizer will attempt to minimize delays when reading records from the file. It might do this at the cost of higher total resources and time used by creating an index or performing a sort. Consequently, it would not be a likely candidate for interactive applications. It is prudent to use *MINWAIT only when benchmark testing proves it to yield the best overall performance.

For interactive applications that use OPNQRYF, such as an inquiry, OPTIMIZE (*FIRSTIO) is usually the best choice. The optimizer attempts to improve the initial time to open the query file and retrieve the first buffer of records from the file. A second element of the OPTIMIZE parameter is used to stipulate the number of records to retrieve for the first buffer. To optimize for an interactive inquiry application that displays returned records in a subfile, make the number of records equal to the subfile page (SFLPAG DDS keyword). For example, if the display file uses SFLPAG(20), specify OPTIMIZE(*FIRSTIO 20).

Note that if either grouping or ordering specifications require that an access path be built, the access path is built completely—even if OPTIMIZE(*FIRSTIO) is specified. In this case, optimization primarily affects the timing of selection processing. Also, be aware that in order to get the benefit of displaying the first screen quickly, *FIRSTIO trades off the total time to process all records in the query. However, there is a reasonable expectation with an inquiry application that not all records will be required.

OPTALLAP. When attempting to find the most efficient way to perform a query, the optimizer normally considers access paths for an internally determined period of time. It operates on the assumption that there is a point of diminishing returns past which additional time spent is not likely to be made up for by a faster query. If there are a large number of access paths over the files being queried, the optimizer may time out before it has considered all the available access paths.

If you specify *YES for the OPTALLAP (Optimize All Access Paths) parameter, the query optimizer will consider all the access paths that exist over the files being queried. Knowing when it is good to use this parameter is tantamount to outsmarting the optimizer. If there are a large number of access paths over the files being queried, it may be useful to run several benchmarks to determine whether OPTALLAP(*YES) could yield a performance benefit.

KEYFLD, JORDER, and ALWCPYDTA Revisited

The KEYFLD parameter specifies the fields that are used to order the records in the query. If the order of the records is not important, specifying KEYFLD(*NONE) can have a very positive effect on performance of processing records through the Open Query File. Consequently, you should never specify KEYFLD unless a specific order is required.

The JORDER parameter allows you to determine whether the join order must match the order specified on the FILE parameter. Consider JORDER(*ANY) if you have specified an inner join (JDFTVAL(*NO)) and the arrangement of the resulting records is not important. JORDER(*ANY) allows Open Query File more flexibility to improve the performance of processing records.

The ALWCPYDTA parameter can be used to improve the total processing time (opening the files and processing the data) for certain types of batch query requests. Specifying ALWCPYDTA(*OPTIMIZE) allows Open Query File to use a sort routine to order the output as requested on the KEYFLD parameter. The sort routine is only used if a sort would improve query performance without conflicting with other OPNQRYF options.

The principal involved in the performance improvement from using a sort is that an application program (or CPYFRMQRYF) can sequentially read a sorted file very quickly. The OPNQRYF command processing itself will typically take longer with a sort (even though time is saved by not creating an access path). However, the total time to perform the OPNQRYF and run a program that reads the opened query file will be shorter. ALWCPYDTA(*OPTIMIZE) should be considered for batch reporting that uses all or most of the records in the queried file and that requires reordering the data.

Using Variable Information in the Selection Criteria

Arguably, the most powerful aspect of Open Query File is its capability to perform an *ad hoc query* (a query that is defined and performed at runtime). Logical files and the Reformat Utility both use predetermined selection criteria and ordering. The most common method of tapping this capability of OPNQRYF is by concatenating CL variables into the expressions used to specify the QRYSLT and GRPSLT parameters. For the sake of simplicity, the remainder of this discussion is limited to QRYSLT, but the principles also apply to GRPSLT as well as any other expression specified for OPNQRYF parameters.

Typically, it is the constant values to be compared to database fields that are supplied by concatenating CL variables into the quoted string. For example, to create the QRYSLT string:

```
'ZIP *EQ "90210"'
```

It is usually the zip code 90210 that is supplied by a variable. A typical example would include the following lines of code:

```
PGM         (&ZIP)
DCL         &ZIP  *CHAR 5
OPNQRYF     FILE(POMAST) +
     QRYSLT('ZIP *EQ "' *CAT &ZIP *CAT '"')
```

There is often confusion centered around the use of expressions on the QRYSLT parameter. It is important to understand that while QRYSLT must contain a relational expression, it is specified as a string. Consequently, like most other CL character parameters, QRYSLT can contain any CL character string expression.

It helps to think of OPNQRYF validation in steps. First, the CL syntax checker will ensure that the value specified for QRYSLT is a valid character string expression—and that is all! Second, the CL interpreter will resolve the expression. In other words, it will replace CL variables with their values and perform any substring and concatenation operations that are not within the quoted string. Neither CL syntax checking nor the CL interpreter are aware of or care whether the QRYSLT string is a valid relational expression.

Then, the Open Query File process gets the string, performs OPNQRYF syntax checking, and validates that database field names exist in the queried files. Finally, when applying the selection test to each record, OPNQRYF resolves the relational expression by replacing database field names with their values and performing any string operations and functions specified in the relational expression. If the relational expression resolves to true, the record is included in the result.

A few simple techniques can make coding OPNQRYF statements easier. When trying to code one of these expressions, it is often helpful to start by writing out a representative example of how the OPNQRYF expression should look. For example, suppose the expression should be:

```
%SST(ZIP 1 2) *EQ "90"
```

This is a valid logical expression. It states that the first two positions of the database field ZIP must equal the characters '90'. At runtime, Open Query File will resolve the substring of the database field ZIP and compare it to '90'. For a PO having ZIP code 90210, the relationship is true and the record will be selected.

OPNQRYF recognizes known tokens such as %SST, *EQ, and parentheses. Anything else in the expression is interpreted as follows:

- Unquoted character values are treated as database field names.
- Values in double quotes are treated as character literals.
- Numeric values are treated as numeric literals.

CL must supply the relational expression to OPNQRYF as a character string expression. If this selection criteria were hard-coded, placing single quotes around it would do the trick. But we want the Z part of the criteria to be supplied by the CL variable &PREFIX. (Angle brackets are used here in place of quotation marks to avoid confusion.) Remember that even though the prefix is supplied as a variable, it is resolved by CL and passed to OPNQRYF as a literal. Open Query File doesn't directly use variables—only field names and literals.

The CL character string must be made up of the variable &PREFIX concatenated between two character literals, < %SST(ZIP 1 2) *EQ " > and the trailing < " >. The expression can be built in steps. Start by writing the first literal, some space, the variable name, some more space, and the second literal:

```
%SST(ZIP 1 2) *EQ "        &PREFIX        "
```

Then, if there were single quotes in the literal, you would change them to double quotes. OPNQRYF lets you use the double quote character instead of requiring two single quotes. Next, place single quotes around each literal:

```
'%SST(ZIP 1 2) *EQ " '        &PREFIX        ' " '
```

Finally, insert the appropriate concatenation symbols between the operands and surround the expression with parentheses:

```
('%SST(ZIP 1 2) *EQ " ' *CAT &PREFIX *CAT ' " ')
```

To interpret this expression, the process is approximately reversed. First, identify the literals. They begin and end with single quotes. The quotes that surround literals are always either immediately:

- Within the parentheses.
- Before or after a concatenation symbol.

Write the expression without the surrounding parentheses and quotes:

```
%SST(ZIP 1 2) *EQ "  *CAT  &PREFIX *CAT  "
```

Then, replace any double quotes with single quotes except for those surrounding variables. In this case, there are none. Next replace the variable with a value that seems reasonable:

```
%SST(ZIP 1 2) *EQ "  *CAT  90 *CAT  "
```

Finally, apply the concatenation operators:

```
%SST(ZIP 1 2) *EQ "90"
```

USING OPNQRYF TO PROCESS OUTFILES

Like any other database file, files created by DSPxxx and WRKxxx commands can be dynamically manipulated with OPNQRYF. To tie all of these features together, a simple CL program is featured in Figure 12.13.

```
 1.00 /****************************************************************/
 2.00 /*  CL Program:  PRTOUTF - print list of OUTFILEs               */
 3.00 /****************************************************************/
 4.00 PGM
 5.00    MONMSG     MSGID(CPF0000) EXEC(GOTO ERR_RTN)
 6.00 /*===========================================================*/
 7.00    DSPFD      FILE(QSYS/QA*) TYPE(*RCDFMT) +
 8.00                 OUTPUT(*OUTFILE) FILEATR(*PF)  +
 9.00                 OUTFILE(QTEMP/OUTFMTS)
10.00
11.00    DSPOBJD    OBJ(QSYS/QA*) OBJTYPE(*FILE) +
```

Figure 12.13: CL program to print a list of outfile names (part 1 of 2).

```
12.00              OUTPUT(*OUTFILE) OUTFILE(QTEMP/OUTFILES)
13.00
14.00   OPNQRYF   FILE((QTEMP/OUTFMTS) (QTEMP/OUTFILES)) +
15.00               FORMAT(OUTFILE) KEYFLD((RFFILE)) +
16.00               QRYSLT('ODOBTX *CT "OUTFILE"') +
17.00               JFLD((OUTFMTS/RFFILE OUTFILES/ODOBNM) +
18.00                    (OUTFMTS/RFLIB  OUTFILES/ODLBNM)) +
19.00               MAPFLD((ODOBTX '%XLATE(OUTFILES/ODOBTX +
20.00                      QSYSTRNTBL)')) OPNID(OUTFILE)
21.00
22.00   CPYFRMQRYF FROMOPNID(OUTFILE) TOFILE(*PRINT)
23.00
24.00   CLOF      OPNID(OUTFILE)
25.00
26.00 RETURN
27.00 /*════════════════════════════════════════════════════════*/
28.00 ERR_RTN:
29.00   CALL      PGM(FWDMSG) PARM('1') /* Forward messages */
30.00     MONMSG  MSGID(CPF0000)  /* <- Very Important! */
31.00 ENDPGM
```

Figure 12.13: CL program to print a list of outfile names (part 2 of 2).

The program in Figure 12.13 (PRTOUTF) creates a list of outfile names, their record format names, and their text descriptions.

The PRTOUTF CL program uses OPNQRYF to join and search two database files (which themselves are OUTFILES). To map the two files, so that only the fields you want are printed, a format file is used. The DDS for the format file is shown in Figure 12.14. To compile the DDS, run the following CL command:

```
    CRTPF  FILE(OUTFILE)  TEXT('Used by OPNQRYF in PRTOUTF')
SeqNoA..........R.Name++++++RLen++TDcB......Functions+++++++++++++++++++
     A          R FORMAT
     A            RFFILE    R                REFFLD(RFFILE QAFDRFMT)
     A            RFNAME    R                REFFLD(RFNAME QAFDRFMT)
     A            RFFILE    R                REFFLD(ODOBTX QADSPOBJ)
```

Figure 12.14: DDS for outfile format file.

The CPYFRMQRYF (Copy from Query File) command allows the records in an OPNQRYF view to be copied to a database physical file or device file. These records then can be further processed by any high-level language program, query tool, or even OPNQRYF. The CPYFRMQRYF command is needed because:

- No program product (i.e., IBM OS/400 utility) can access files through a shared ODP.

- The CPYF (Copy File) command cannot copy an OPNQRYF view.

- The OPNQRYF view goes away when the job ends or when the file is closed. Therefore, copying the data from it can save time later, should the same view of the data be needed again.

In this example, the output is directed to *PRINT, creating a listing of the outfiles.

AN ENHANCED INITIAL PROGRAM

A generalized initial program, INLPGMCL is featured in chapter 11. In this chapter, alternative techniques are considered and illustrated in the CL program INLPG2CL featured in Figure 12.15.

```
 1.00   /*****************************************************/
 2.00   /* Program Name: INLPG2CL - General initial program for end-user */
 3.00   /*****************************************************/
 4.00
 5.00 PGM
 6.00    DCL        &WSID      *CHAR 10
 7.00    DCL        &USER      *CHAR 10
 8.00    DCL        &MENU      *CHAR 10
 9.00    DCL        &USRCLS    *CHAR 10
10.00    DCL        &MENURUN   *LGL
11.00    DCL        &ERROR     *LGL
>11.01   DCL        &JOBNBR    *CHAR    6
12.00    DCLF       INLPGMDF
13.00
14.00    MONMSG     CPF9999 EXEC(GOTO ERROR_RTN)
15.00
16.00 CHKFOR_BYE:
>17.00   RTVJOBA    JOB(&WSID) USER(&USER) NBR(&JOBNBR)
18.00    IF         (&USER = BYE) SIGNOFF *NOLIST
19.00
```

Figure 12.15: Enhanced generalized initial program (part 1 of 3).

```
  20.00 SETUP:
  21.00   SNDF       RCDFMT(SIGNON )
  22.00   RTVUSRPRF  USRCLS(&USRCLS) INLMNU(&MENU)
 >23.00   ADDLIBLE   LIB(&USER) POSITION(*AFTER ASPUTIL)
  24.00   CHGJOB     OUTQ(&USER) PRTTXT('Print by:' *BCAT &USER)
  25.00   IF         (%SST(&WSID 1 4) *EQ 'DIAL') +
  26.00                RMVMSG  MSGQ(&WSID) CLEAR(*ALL)
  27.00   CHGMSGQ    MSGQ(*WRKSTN)  DLVRY(*BREAK)
  28.00   OVRPRTF    FILE(*PRTF) OUTPTY(3) USRDTA('For' *BCAT %SST(&USER 1 6))
  29.00   STRCMTCTL  LCKLVL(*CHG) NFYOBJ(ERRORSMQ *MSGQ)
  30.00   CALL       LODLDACL /* load the LDA */
  31.00
 >31.01 BRKMSG:
 >31.02   STRMSGCMD  MSGLIB(GENLIB)
  32.00 SPECIAL:     /* Call a pgm for special user setup */
  33.00   CALL       PGM(USERPGMS/&USER)
  34.00     MONMSG   MSGID(CPF0001)
  35.00 /*==================================================================*/
  36.00 OPENFILES:
  37.00   IF         (&USRCLS *EQ '*USER') +
  38.00                CALL   OPNFILCL
  40.00 GO_MENU:
  41.00   RCLRSC
  42.00   CHGVAR     &MENURUN '1'
  43.00   IF         (&MENU *NE '*SIGNOFF')  GO &MENU
  44.00   ELSE       IF   (&USRCLS *NE '*USER')  CALL QCMD
  45.00   ELSE       CHGVAR &ERROR '1'
  47.00 SIGNOFF:
  48.00   SNDF       RCDFMT(SIGNOFF)
  49.00   IF         (*NOT &ERROR)  SIGNOFF LOG(*LIST)
  50.00 /*==================================================================*/
  51.00 ERROR_RTN:
  52.00   IF         &ERROR DO
  53.00              /* in an error loop */
  54.00              SNDPGMMSG  MSGID(CPF9898) MSGF(QCPFMSG) MSGDTA(&USER +
  55.00                          *BCAT 'cannot sign on at device' *BCAT +
  56.00                          &WSID) TOMSGQ(QSYSOPR) MSGTYPE(*ESCAPE)
  57.00               MONMSG CPF0000
  58.00              SNDPGMMSG  MSGID(CPC2402) MSGF(QCPFMSG) TOPGMQ(*PRV QCMD) +
  59.00                          MSGTYPE(*ESCAPE)
  60.00               MONMSG CPF0000
  61.00   ENDDO /* in an error loop */
  61.10
  62.00 FIRST_ERR:
  63.00   CHGVAR     &ERROR '1'
  64.00   CHGJOB     LOG(4 00 *SECLVL)
  65.00   IF         (&USRCLS *EQ '*USER') +
  66.00              DO     /* end-user? */
  67.00              IF   (*NOT &MENURUN)  GOTO SIGNOFF
  68.00              ELSE  GOTO GO_MENU
  69.00              ENDDO  /* end-user */
```

Figure 12.15: Enhanced generalized initial program (part 2 of 3).

```
70.00    ELSE      DO  /* Technical user */
71.00              SNDPGMMSG MSG('ERROR: /* Errors in INLPGMCL! +
72.00                See previous messages in the job log. */') +
73.00                TOPGMQ(*EXT) MSGTYPE(*RQS)
74.00              CALL QCMD
75.00              ENDDO /* Technical user */
76.00 ENDPGM
```

Figure 12.15: Enhanced generalized initial program (part 3 of 3).

Using the ADDLIBLE Command

In the original CL program, the CHGLIBL command is used to modify the job's library list. Another way to change the library list is to use the ADDLIBLE (Add Library List Entry Command. There are differences between CHGLIBL and ADDLIBLE. For example, the CHGLIBL command replaces the entire library list while the ADDLIBLE command can add only a single library name to the library list. The library can be added to the beginning of, to the end of, or before, after, or replacing a library that is currently in, the library list.

At line 23.00 of CL program INLPG2CL, the library list is changed using the ADDLIBLE command. The LIB (Library) parameter specifies the name of the library added to the user library list. In INLPG2CL, the name of the library being added is stored in the CL variable &USER. The POSITION (List Position) parameter specifies the position in the user library list where the library is inserted. Valid values for the POSITION parameter are as follows:

- *FIRST—The library is inserted in front of the libraries existing in the user portion of the library list.
- *LAST—The library is added to the end of the user portion of the library list.
- *AFTER—The library is inserted into the library list following the reference library.
- *BEFORE—The library is inserted into the library list before the reference library.
- *REPLACE—The library is inserted into the library list in the position currently taken by the reference library.

The reference library must be specified when *AFTER, *BEFORE, or *REPLACE is specified and must exist in the user portion of the library list.

```
 1.00 /*************************************************************/
 2.00 /* Program Name: WENDYFV - Initial user code module          */
 3.00 /*************************************************************/
 4.00
 5.00 PGM
 6.00    MONMSG      CPF9999 EXEC(GOTO ERROR_RTN)
 7.00
 8.00    ADDLIBLE    PAYROLLIB
 9.00    OVRDBF      GLTRAN00 MBR(SOUTHWEST) OVRSCOPE(*JOB)
10.00    RETURN
11.00 /*==========================================================*/
12.00 ERROR_RTN:
13.00    DMPCLPGM
14.00    CALL        ERRORMGR
15.00     MONMSG     MSGID(CPF0000)
16.00 ENDPGM
```

Figure 12.16: Enhanced initial user code module.

Running Overrides in a Called Program

One of the keys to successfully generalizing an initial program is being able to perform special functions for a specific user during the initial program. The original example of a generalized initial program called a separate CL program with the same name as the user profile. Prior to ILE and override scoping, it was difficult to issue overrides specific to a user using this approach. This is because the overrides issued in the called CL program were no longer in effect when the program ended.

Because of the scoping concepts that are part of ILE, OPM programs can take advantage of job level override scoping to issue user-specific overrides. For example, the user with the profile WENDYFV is one of only two users who need the payroll library in their library list and who require that the file GLTRAN00 be overridden to member SOUTHWEST. CL program WENDYFV, shown in Figure 12.16, will be called by INLPG2CL each time that user WENDYFV signs on.

At line 8.00, the library PAYROLLIB is added to the library list. At line 9.00, the override to GLTRAN00 remains in effect for the duration of the job.

REVIEW QUESTIONS

1. A program that allows user applications to take control when a message arrives on a message queue in break mode is called a _____-_____ program.

2. _____ _____ is information about the sender of a message that can be copied into a CL return variable of the RCVMSG command.

3. The message data record that provides the _____ values used in the text of most pre-defined messages can be copied into a CL return variable using the _____ parameter of RCVMSG. The message data is received as a _____ with a maximum length of 512 characters.

4. The SNDUSRMSG command can be used to send an _____ and wait for a _____.

5. The SNDUSRMSG command allows specification of a list of valid _____ _____.

6. Some display and "work with ..." commands allow their output to be directed to a database file, referred to as an _____.

7. The _____ command provides field-level information for one or more files.

8. Spooled file data from display commands that do not support an outfile can be copied to a user-defined physical database file through the _____ command, creating a _____ outfile.

9. The OPNQRYF command opens a database file to a particular _____ of the data.

10. When a file is opened using OPNQRYF, the records in the file are accessed by high-level language programs that share the _____ _____ _____.

11. Open Query File request can perform any combination of the following database functions:

    a. _____ _____ from more than one file, member, and record format.

    b. Calculate _____ _____ _____ using numeric and character operations.

    c. Group records by like values of one or more fields, and calculate _____ _____, such as minimum field value and average field value, for each group.

    d. Select a _____ of the available records, with selection both before and after grouping the records.

    e. Arrange result records by the value of one or more ___ _____.

12. The primary purpose of Open Query File is to provide an interface to the Query Component for use by your application. Your application must provide the _____-_____.

13. If a subset of the fields are used, a file that has exactly the fields needed on the query, sometimes referred to as a _____ ____, must exist.

14. If the file being queried does not have SHARE(*YES) specified, or if a format file is used, an _____ command must be processed ahead of the OPNQRYF command.

15. Arguably, the greatest benefit of Open Query File lies in its ability to perform an _____ _____ query. The most common method of tapping this capability is by concatenating CL variables into the expressions used to specify the _____ parameter.

13

CL IN THE INTEGRATED LANGUAGE ENVIRONMENT

T he programming environment that was part of OS/400 when the AS/400 was introduced is now referred to as the *Original Program Model* (OPM). In Release 2 of OS/400, the *Extended Program Model* (EPM) was introduced to provide support for Pascal, the initial version of C, and any other languages that use *procedures* (or *functions* in C). The EPM is implemented as an additional layer that sits on top of the operating system.

The Integrated Language Environment (ILE), introduced in Version 2, Release 3, is the latest programming model. Just as OPM is, ILE is integrated into OS/400. ILE has greatly extended the procedure support provided by EPM and has provided for the tight interoperability of RPG, COBOL, and C. ILE has driven the development of separate, ILE versions of RPG and COBOL. As of Version 3, Release 1, when CL first received ILE support, ILE also has required changes to the CL programming language.

This chapter addresses when and why you might want to use ILE CL, the application of ILE terminology to CL, and converting OPM CL to ILE. The chapter also includes an ILE Sample Application as well as examples of ILE techniques. It is beyond the scope of this text to fully explain ILE concepts. For readers not familiar with ILE concepts, I recommend reading the IBM manual, AS/400e series *ILE Concepts*.

REASONS TO USE ILE CL

Why would you want to use ILE CL? The answer would be easy if the question were "Why would you want to use RPG IV?" RPG IV is a far superior language to RPG III. I have observed that most programmers who are using RPG IV don't really even understand ILE concepts. The programmers simply want to take advantage of the many enhancements to the RPG language that are found only in RPG IV.

If you are hoping to discover an all-new-and-improved version of CL for ILE, you will be sorely disappointed. The changes to CL for ILE are merely changes to a few commands so that they support the ILE model. It is often impossible to tell ILE CL from OPM CL. Does that mean you should stop reading right here? Not at all. There are still two reasons to understand and use ILE CL.

The first reason is that you want to use CL procedures in a true ILE environment, statically calling or called by other ILE languages in a bound program. What if the question posed at the beginning of this section were rephrased as, "Why would you want to use ILE at all?" The answer would involve a lengthy discourse on the benefits of ILE. If you don't understand these benefits already, I again refer you to the IBM manual, AS/400e series *ILE Concepts*. If you already know you want to use CL procedures in an ILE environment, read on. Though the changes for ILE CL are few, understanding them is crucial to overall ILE success.

The second reason for using ILE CL is to take advantage of the *bindable APIs* in a CL program. The bindable APIs are math, date, and miscellaneous other convenient APIs (think of them as functions) available only to ILE programs. If you need or want to access them from CL, you should read this chapter.

Enhancements to CL for ILE

Static Calls. The only CL command allowed exclusively in ILE is CALLPRC (Call Procedure). CALLPRC is used to perform a *static call* to a procedure. In other words, the called procedure must have been bound to the calling procedure during the binding process that occurs when an ILE program is created. The benefit of binding the modules together is that it reduces the overhead associated with calling programs. This speeds up the call. The OPM call mechanism is referred to as a *dynamic* or *external program call*, and the ILE method is referred to as a *static* or *bound procedure call*.

Variable Length Parameter Lists. As mentioned in chapter 5, the parameter lists of the calling and called OPM CL programs must correspond in number of parameters and order of specification. The operating system prevents you from calling a CL program with more or fewer parameters than the program expects. ILE CL procedures, however, are more flexible; the system doesn't check the number of parameters that are passed on the call. Consequently, you can write procedures that have variable-length parameter lists. Of course, this opens the possibility for unpredictable results when parameters are inadvertently not passed. It is the programmer's responsibility to ensure that the procedure does not attempt to reference an unpassed parameter.

Optional Parameters. When calling a procedure that accepts parameters, you can pass the special value *OMIT for a parameter that you want to omit from the parameter list. In this case, the procedure is passed a null pointer. Again, it is the programmer's responsibility to ensure that the procedure correctly handles an omitted parameter. The first reference to an omitted parameter generates the exception MCH3601. If omitted parameters are possible, you should monitor for MCH3601 and take appropriate action.

ILE Terminology

Since ILE was introduced, there have been several changes in terminology related both to ILE object differences and to the significant operating system changes required to support ILE. More recent versions of the AS/400e series *CL Programming* manual have become very oriented toward ILE. If your experience is primarily in OPM, you will have to adapt your language to discuss CL programming from an ILE perspective.

ILE Building Blocks

In OPM, applications are built from programs. In ILE, applications are built from programs, programs are built from modules, and modules are built from procedures. Again, without attempting to fully explain ILE concepts, I define here the basic ILE building blocks and relate them to CL programming.

Procedures. A procedure is the smallest meaningful block in the ILE program structure. It is a set of high-level language statements that performs a single function and may return a value to its caller. A procedure can declare *local variables* (variables that are only addressable from within the procedure). A special procedure called the *program entry procedure* (PEP) is created by the system for each ILE program. When the ILE program is dynamically called, the PEP receives control. The PEP then passes control to the procedure defined as the entry point by the programmer. There is no command to create a procedure; procedures are only coded within modules.

Will the real PEP please stand up?: *Strictly speaking, each CL, RPG, and COBOL module has a PEP generated by the compiler. The PEP for the module specified as the entry module (ENTMOD parameter) then becomes the real program entry procedure when multiple modules are bound together.*

Module. A *module* is the object created by an ILE compiler. It can consist of one or more procedures. The exception is a CL module, which always contains one and only one procedure (other than the PEP). Consequently, an OPM CL program is equivalent to both an ILE module and an ILE procedure. Even though a module is compiled, it is not executable. The procedures in a module must be bound into an ILE program or service program to be run.

ILE Program. An ILE program contains one or more modules and is created using the CRTPGM (Create Program) or CRTSRVPGM (Create Service Program) command. An ILE CL program can be created directly from a CLLE source member with the CRTBNDCL (Create Bound CL program) command. When you use CRTBNDCL, the system first creates a temporary module from your source and then creates a program.

Other ILE Terminology

Other terms that have been adapted to ILE and its attendant operating system changes include *call stack* and *call message queue.*

Programmers who have worked on the AS/400 for some time might be familiar with the term "program invocation stack." This has traditionally been considered the stack of programs that are active in a job. Because of ILE, this stack can contain both programs and procedures. Consequently, it has been renamed the call stack.

Correspondingly, the *program message queue* has traditionally been considered the portion of the job message queue that contains messages specific to a program. With ILE, this message queue can contain messages for either programs or procedures and consequently has been renamed the call message queue.

CONVERTING TO ILE CL

Throughout this text, I generally refer to CL programs. Except where I have pointed out special considerations for ILE, all discussions are equally applicable to ILE procedures. Nearly every OPM CL program could be recompiled as an ILE module or bound CL program with no changes. Actually, there is only one command that would cause a compiler error: The TFRCTL command serves no useful function in an ILE environment and, therefore, is not supported. However, TFRCTL is so seldom used in applications that you could safely count on converting 100 percent of the CL programs for any given application.

That is not to say that all converted CL procedures would run as expected. There are several reasons that a converted CL program could cause unexpected results. Some of the considerations for converting from OPM to ILE follow.

All ILE programs are activated within a substructure of a job called an *activation group.* Actually, even OPM programs run in an activation group called "the default activation group." And, under certain conditions, even ILE programs can run in the default activation group. Generally, however, ILE programs run in a *named activation group* that delineates the application from other applications. The concept of activation groups introduces the requirement for additional scoping capabilities that affect parameters on several CL commands. The most significant of these are the override file (OVR*xxx*F) commands.

Override Commands. In the traditional OPM environment, overrides are scoped to the call level. In other words, an override is in effect for the program that issued it and all called programs. The effect of the override ends when the program that issued it ends. The ILE model provides for overrides to be scoped to the activation group. The effect of the override remains until the activation group in which it was issued ends.

The scoping for overrides is determined by the OVRSCOPE (Override Scope) parameter. The default value *ACTGRPDFN specifies that override scoping is defined by the activation group the issuing program is running in. If the program is running in the default activation group (OPM or ILE programs), the override is scoped to the call level. If the program is running in a named activation group (ILE programs only), the override is scoped to the activation group.

> **NOTE:**
> For ILE CL programs created by the CRTBNDCL command with the default DFTACTGRP (*YES) specified, overrides are scoped to the call level, as in OPM programs.

To use call level override scoping in an ILE program in a named activation group, specify OVRSCOPE (*CALLLVL) on any override command. The effect of the override will end when the procedure that issued the override ends.

File Opens. Like overrides, file opens in the OPM environment are scoped to the call level. Also like overrides, file opens in an ILE application can be scoped to the activation group. The scoping for file opens is determined by the OPNSCOPE (Open Scope) parameter on the OPNDBF (Open Database File), OPNQRYF (Open Query File), and all override file commands. The default value *ACTGRPDFN specifies that the scope of the open data path (ODP) is defined by the activation group of the issuing program. If the program is running in the default activation group, the ODP is scoped to the call level. If the program is running in a named activation group, the ODP is scoped to the activation group. To open a file with job level scoping, you can specify OPNSCOPE(*JOB). If issued in the default activation group, OPNSCOPE(*ACTGRP) scopes the ODP to the activation group. However, you cannot override a file in a named activation group to be opened at the call level.

RCLRSC. Another consideration related to activation groups involves use of the RCLRSC (Reclaim Resources) command. In a traditional OPM environment, the RCLRSC command is often used to close open files and free static storage for RPG programs that have returned without ending or have ended abnormally. But, RCLRSC affects programs only in the default activation group.

For ILE programs that are created by the CRTBNDCL or CRTBNDRPG command with DFTACTGRP(*YES) specified, RCLRSC frees static storage just as in OPM programs. For other ILE programs in the default activation group, the RCLRSC command reinitializes programs that have returned without ending, but doesn't close files or free static storage. RCLRSC doesn't reinitialize static storage of service programs.

ILE Message Handling

The last and perhaps most crucial consideration for converting to ILE CL relates to message and exception handling. ILE message handling is significantly more complex than OPM message handling. At least the structure and theory is that complex. Fortunately, most ILE programmers will not have to deal with all the intricacies for which IBM has provided. It was a challenge for and is a credit to IBM Rochester that they integrated ILE system-wide while allowing message-handling commands to function in OPM without change. Because this section re-addresses some of the concepts introduced in chapter 6, but from an ILE perspective, you might want to review that chapter before continuing.

A single job message queue structure supports both the OPM and ILE program models. You will recall that the job message queue is logically partitioned into an external message queue for the job and a call message queue for each program invocation in the job. Actually, the job message queue contains a call message queue for each OPM program and each ILE procedure that is called within the job, including the PEPs for each ILE program.

The job message queue thus facilitates the sending and receiving of messages between the programs and procedures running on the call stack. The call message queue is referenced by the name of the OPM program or ILE procedure to which it is related.

This has a direct bearing on the TOPGMQ parameter of the SNDPGMMSG command. TOPGMQ is specified as a list of two values, relationship (or *offset entry*) and call stack entry. As mentioned in chapter 6, the second value, call stack entry, can be the name of an OPM program that is currently in the job's call stack, or the default, predefined value '*' that implies the name of the OPM program sending the message. However, the call stack entry also can refer to the call message queue of an ILE procedure. And therein lies the rub. ILE procedure names aren't necessarily unique. Consequently, procedure names can be qualified by their module or ILE program names.

The preceding can best be illustrated by looking at some examples of sending messages in an ILE environment. Refer to Figure 13.1 while considering the next several examples. Figure 13.1 is a representation of the job message queue and the call message queues that result when OPM program CLPGMA is called. (Mixed case names are used in the examples for readability.) CLPGMA calls ILE program PGMB. The program entry module for PGMB is the CL module PROC1. Procedure _CL_PEP is the PEP for PGMB that was created by the system when PGMB was created.

PROC1 performs a dynamic call to ILE program PGMC. The program entry module for PGMC is the RPG module RPG2. Procedure _QRNP_PEP_RPG2 is the PEP for PGMC that was created by the system when PGMC was created. It is shown in the example preceded by a '<' symbol to indicate that the first several characters of the procedure name have been truncated.

Job Message Queue		
*EXTERNAL		
OPM Pgm or Proc	Module	ILE Pgm
CLPgmA		
_CL_PEP	Proc1	PgmB
Proc1	Proc1	PgmB
<_PEP_RPG2	RPG2	PgmC
RPG2	RPG2	PgmC
Proc2	RPG2	PgmC
Proc1	Proc1	PgmC
Proc2	Proc2	PgmC
Proc9	Proc9	PgmC

Figure 13.1: Call message queues for ILE Procedures.

Procedure RPG2 is the main procedure for module RPG2. RPG2 contains a bound call to procedure PROC2 in the same RPG module. PROC2 calls PROC1in CL module PROC1. Note that PROC1 is now in the call stack twice. This could be either the same CL procedure bound into two ILE programs or separate CL procedures with the same name. It is not important here.

Procedure PROC1 calls PROC2 in CL module PROC2. Now PROC2 is in the call stack twice. These are different procedures with the same name. The first is in the RPG module RPG2. PROC2 calls procedure PROC9 in CL module PROC9. Procedure PROC9 in ILE program PGMC currently has control.

Sending Messages to Call Message Queues for ILE Procedures

Presume that procedure PROC9 needs to send a message to the call message queue of procedure PROC2 in module PROC2 of PGMC. To support sending messages to the call message queue of an ILE procedure, the call stack entry value is made up of three items. The items are the:

- Procedure name.
- Name of the module into which the procedure was compiled.
- Name of the program into which the module was bound.

If the call stack entry is a *simple name*, that is, only the first item is specified, it references the call message queue of the nearest (most recently called) program or procedure that matches the specified name. For example, procedure PROC9 can send a message to the call message queue of procedure PROC2 in module PROC2 of PGMC using the command:

```
SNDPGMMSG  MSG('Any message') TOPGMQ(*SAME PROC2)
```

Although PROC2 appears twice in the call stack, the message is sent to the nearest invocation because a simple name was used for the call stack entry.

For PROC9 to send a message to the call message queue of PROC2 in module RPG2 of PGMC, the call stack entry would have to be specified as a complex name. A complex name uses at least two of the three items. The procedure name is always required. The module name, program name, or both can be specified as required to uniquely identify the desired call message queue. For example, procedure PROC9 can send a message to the call message queue of procedure PROC2 in module RPG2 of PGMC using the command:

```
SNDPGMMSG  MSG('Any message') TOPGMQ(*SAME (PROC2 RPG2))
```

The combination of procedure and module name is sufficient to uniquely identify PROC2 in module RPG2. Also, note that you must surround complex names with parentheses. Procedure PROC1 also appears twice in the call stack. PROC9 can send a message to the call message queue of PROC1 in module PROC1 of PGMB using either of the following commands:

```
SNDPGMMSG  MSG('Any message') TOPGMQ(*SAME (PROC1 PROC1 PGMB))
```
or
```
SNDPGMMSG  MSG('Any message') TOPGMQ(*SAME (PROC1 *NONE PGMB))
```

Because the combination of procedure and program name is sufficient to uniquely identify PROC1 in program PGMB, the module name is not required. If the module name is omitted, however, the placeholder *NONE must be specified for the second item of the call stack entry.

Specifying *PRV for the relationship works, as expected, with one exception. The message will be sent to the caller of the procedure identified in the second value unless the caller is the PEP for the ILE program. In that case, the PEP is skipped and the message is sent to the caller of the ILE program.

There are three special values for call stack entry that can be very useful in an ILE or mixed ILE and OPM environment: *PGMNAME, *PGMBDY, and *CTLBDY. Each value is discussed in the text that follows.

Help Wanted for Online Help:

The online help for the TOPGMQ parameter of SNDPGMMSG describes the syntax for specifying nested procedure names. This has been the cause of some confusion. Prior to Version 4, Release 4 of OS/400, no languages that support nested procedures were available to AS/400 customers. Internally, IBM has used languages on the AS/400 that take advantage of nested procedures. As of V4-R4, ILE COBOL nested calls are implemented as nested procedures.

Sending Messages to an ILE Program

Recall that the call stack entry value can specify the name of either an OPM program or an ILE procedure, but not an ILE program. There is no call stack entry and, hence, no call message queue for an ILE program. But what if you only know the name of an ILE program and not a procedure name within the program? The special value *PGMNAME allows sending a message to the most recently called procedure in the specified program. For example, procedure PROC9 can send a message to the most recently called procedure in PGMB using the command:

```
SNDPGMMSG  MSG('Any message') TOPGMQ(*SAME (*PGMNAME *NONE PGMB))
```

The message will be sent to the most recently called procedure in program PGMB (PROC1).

If a module name is specified for the second item, the message is sent to the most recently called procedure in the specified module. For example, procedure PROC9 can send a message to the most recently called procedure in module RPG2 of PGMC using the command:

```
SNDPGMMSG  MSG('Any message') TOPGMQ(*SAME (*PGMNAME RPG2 PGMC))
```

The message will be sent to procedure PROC2.

If you don't know whether the specified program is an OPM or an ILE program, *PGMNAME is particularly useful. If *PGMNAME is used with an OPM program name, the effect is the same as if you just used the simple name. The following commands are equivalent:

```
SNDPGMMSG  MSG('Any message') TOPGMQ(*SAME CLPGMA)
SNDPGMMSG  MSG('Any message') TOPGMQ(*SAME (*PGMNAME *NONE CLPGMA))
```

In either case, the message will be sent to CLPGMA. The advantage to using *PGMNAME is that the first command only works if CLPGMA is an OPM program. The second command works whether CLPGMA is OPM or ILE.

Sending Messages to an ILE Program's Caller

The special value *PGMBDY is particularly useful in error-handling routines. *PGMBDY is used to identify the PEP of an ILE program. It is usually used to send a message from within a CL procedure outside the boundary of the program that contains the procedure. For example, procedure PROC9 can send a message to the caller of PGMC using the command:

```
SNDPGMMSG  MSG('Any message') TOPGMQ(*PRV *PGMBDY)
```

The message will be sent to the most recently called procedure in program PGMB (PROC1).

*PGMBDY also can be used with a program name. Procedure PROC9 can send a message to the caller of PGMB using the command:

```
SNDPGMMSG  MSG('Any message') TOPGMQ(*PRV (*PGMBDY *NONE PGMB)
```

The message will be sent to CLPGMA.

Sending Messages to an ILE Application's Caller

When named activation groups are implemented as part of an overall ILE design strategy, the activation group is often used to delineate an application. The special value *CTLBDY can be used within a CL procedure to send a message outside the boundary of the activation group or application that contains the procedure. The *control boundary* is the boundary between call stack entries that are running in different activation groups or between any ILE program and an OPM program. The entry identified by *CTLBDY is the entry running in the same activation group as the entry that is sending the message. For example, presume that PGMB and PGMC are both running in an activation group named DEMO. Procedure PROC9 can send a message to the caller of the activation group using the command:

```
SNDPGMMSG  MSG('Any message') TOPGMQ(*PRV *CTLBDY)
```

The message will be sent to CLPGMA.

Receiving Messages in an ILE Environment

Call Stack Entry. Unfortunately, the RCVMSG command doesn't offer the same flexibility in an ILE environment as SNDPGMMSG. The RCVMSG command uses the same, three-part structure for the call stack entry as SNDPGMMSG, but does not allow the special values of *PGMNAME, *PGMBDY, or *CTLBDY. This throws a monkey wrench into some message-handling techniques.

ERRORMGR, the generic error-handler program described in chapter 7, uses the technique of sending a message to a call message queue, receiving the message, and determining the name of the program (or call stack entry) the message was sent to by interrogating the sender data. This technique works with ILE programs most of the time, but not if the special values for call stack entry are used. For instance, if in an ILE CL procedure you wanted to know the name of the PEP procedure for the ILE program, you could send a message to (*SAME (*PGMBDY)). However, you have no sure way to receive that message.

> **NOTE:**
>
> When specifying the special value *PGMBDY, if the third item is the name of an OPM program, it is the same as specifying the OPM program as a simple name. If the OPM program in this case has called itself recursively, the message will be sent to the first invocation of the program.

Sender Data. Chapter 12 discusses the SENDER parameter of RCVMSG and using the short format for sender data. When receiving messages from call message queues in an ILE environment, however, the short format for sender data is not usually adequate. A longer format is required to capture procedure, module, and program information about the sender and the target message queue. To meet this requirement and still keep ILE CL nearly 100 percent compatible with OPM CL, IBM very cleverly added one new parameter—SENDERFMT (Sender Format)—to the RCVMSG command. You use SENDERFMT to specify which format of sender data you want returned in the CL variable specified for the SENDER parameter. The default is *SHORT. If you specify *LONG, you must declare the variable long enough to hold 720 bytes of data. Table 13-1 lists the *LONG format of the sender data.

Table 13.1: *LONG Format of the Sender Parameter.

From	To	Size	Description
1	10	10	Job name
11	20	10	Job user profile ID
21	26	6	Job number
27	33	7	Date sent (cyymmdd)
34	39	6	Time sent (hhmmss)
40	40	1	Sender program type 0 = OPM or SLIC <= 12 1 = ILE Proc <= 256 2 = ILE Proc > 256 3 = SLIC > 12
41	41	1	Sent-to program type 0 = OPM 1 = ILE Proc <= 256 2 = ILE Proc > 256
42	53	12	Sender program name
54	63	10	Sender module name
64	319	256	Sender procedure name
320	320	1	Blank
321	324	4	Number of STMT numbers for sender
325	354	30	Sender STMT numbers (10 each)
355	364	10	Sent-to program name
365	374	10	Sent-to module name
375	630	256	Sent-to procedure name
631	640	10	Blank
641	644	4	Number of STMT numbers for sent-to
645	674	30	Sent-to STMT numbers (10 each)
675	720	46	Reserved for future use

RMV Parameter. In addition to *YES and *NO, the RMV parameter of RCVMSG supports the special value *KEEPEXCP. The ILE exception-handling model (see the subheading ILE Exception Handling) allows the programmer to decide whether to handle a specific exception in the user-written, exception-handling routine or to let the system continue exception processing by attempting to locate another exception handler. When you receive an exception message, you can leave the exception unhandled by specifying RMV(*KEEPEXCP) on the RCVMSG command.

After examining the message, if you decide to handle it in this routine, you can receive the message again as a *EXCP message specifying RMV(*YES) or RMV(*NO). I don't recommend using this option unless you have implemented a thorough ILE exception-handling strategy.

Other Differences between OPM and ILE CL

- ILE CL source members have a source type of CLLE. PDM option 14 runs the CRTBNDCL command against the member. Option 15 runs the CRTCLMOD command.

- The source for ILE CL programs or modules cannot be retrieved through RTVCLSRC (Retrieve CL Source).

- The CRTBNDCL command doesn't support the GENOPT(*LIST) function for creating a listing of the intermediate code.

A Sample ILE Application

As shown in Figures 13.2 and 13.3, the List logical files application uses messages to list physical files in a specified library, and all of their dependent logicals. If the application is called from the Command Entry display, the messages will all follow the line containing the CALL command, providing a sort of "poor man's subfile." The example is admittedly contrived. Although there is not much gained by creating this simple utility as an ILE program instead of two OPM CL programs, it serves to illustrate the differences in coding practices between OPM and ILE CL programming.

The application has two procedures. The first uses DSPOBJD (Display Object Description) to create an outfile of physical files in a library. It then reads the file and for each record:

- Uses DSPDBR (Display Database Relations) to create a second outfile of the dependent logicals.

- Calls the second procedure.

The second procedure reads the database relations outfile and sends nicely formatted program messages that list the physical files, the dependent logicals, and the library of each logical.

The code is almost identical to that of an OPM version of the same utility but, there are a few differences worth noting. Figure 13.2 shows the source for procedure LSTLGL101. The global MONMSGS at statement 8.00 and 8.10 monitor for CPF9897 as well as CPF9999. Due to the nuances of ILE exception handling, the strategy for a generic error handler is slightly modified. Accordingly, the error routine calls ERRORMGRLE instead of ERRORMGR as discussed in chapter 7. ILE error handling and the ERRORMGRLE program are discussed under the subheading, A Generic ILE/OPM Exception Handler.

At statement 23.00, the CALLPRC (Call Procedure) command is used to perform a static or bound call to procedure LSTLGL102. If there is one advantage to creating this as an ILE application, it is that there can be a significant performance benefit for bound calls that are repeated many times.

```
1.00   /****************************************************************/
2.00   /* Program Name: LSTLGL101 - List logical files - Main Procedure    */
3.00   /****************************************************************/
4.00   PGM         &LIB
5.00     DCL       &LIB        *CHAR    10
6.00     DCL       &RCDCOUNT   *DEC     10
7.00     DCLF      QADSPOBJ
8.00     MONMSG    (CPF9897) CMPDTA('We have discovered') EXEC(GOTO ERROR)
```

Figure 13.2: List logical files utility—main procedure (part 1 of 2).

```
 8.10    MONMSG     (CPF9897) EXEC(GOTO ERROR)
 9.00   /*═══════════════════════════════════════════════════════════════*/
10.00   ONE_TIME:
11.00    DSPOBJD    OBJ(&LIB/*ALL) OBJTYPE(*FILE) +
12.00                 OUTPUT(*OUTFILE) OUTFILE(QTEMP/ALLFILES)
13.00    OVRDBF     QADSPOBJ    ALLFILES
14.00   /*═══════════════════════════════════════════════════════════════*/
15.00   READ:
16.00    RCVF
17.00      MONMSG   CPF0864     EXEC(RETURN)
18.00
19.00    IF         (&ODOBAT = 'PF')   +
20.00      DO       /* List the logicals */
21.00        DSPDBR   FILE(&LIB/&ODOBNM) OUTPUT(*OUTFILE) +
22.00                   OUTFILE(QTEMP/PHYSFILES)
23.00        CALLPRC  LSTLGL102
24.00        ENDDO  /* List the logicals */
25.00    GOTO       READ
26.00   /*═══════════════════════════════════════════════════════════════*/
27.00   ERROR:
28.00    CALL       ERRORMGRLE
29.00      MONMSG   CPF0001
30.00   ENDPGM
```

Figure 13.2: List logical files utility—main procedure (part 2 of 2).

In the second procedure, LSTLGL102 (see Figure 13.3), all the SNDPGMMSG commands that provide the "poor man's subfile" (e.g., line 15.00) use the *PGMBDY
special value for the call stack entry. This technique causes the messages to be
sent to the caller of the ILE program (the Command Entry display in this case),
and not the caller of the procedure. Philosophically, this approach treats the utility as an application. To do the same thing in an OPM version of this application
would require sending the messages to the caller of the named program
LSTLGL101. The philosophical advantages of the ILE model begin to show here.

```
 1.00   /****************************************************************/
 2.00   /* Program Name: LSTLGL102 - List logical files - Sub-Procedure    */
 3.00   /****************************************************************/
 4.00   PGM
 5.00    DCLF      QADSPDBR
 6.00    MONMSG    (CPF9897) CMPDTA('We have discovered') EXEC(GOTO ERROR)
 6.10    MONMSG    (CPF9897) EXEC(GOTO ERROR)
 7.00   /*═══════════════════════════════════════════════════════════════*/
 8.00    OVRDBF    QADSPDBR    PHYSFILES
```

Figure 13.3: List logical files utility—sub-procedure (part 1 of 2).

```
 9.00   /*════════════════════════════════════════════════════*/
10.00    RCVF
11.00      MONMSG   CPF0864     EXEC(RETURN)
12.00    IF          (&WHNO = 0) RETURN
13.00   /*════════════════════════════════════════════════════*/
14.00
15.00    SNDPGMMSG  MSG('Phys file  Lgl file   Library') +
16.00                 TOPGMQ(*PRV (*PGMBDY))
17.00    SNDPGMMSG  MSG('─── ─── ───') +
18.00                 TOPGMQ(*PRV (*PGMBDY))
19.00
20.00   /*════════════════════════════════════════════════════*/
21.00   DO_UNTIL:
22.00    SNDPGMMSG  MSG(&WHRFI || ' ' || &WHREFI || ' ' || &WHRELI) +
23.00                 TOPGMQ(*PRV (*PGMBDY))
24.00    RCVF
25.00      MONMSG   CPF0864     EXEC(GOTO EOF)
26.00    GOTO        DO_UNTIL
27.00   /*════════════════════════════════════════════════════*/
28.00   EOF:
29.00    SNDPGMMSG  MSG('═══════════════════════════════') +
30.00                 TOPGMQ(*PRV (*PGMBDY))
31.00    RETURN
32.00   /*════════════════════════════════════════════════════*/
33.00   ERROR:
34.00    CALL ERRORMGRLE
35.00          MONMSG CPF0001
36.00   ENDPGM
```

Figure 13.3: List logical files utility—sub-procedure (part 2 of 2).

Creating the Program

To create the list logical files application requires running the following three
commands:

```
CRTCLMOD   MODULE(LSTLGL101) SRCFILE(QCLSRC)
CRTCLMOD   MODULE(LSTLGL102) SRCFILE(QCLSRC)
CRTPGM     PGM(LSTLGL100) MODULE(LSTLGL*)ENTMOD(LSTLGL101) ACTGRP(*CALLER)
```

The CRTCLMOD (Create Control Language Module) command creates a CL module from the specified CL source member. The CRTPGM command creates a
bound, ILE program from the list of modules specified on the MODULE parameter. In this case, it includes all modules in the library list that begin with the characters "LSTLGL." The ENTMOD (Program Entry Procedure Module) specifies that
LSTLGL101 is the module that contains the program entry procedure specifica-

tions to be used for this program. Parameters required by this procedure should be provided on the call to the ILE program. The ACTGRP (Activation Group) parameter specifies that the created program is to run in the activation group of its caller. For a utility like this one, avoiding the creation of a new activation group will reduce unnecessary overhead.

ILE Exception Handling

One of the more complex components of ILE is exception handling. In addition to user-written and HLL-specific exception handling, the ILE exception-handling model addresses ILE-only constructs of Direct Monitor Handlers, Condition Handlers, Handle Cursors and Resume Cursors, Unhandled Exception Messages, and Exception Percolation. A complete description of the ILE exception-handling model is well beyond the scope of this chapter. This discussion is limited to user-written exception handling in ILE CL programs. For more information, see the IBM manual AS/400e series *ILE Concepts.*

A Generic ILE/OPM Exception Handler

The goals and methods of exception handling for a CL procedure are virtually the same as for a CL program. Some of the coding techniques, however, have to be adapted to the ILE exception-handling model. Chapter 7 presents ERRORMGR, a prototype for a generic error- handling program. ERRORMGRLE (see Figure 13.4) is presented here as an ILE version of the program designed to handle errors for either OPM or ILE applications. ERRORMGRLE is almost identical to ERRORMGR and can be substituted for it freely. Because this prototype is suitable for both ILE and OPM programs, you could simply name it ERRORMGR and use it instead of the program described in chapter 7. Like ERRORMGR, ERRORMGRLE is complex. If you don't thoroughly understand the rationale, concepts, and functions of a generic error handler in general and ERRORMGR specifically, I strongly recommend that you review chapter 7 before continuing.

```
 1.00   /************************************************************************/
 2.00   /* Program Name: ERRORMGRLE - Generic Error Handler for ILE & OPM    */
 3.00   /************************************************************************/
 4.00 PGM
 5.00 DCL     &MSG            *CHAR      512
 6.00 DCL     &MSGID          *CHAR        7
 7.00 DCL     &MSGKEY         *CHAR        4
 8.00 DCL     &SENDER         *CHAR      720
 9.00 DCL     &PGMNAME        *CHAR       10
10.00 DCL     &PGMTYPE        *CHAR        1
11.00 DCL     &USER           *CHAR       10
12.00 DCL     &WRKSTN         *CHAR       10
13.00 MONMSG CPF9999 EXEC(GOTO POLITE_MSG)
14.00 /*=====================================================================*/
15.00 GETNAME:      /* Find out what program got the error (my caller) */
16.00   SNDPGMMSG  MSG('Get program name') KEYVAR(&MSGKEY)
17.00   RCVMSG     PGMQ(*PRV) MSGKEY(&MSGKEY) SENDER(&SENDER)
18.00
19.00   CHGVAR     &PGMTYPE   VALUE(%SST(&SENDER 71   1))
20.00   CHGVAR     &PGMNAME   VALUE(%SST(&SENDER 56  10))
21.00 /*=====================================================================*/
22.00 RCV_ERR:     /* Receive the offending error message */
23.00   RCVMSG     PGMQ(*PRV) MSGTYPE(*EXCP) RMV(*NO) +
24.00               KEYVAR(&MSGKEY) MSG(&MSG) MSGID(&MSGID)
25.00
26.00   IF         (&MSGID = CPF9999 *AND &PGMTYPE = '0') +
27.00              /* OPM function check */ GOTO RCV_ERR
28.00
29.00 /*=====================================================================*/
30.00 TIME1TEST:   /* Check if Original error or just percolating  */
31.00   IF         (&MSGID = CPF9897 +
32.00     *AND     %SST(&MSG 1 18) = 'We have discovered') +
33.00              GOTO POLITE_MSG
34.00
35.00 /*=====================================================================*/
36.00 NOTIFY:      /* Original error, Notify IS & other 1-time actions */
37.00   CHGJOB     LOGCLPGM(*YES) LOG(4   *SECLVL)
38.00   RTVJOBA    USER(&USER) JOB(&WRKSTN)
39.00   SNDPGMMSG  MSG('An error occurred in' *BCAT &PGMNAME +
40.00               *BCAT 'for user' *BCAT &USER *BCAT 'at' +
41.00               *BCAT &WRKSTN *CAT '.  The error was:' +
42.00               *BCAT &MSG) TOUSR(QSYSOPR) MSGTYPE(*DIAG)
43.00
44.00   SNDBRKMSG  MSG('An error occurred in' *BCAT &PGMNAME +
45.00               *BCAT 'for user' *BCAT &USER *BCAT 'at' +
46.00               *BCAT &WRKSTN *CAT '.  The error was:' +
47.00               *BCAT &MSG) TOMSGQ(DSP01 HELPDESK)
48.00     MONMSG CPF0000
49.00
50.00 /*=====================================================================*/
```

Figure 13.4: A generic error handler for ILE & OPM programs (part 1 of 2).

```
51.00 POLITE_MSG:   /* Percolate a polite error message up the call stack */
52.00   SNDPGMMSG   MSGID(CPF9897) MSGF(QSYS/QCPFMSG) MSGDTA('We +
53.00                 have discovered a problem in your +
54.00                 application. MIS will contact you.') +
55.00                 TOPGMQ(*PRV (*PGMBDY *NONE &PGMNAME)) +
56.00                 MSGTYPE(*ESCAPE)
57.00       MONMSG CPF0000
58.00
59.00 /*============================================================*/
60.00 ERROR:
61.00   SNDPGMMSG   MSGID(CPF9897) MSGF(QCPFMSG) MSGDTA('Please +
62.00                 notify I.S. immediately! Thank you.') +
63.00                 TOPGMQ(*EXT) MSGTYPE(*INFO)
64.00       MONMSG CPF0000
65.00 ENDPGM
```

Figure 13.4: A generic error handler for ILE & OPM programs (part 2 of 2).

In comparison to ERRORMGR, there are really only two differences. The first difference is the declaration and use of an additional variable, &PGMTYPE. The sent-to program type is extracted from the sender data into &PGMTYPE at line 19.00. Then, after the caller's exception message is received, it is used at line 26.00 to condition a branch.

Recall that in the OPM-only version of this program, if the message identifier is CPF9999, the prior exception message is received. Reviewing the rationale for this technique, OPM programs that implement ERRORMGR as their exception handler globally monitor CPF9999. As a result, there are two unhandled exception messages—the original exception and the function check—in the call message queue

> **Review—The role of the function check:** Many programmers are accustomed to using CPF0000 on a global monitor. You could monitor for the generic CPF0000, but there are advantages to using CPF9999: If an exception message arrives on the call-message queue and is not monitored, the function check message, CPF9999, is sent. This message contains the statement number of the failing statement, which is very useful information to have when diagnosing a problem. More important, there are error messages other than CPFxxxx messages that can cause a CL program to terminate (MCHxxxx, CEExxxx, etc.). By allowing the function check to occur, the problematic code is easier to locate, and you never have to worry about additional error-message groups.

at the time ERRORMGR is called. In ERRORMGR, because you want to send the text of the original exception to the help desk, you receive the last exception, find that it is CPF9999, and then receive the prior exception.

The technique works differently in ILE programs. The ILE exception-handling model adds a twist that complicates the scheme. When unmonitored escape messages are sent to ILE procedures, the function check is not immediately sent. Instead, the exception is first percolated by the system, up the call stack, one procedure after another, in search of a procedure that will handle that exception. If the exception reaches the control boundary (the boundary between activation groups) unhandled, the function check is sent. If after receiving the CPF9999 message in an ILE procedure, ERRORMGRLE attempted to receive the prior exception, it would not be found. The original exception would have percolated up to the control boundary.

Consequently, it is extremely difficult for a generic error handler to receive the original exception message. The approach taken in ERRORMGRLE is a compromise. If the caller of ERRORMGRLE is an OPM program, the original exception will be received and its message text sent to the help desk. If the caller of ERRORMGRLE is an ILE procedure, the message text of the function check will be sent to the help desk. Therefore, the GOTO at line 27.00 is performed only if the sent-to program type is '0' (OPM).

ILE System Percolation:

When the system percolates an exception, it effectively moves the message from one call message queue to another. It doesn't remove and re-send the message. The sender data for a percolated exception indicates the message queue the message was originally sent to, and not the message queue it is in.

A second difference is in how the polite escape message is sent (51.00 – 56.00). TOPGMQ is specified as (*PRV (*PGMBDY *NONE &PGMNAME)). Recall that when specifying the special value *PGMBDY, if the third item is the name of an OPM program, it is the same as specifying the OPM program as a simple name. That takes care of errors in OPM programs just fine. From the ILE perspective, this line of code reveals the exception-handling strategy supported by the generic error handler. Specifying *PGMBDY here for an ILE procedure indicates that control will be returned to the caller of the ILE program containing the failing procedure, and not to the caller of the failing procedure.

ERRORMGRLE can be created as either an OPM program or a bound CL program. It could even be created as a module and bound into a service program. It can be created as a bound CL program that runs in the activation group of its caller with the following command:

```
CRTBNDCL   PGM(ERRORMGRLE) SRCFILE(BOOKSRC) +
           DFTACTGRP(*NO) ACTGRP(*CALLER)
```

When you use CRTBNDCL, the system first creates a temporary module from your source and then creates a program.

You should understand that the exception-handling strategy supported by ERRORMGRLE might not be the strategy you want to support. Remember, ERRORMGRLE is a prototype rather than a canned solution. Perhaps you would prefer to use the control boundary as the scope of your user-written exception handling. Or, if you want to implement exception handling at a procedure level, you could modify the GETNAME section of ERRORMGRLE to use the *LONG sender data format so that you could extract the procedure and module name of the caller. You could even include user-written exception-handling logic in the user entry procedure only and let ILE percolate the exceptions to a single point. The additional complexity of the ILE model offers additional flexibility and more decisions to make!

USING THE BINDABLE APIs

Even if you don't want to use CL procedures in a true ILE environment, an excellent reason for using ILE CL is to take advantage of the ILE bindable application programming interfaces in a CL program. The bindable APIs, or ILE CEE APIs as they are sometimes called, are program interfaces (or functions) that supplement the function of CL or any other particular HLL. You can think of them as procedures in an ever-present service program. Additionally, all ILE C runtime functions can be called in ILE CL with a bound call. Of course, there are also numerous bindable APIs other than the CEE APIs; many system APIs are provided in bindable forms (i.e. service programs). However, these can be called from either ILE or OPM programs.

Of course, if you are already in an ILE environment, there is no particular need to use ILE CL just to use a bindable API. The bindable APIs are available to all of the ILE HLLs. But what if you are writing a program to manage the daily backup procedure which, incidentally, requires special processing on Wednesdays and Sundays? CL is the obvious language of choice but, you need a way to determine the day of the week for the current date and, CL doesn't provide that function. Enter the bindable APIs! CEEDYWK is a bindable API that provides the required function. The only additional requirements for the program are that its source type is CLLE and that it is created using the CRTBNDCL command (or the combination of CRTCLMOD and CRTPGM).

As shown in Figure 13.5, the ILE CL program DAYOFWEEK demonstrates calling two commonly used bindable APIs: CEEDYWK and CEEDAYS. The specifications for these and all the other bindable APIs can be found in AS/400e series *System API Reference, OS/400 Integrated Language Environment (ILE) CEE APIs* manual. This program is also an example of using %BIN and of array processing in CL. (The %BIN built-in function is discussed in chapter 3.)

```
 1.00 /*****************************************************************/
 2.00 /* Program Name: DAYOFWEEK - Return day of week for a mm/dd/yyyy    */
 3.00 /*****************************************************************/
 4.00 PGM           (&Date)
 5.00 DCL           &Date        *CHAR    10    /* Input mm/dd/yyyy       */
 6.00 DCL           &LDateB      *CHAR     4    /* Lilian date (binary)   */
 7.00 DCL           &LDateN      *DEC     15    /* Lilian date (decimal)  */
 8.00 DCL           &DaysArray   *CHAR    63 +
 9.00               ('Sunday    Monday    Tuesday   Wednesday+
10.00                   Thursday  Friday    Saturday ')
11.00 DCL           &IndexB      *CHAR     4    /* Array index (binary)   */
12.00 DCL           &IndexN      *DEC     15    /* Array index (decimal)  */
13.00 DCL           &Start       *DEC     15
14.00 DCL           &DayOfWeek   *CHAR     9
15.00 DCL           &Msg         *CHAR   100
16.00 MONMSG        CEE0000   EXEC(GOTO CEE_ERROR)
17.00 MONMSG        CPF9897   CMPDTA('We have discovered') EXEC(GOTO ERROR)
```

Figure 13.5: An example of a bindable API (part 1 of 2).

```
18.00   MONMSG     CPF9999  EXEC(GOTO ERROR)
19.00 /*===============================================================*/
20.00 /* Convert Date 1 to Lillian */
21.00   CALLPRC    CEEDAYS  (&Date 'MM/DD/YYYY' &LDateB *OMIT)
22.00
23.00 /* Determine day of week */
24.00   CALLPRC    PRC(CEEDYWK) PARM(&LDateB &IndexB *OMIT)
25.00   CHGVAR     &IndexN  (%BIN(&IndexB))
26.00
27.00 /* Lookup and display day of week */
28.00   CHGVAR     &Start      (&IndexN  * 9 - 8)
29.00   CHGVAR     &DayOfWeek  %SST(&DaysArray &Start 9)
30.00   SNDPGMMSG  (&DATE |> 'Falls on' |> &DayOfWeek |< '.') +
31.00                TOPGMQ(*PRV *PGMBDY)
32.00
33.00 RETURN
34.00 /*===============================================================*/
35.00 CEE_ERROR:
36.00   RCVMSG     MSGTYPE(*EXCP) RMV(*NO) MSG(&MSG)
37.00   SNDPGMMSG  MSGID(CPF9897) MSGF(QCPFMSG) MSGDTA(&MSG) MSGTYPE(*ESCAPE)
38.00 /*===============================================================*/
39.00 ERROR:
40.00    CALL ERRORMGRLE
41.00 ENDPGM
```

Figure 13.5: An example of a bindable API (part 2 of 2).

DAYOFWEEK accepts a date in "mm/dd/yyyy" format and sends a message containing the day of the week to its caller. Both CEEDYWK and CEEDAYS require parameters with a binary data type. Because CL doesn't support the binary data type directly, the character variables &LDATEB and &INDEXB are used to store the binary values. The 63-byte character variable &DAYSARRAY serves as a pseudo-array having 7 elements of 9 bytes each. It is initialized to contain the seven days of the week.

The CEEDYWK API requires a Lilian date in binary format. That's where CEEDAYS comes in. At statement 21.00, a bound procedure call to CEEDAYS passes a calendar date and a *picture string* (or format of the date), and returns the Lilian date as a binary number into &LDATEB. At statement 24.00, the Lilian date is passed to CEEDYWK, which returns the day of week into &INDEXB as a binary number from 1 to 7. You can't directly use the binary number as an index to &DAYSARRAY. Therefore, at line 25.00, %BIN is used to convert it to a decimal value. Statements 28.00 and 29.00 represent the CL version of an array lookup.

The DAYOFWEEK example includes some specialized error handling. All ILE CEE APIs use a special group of exception messages beginning with CEE. For example, CEEDAYS will send escape messages with message identifiers of CEE2508 (The value for day is not valid), CEE2521 (The value for year is not valid), etc. In this particular example, these are anticipated exceptions that would normally be monitored at the command level. They are monitored globally as a matter of convenience. If the generalized error handler ERRORMGRLE handled these exceptions, the user would get a general notification of a problem instead of the useful feedback in the message text.

> **Lilian Date:**
>
> The Lilian date *is named for the 16th century King of Wales, Li'l Ian, who was crowned on October 14, 1582 and on that day declared, "Time begins today!" Hence, the Lilian date is the number of days since October 14, 1582. The AS/400 implementation of Lilian date does not support dates before October 14, 1582 nor dates after December 31, 9999. Consequently, programs that refer to Lilian date will no longer work on January 1, 10,000. This is sometimes referred to as the Y10K bug.*

REVIEW QUESTIONS

1. *The programming model that was part of OS/400 when the AS/400 was introduced is referred to as the _____ _____ _____, or OPM. The _____ _____ _____,or ILE, is the latest programming model.*

2. *A _____ is the smallest meaningful block in the ILE program structure. It is a set of high-level language statements that performs a single function and may return a value to its caller.*

3. *A special procedure called the PEP, or _____ _____ _____, is created by the system for each ILE program. It receives control when the ILE program is dynamically called.*

4. *A _____ is the object created by an ILE compiler.*

5. All ILE programs are activated within a substructure of a job called an

    _____ _____.

6. To support sending messages to the call message queue of an ILE procedure, the call stack entry value is made up of three items: the _____name, the name of the _____, and the name of the _____.

7. If the call stack entry is a _____ _____, that is, only the first item is specified, it references the call message queue of the _____ _____ _____ program or procedure that matches the specified name.

8. The special value *PGMNAME for the call stack entry parameter of SNDPGMMSG allows sending a message to the _____ _____ _____ procedure in the specified program or an _____ program.

9. The special value *PGMBDY is used to identify the ____ of an ILE program. It is usually used to send a message from within a CL procedure outside the boundary of the program which contains the procedure.

10. The special value *CTLBDY can be used to send a message from within a CL procedure outside the boundary of the _____ _____ that contains the procedure.

11. The _____ _____ is the boundary between call stack entries that are running in different activation groups or between any ILE program and an OPM program.

12. When you create an ILE CL program using CRTBNDCL, the system first creates a _____ _____ from your source and then creates a program.

13. An excellent reason for using ILE CL is to take advantage of the ____ _____ ____, or ILE CEE APIs in a CL program. These are program interfaces, or functions that may supplement the function of CL or any other particular HLL.

14

CREATING USER-WRITTEN COMMANDS

Thr AS/400 Control Language is made up of a set of command statements. Just to mention a few, there are commands for changing a program variable, opening, copying and reading a file, calling a program, and submitting another command to the batch job queue. The CL language has one advantage over most other languages in that it is extensible. This means that an application programmer can create new CL commands and use those commands anywhere they are needed. Unlike most other languages, however, CL doesn't support macros. Instead, CL allows you to use command statements to create new commands.

A CL command is an AS/400 object. It has an object type of *CMD and is referred to as a *Command Definition Object* (CDO). Some prefer to use the simpler term *Command* when referring to a CDO.

Command definition objects are created by compiling a series of *command definition statements*. These command definition statements are special CL commands that differ from most CL commands in that they can be specified only within a CMD source file member. Command definition statements are compiled

with the CRTCMD (Create Command) command. The six command definition
statements that can be used to create user-written CL commands are:

- CMD (Command Definition).
- PARM (Parameter Definition).
- QUAL (Qualifier Definition).
- ELEM (Element Definition).
- PMTCTL (Prompt Control Definition).
- DEP (Dependency Definition).

The order in which the above command definition statements appear is the chro-
nological order of the statements as they would appear in a typical command. Although the order isn't rigid, it is customary to specify them in this order.

User-written commands can simplify many programming functions, including
parameter passing, prompting, and dependency checking. For example, a
user-written command can simplify an accounting application where an aged trial
balance needs to be printed. A command can be created to allow accounting personnel to specify the starting and ending dates for the report. Dependency checking between the two dates can be performed and special values, such as
*CURRENT (meaning "today's date"), are supported.

As you can see in Figure 14.1, command definition source is very similar to CL
program source. Actually, the command definition statements are CL commands
themselves. They have parameters with keywords and can be prompted with the
CL prompter.

```
AGING:    CMD  PROMPT('Aged Trial Balance Report')

      /*  Command processing program is ARTRLBAL  */

          PARM  KWD(FROM) TYPE(*DATE) +
                DFT(*START)  SPCVAL((*START 000000)) +
                PROMPT('Starting date for report')

          PARM  KWD(TO) TYPE(*DATE) +
                DFT(*CURRENT)  SPCVAL((*CURRENT 000000)) +
                PROMPT('Ending Date for Report')
```

Figure 14.1: User-written command source.

Creating a user-written command is similar to compiling a high-level language program. The command compiler is invoked by the CRTCMD (Create Command) command.

Command definition objects provide only prompting and a parameter-formatting mechanism; they don't actually "run" by themselves. A command processing program is associated with the command. This program is invoked by the command processor when the command is run. To create the example command listed in Figure 14.1, run the following command:

```
CRTCMD  CMD(AGING) PGM(ARTRLBAL) SRCFILE(CLBOOK/QCMDSRC) +
           SRCMBR(AGING)
```

The PGM (Program to Call) parameter identifies the *command processing program* (CPP). The CPP runs when the command is successfully entered into the system.

Once the command is compiled, it can be run from any of the normal command processing entry points on the system. These entry points include the command entry display, the command line, batch through SBMJOB, or as part of a compiled CL program.

The command-processing program for the AGING command can be written in any AS/400 language. The only requirement is that it receive the appropriate parameters. Figure 14.2 shows an excerpt from a CL program used as the CPP for the aging command.

```
4.00 ARTRLBAL:
5.00    PGM        PARM(&FROM  &TO)
6.00    DCL        &FROM  TYPE(*CHAR)  LEN(7)  /* From date */
7.00    DCL        &TO    TYPE(*CHAR)  LEN(7)  /* To date */
```

Figure 14.2: CL code to receive command parameters.

A unique feature of command definitions is the prompter. OS/400 provides a dynamic prompt for every command whether it is a system command, an in-line CL command, a command definition statement, or a user-written command. As shown in Figure 14.1, the Aged Trial Balance Report command produces the prompt listed in Figure 14.3.

```
*...v... 1 ...v... 2 ...v... 3 ...v... 4 ...v... 5 ...v... 6 ...v... 7 ...v... 8
                    Aged Trial Balance Report (AGING)

Type choices, press Enter.

Starting date for report . . . .   *START       Date, *START
Ending date for report . . . . .   *CURRENT     Date, *CURRENT




                                                                    Bottom
F3=Exit   F4=Prompt   F5=Refresh   F12=Cancel   F13=How to use this display
F24=More keys
```

Figure 14.3 Prompted aging command.

COMMAND DEFINITION STATEMENTS

Every command is defined by one or more *command definition statements*. The statements define the prompter text, parameter keywords, and parameter dependencies for the command. The six command definition statements used to define a user-written command are listed in Table 14.1.

CMD STATEMENT

The CMD statement is used to define the text that is used for the title on the prompt display. The CMD statement is required, but the prompt text itself is not. The CMD statement can appear anywhere in the command definition source member, but traditionally appears first.

In addition, a label can be specified for the CMD statement, but has no effect on the command definition. Traditionally, the label for the CMD statement is used to identify the name of the command. Consequently, the label for the CMD statement is the same as the name of the source file member.

Table 14.1: Command Definition Statements.	
Command Statements	**Description**
CMD	Used to define the title (prompter text) for the command. It is always the first statement in a command-definition source member.
PARM	Used to define each parameter for the command. A PARM statement defines the parameter. PARM statements can refer to QUAL or ELEM statements to further define the parameter.
QUAL	Used to further define a PARM and, sometimes, an ELEM statement as a qualified AS/400 name. A minimum of two QUAL statements is required in order to create a valid qualified name.
ELEM	Used to define an element of a mixed list. ELEM statements allow a parameter to be composed of multiple unlike values, similar to a data structure in RPG or COBOL.
PMTCTL	Used to control which parameters are displayed based on the value of other parameters. This statement is how conditional prompting is controlled within the CDO.
DEP	Used to test dependencies between parameters and issue messages during prompting or when the command is entered.

CMD Statement Parameters

The CMD statement contains one parameter, PROMPT, to defined the prompt text for the command. All other command definition statements have multiple parameters.

PROMPT Parameter

The PROMPT parameter defines the prompt text associated with the command when the command is prompted. The name of the command is concatenated to this text to form the prompt title. For example, in the AGING command, the prompt text is Aged Trial Balance Report (AGING). See Figure 14.3.

In addition to a quoted text string, a message identifier can be specified for the PROMPT parameter. At compile time, the text for the message identifier is retrieved from the message file specified on the PMTFILE parameter of the CRTCMD command. Typically, message IDs are used only by IBM for system commands.

PARAMETER DEFINITION STATEMENTS

The PARM, QUAL, and ELEM statements are used to define each parameter of a user-written command. These command statements are referred to as *parameter definition statements* (PDS). The PARM statement is the primary descriptor, while QUAL and ELEM statements are subordinate to a PARM statement. Only PARM statements are required to define a parameter keyword; ELEM and QUAL statements are only used when the parameter is a mixed list or a qualified name, respectively. The PARM statement is optional in a command. However, if no PARM statements are specified, no parameters are passed to the command-processing program.

Common PARM, QUAL, and ELEM Keywords

The parameter definition statements share many parameters. Rather than go through a list of the keywords for each parameter definition statement, a single list of keywords common to the three statements is provided. Then the keywords unique to each statement are listed separately.

TYPE (Data Type)

The TYPE parameter is used to define the data-type of the value being specified. Any data type can be specified, including *CHAR, *DEC, and *NAME. Table 14.2 lists the possible data types and meanings.

In addition, the statement label of a QUAL or ELEM statement can be specified for the TYPE parameter to further define the parameter. For example, instead of specifying TYPE(*CHAR) for a particular parameter, TYPE(FILENAME) can be used to identify the label of a pair of QUAL statements. This allows the parameter to be defined as a qualified name. (See Figure 14.4.) This same technique is used to define a parameter consisting of ELEM statements and is referred to as a mixed list.

```
           PARM  TYPE(FILENAME) MIN(1) PROMPT('File name')

FILENAME:  QUAL  TYPE(*NAME) EXPR(*YES) MIN(1)
           QUAL  TYPE(*NAME) EXPR(*YES) DFT(*LIBL) +
                   SPCVAL((*LIBL) (*CURLIB *CURLIB)) +
                   PROMPT('Library')
```

Figure 14.4: Sample qualified name declaration.

Table 14.2: Valid Data Types For TYPE Parameter.

Data Type	Description
*CHAR	Character data.
*CMDSTR	A valid command. For example, the CMD parameter of the sbmjob command.
*DATE	Valid date.
*TIME	Valid time.
*DEC	Packed decimal data. (There is no "zoned" data type.)
*GENERIC	Generic name. For example: OBJ(ABCD*)
*INT2	Two-byte binary integer.
*INT4	Four-byte binary integer.
*HEX	Valid hexadecimal values only (0 to 9 and A to F).
*LGL	Logical '1' or '0'.
*NAME	Valid OS/400 name. The name must begin with A to Z, $, @, or # and may contain the characters (.) and _. If the name contains any other special characters, it must be enclosed in apostrophes. For example: 'AS/Name!'
*SNAME	Simple name. Must begin with A to Z, $, @, or #. The rest of the name can contain these same characters as well as the numbers 0 to 9 and an underscore (_).
*CNAME	Communication name. Must begin with A to Z, $, @, or #. The rest of the name can contain these same characters as well as the numbers 0 to 9.
*PNAME	Path name string. If the path name string contains any special characters (not including an asterisk (*)), it must be enclosed in apostrophes.
*NULL	A null pointer. Typically used as a "place-holder" for a parameter that isn't used by the command, but is required by the command processing program.
*ZEROELEM	Zero element. The value sent to the command processing program is zero for an ELEM list. Typically, this is used only when multiple commands use the same command processing program.
stmt-label:	A label for a QUAL or ELEM statement. Used to further define the parameter as either a qualified name or an element list, or both.

LEN (Length of Parameter)

The LEN parameter is used to define the length of the parameter. This value represents the length of the data that is passed to the CPP, not the length that is allowed to by typed in by a user. The LEN parameter is optional for most data types. For *DATE, *TIME, *INT2, *INT4, and *ZEROELEM, the LEN parameter cannot be specified because these data types have an implied length. Table 14.3 lists the default size for data types when LEN is not specified as well as the range limit when LEN is specified.

Table 14.3: Data Type Size Limits.

Data Type	Default Length	Range Min/Max
*DEC	(15 5)	(1 0) to (24 9)
*LGL	1	1 to 1
*CHAR	32	1 to 3000
*NAME	10	1 to 256
*SNAME	10	1 to 256
*CNAME	10	1 to 256
*PNAME	32	1 to 5000
*GENERIC	10	1 to 256
*HEX	1	1 to 256
*CMDSTR	256	1 to 6000

CONSTANT (Constant Value)

The CONSTANT parameter allows you to specify a constant value that will always be passed to the command-processing program for this parameter. The constant value can be any data type, but the total length is restricted to 32 characters. When a value is specified for CONSTANT, the parameter cannot be specified when the command is run.

RTNVAL (Return CL Value)

The RTNVAL parameter specifies whether a value can be returned through this parameter. If RTNVAL(*YES) is specified, then a CL variable must be specified for the parameter when the command is run. Specifying RTNVAL(*YES) requires that the command environment be restricted when the user-written command is created. Specifically, the ALLOW parameter of the CRTCMD command must be set to ALLOW(*IPGM *BPGM *IMOD *BMOD) only. If RTNVAL(*NO) is specified, any value can be specified for the ALLOW parameter of the CRTCMD command.

RSTD (Restrict Values)

The RSTD parameter controls whether the values specified for this parameter are restricted to the SPCVAL, SNGVAL, or VALUES parameter values. If RSTD(*YES) is specified, then the values are restricted; RSTD(*NO) allows any value of the data TYPE defined by the type parameter to be specified.

DFT (Default Value)

The DFT parameter can be used to specify a default value for the parameter being defined. The default value is displayed when the user-command is prompted, and it is passed to the CPP, if no value is specified for the parameter, when the user-command is run.

VALUES, REL, and RANGE

The VALUES, REL, and RANGE parameters each provide controls for the allowable values that can be specified for the parameter being defined.

The VALUES parameter accepts a list of values. For example, VALUES(1 2 3 5 7 11 13) restricts the values to several prime numbers. This is similar to the VALUES keyword in DDS. When the VALUES parameter is specified, RSTD(*YES) is required.

The REL parameter allows a relationship test to be performed. For example, REL(*GT 100) if the value must be greater than 100. This is similar to the COMP keyword in DDS.

The RANGE parameter allows a range test to be performed. For example, RANGE('A' 'Z') restricts the values to the letters 'A' through 'Z' (in uppercase). This is similar to the RANGE keyword in DDS.

SPCVAL and SNGVAL

The SPCVAL and SNGVAL parameters allow a list of values to be specified that can be used to:

- Define a special value that may be specified for the parameter.
- Translate the specified value to the value passed to the command-processing program.

For example, for a parameter that accepts a number in the range 1–10, the special value *MAX may be translated to 10.

The principle difference between SPCVAL and SNGVAL is that SNGVAL is used when a single, special value may be specified for a parameter that normally accepts multiple values (i.e., the value specified for the MAX parameter is greater than 1). When the value exists as a SPCVAL, it can be specified multiple times. When the value exists as a SNGVAL, it must be the only value specified for the parameter.

The SNGVAL parameter is not supported by the QUAL command definition statement.

MIN and MAX (Number of Values Required)

The MIN and MAX parameters control the minimum and maximum number of values that can be specified for a parameter. The MIN parameter traditionally is used to indicate that a parameter value is required. For example, MIN(1) indicates that the parameter value must be specified. If MIN(>=1) is specified, no default value can be specified. The value specified for MIN always must be less than or equal to the value specified for MAX.

The QUAL command definition statement restricts the value of MIN to 0 or 1. This defines the QUAL value as optional or required, respectively.

The MAX parameter can be used to define the parameter value as a simple list. For example, MAX(10) indicates that up to 10 elements can be specified for this parameter value. The MAX parameter is not supported by the QUAL command definition statement.

ALWUNPRT (Allow Unprintable Characters)

The ALWUNPRT parameter controls whether the parameter entry can accept unprintable characters. The default is ALWUNPRT(*YES). This parameter applies only when TYPE(*CHAR) is specified.

ALWVAR (Allow CL Variables)

The ALWVAR parameter controls whether the parameter entry will accept CL variable names for the parameter. CL variable names can be specified only in CL programs and must begin with an ampersand (e.g., &AMOUNT). The default is ALWVAR(*YES).

PGM (Program Verification)

The PGM parameter indicates whether a value specified for this parameter is a program name. This information is used only by the OS/400 DSPPGMREF command for cross-reference purposes. The default is PGM(*NO)

DTAARA (Data Area Verification)

The DTAARA parameter indicates whether the value specified for this parameter is a data area name. This information is used only by the OS/400 DSPPGMREF command for cross-reference purposes. The default is DTAARA(*NO).

FILE (File Usage)

This FILE parameter indicates whether the value specified for this parameter is a file name and how the file is used by the command's CPP. This information is used only by the OS/400 DSPPGMREF command for cross-reference purposes. The default is FILE(*NO). Other valid options are:

- *IN — The value is a file used for input.
- *OUT — The value is a file used for output.
- *UPD — The value is a file used for update.
- *INOUT — The value is a file used for input and output.
- *UNSPFD — The value is a file, but its usage is unspecified.

FULL (Full Parameter Required)

The FULL parameter indicates whether or not the entire parameter must be filled in when it is specified. For example, if a parameter's length is 8 characters, and FULL(*YES) is specified, then 8 characters must be specified for the parameter. The default is FULL(*NO).

EXPR (Allow Expression Values)

The EXPR parameter is important for character-type parameters. EXPR allows the use of *CAT, *BCAT, *TCAT, %SST, and %BIN when the command is used in a CL program. The default is EXPR(*NO).

When defining a parameter with a type of *CHAR, *GENERIC, *NAME, *SNAME, *CNAME, or *CMDSTR, be sure to specify EXPR(*YES) or the string functions will not be available for the parameter.

VARY (Pass Length to CPP)

The VARY parameter indicates whether the value passed to the CPP for the parameter should contain a 2-byte binary value prefix that indicates the length of the data specified for the parameter. The default is VARY(*NO).

For example, a parameter where the length is defined as 10 bytes has an 8-character value specified for it. The total number of bytes passed to the CPP is 12. Bytes 1 and 2 contain the binary length of the data being passed (i.e., X'0008') followed by bytes 3 through 12 (the 8 characters of data, and the 2 remaining unused characters.)

DSPINPUT (Display Input Value)

The DSPINPUT parameter controls how the parameter value is displayed when the command is run. A value of DSPINPUT(*YES) will display the input value on the prompter, and log the value to the job log. A value of DSPINPUT(*PROMPT) will display the input value on the prompter, but not log the value to the job log. A value of DSPINPUT(*NO) makes the parameter attribute non-display, both on the prompter and in the job log. This is typically used for security reasons, such as in the case where a user is required to type a password into a command parameter.

CHOICE (Choice Text)

The CHOICE parameter controls what values are displayed to the right of the input parameter when the command is prompted. The default is CHOICE(*VALUES). This causes the command compiler to build choice text using the values specified by the REL, RANGE, VALUES, SPCVAL, and SNGVAL parameters. CHOICE(*NONE) causes no choice text to be displayed when the command is prompted. A message identifier also can be specified. At compile time, the text for the message identifier is retrieved from the message file specified on the PMTFILE parameter of the CRTCMD command.

In addition, if CHOICE(*PGM) is specified, a user-written program can be called to build the choice text dynamically at runtime. The program is specified on the CHOICEPGM parameter. In addition, the permissible values—the text that appears when F4 is pressed while the cursor in located on the parameter—also can be generated by the choice program.

CHOICEPGM (Choice Text Program to Call)

The CHOICEPGM parameter is used to name the program to be called when CHOICE(*PGM) is specified. This user-written program is used to build the normal and extended (i.e., second-level) choice text. For more information and an example of a *choice program*, see the subheading User-Written Choice Program.

PROMPT (Prompt Text)

The PROMPT parameter is used to specify the prompter text that appears to the left of the parameter value. Up to 30 characters of descriptive text can be specified for each PARM, QUAL, or ELEM statement.

In addition, a second value, the *Relative Prompt Number*, can be specified. This value indicates the order that the parameter appears when the command is prompted. Typically, this value is used only when a new parameter is added to an existing command. The new parameter may, logically, need to appear before other parameters that are already defined.

UNIQUE PARM KEYWORDS

In addition to the command keywords just described, the PARM statement has several unique keywords.

KWD (Keyword)

The KWD parameter is used to name the parameter of the user-written command. For example, in the following command, the parameters FROM and TO are specified:

```
AGING   FROM(010191)   TO(123191)
```

These parameter names are specified on the KWD parameter of the PARM statements listed in Figure 14.1.

PMTCTL (Prompt Control)

The PMTCTL parameter is used to control which parameters are displayed when the command is prompted. If PMTCTL(*NONE) is specified, the parameter is always displayed. If PMTCTL(*PMTRQS) is specified, the parameter is displayed only when it is changed or when the user presses F10 or F9 while the command is prompted. This is the simplest form of prompt control.

If PMTCTL(*label*) is specified, the prompt control for this parameter is based on the result of a condition test. This condition test is performed by a PMTCTL command definition statement having the *label* that is specified for this keyword.

PMTCTLPGM (Prompt Control Program)

The PMTCTLPGM identifies a program to be called that is used to translate the value specified for the parameter being defined. The translated value is the value that is used by a PMTCTL statement.

KEYPARM (Key Parameter)

The KEYPARM parameter controls whether the parameter is initially displayed when the command is prompted and a prompt override program is specified. For more information on this keyword, see the subheading User-Written Prompt Override Program.

PROMPT CONTROL DEFINITION STATEMENTS

If a label is specified for the PMTCTL parameter of a PARM statement, the prompt control for the parameter is based on the result of a condition test. The condition test is performed by a PMTCTL command definition statement with the label. More than one PARM statement can refer to the same label.

The PMTCTL statement uses a rather awkward syntax to specify the name of the controlling parameter, one or more conditions to be tested, and the number of conditions that must be true to select the conditioned parameters for prompting.

A common example is a display command that has an OUTPUT parameter that supports an outfile. The OUTFILE parameter is only displayed if OUT-PUT(*OUTFILE) has been specified. This function is enabled by specifying a PMTCTL label on the OUTPUT PARM statement:

```
PARM    OUTFILE SPCVAL((*OUTFILE F)) PMTCTL(OUTFILE) …
```

The PMTCTL statement with the matching label is used to control the prompt of the OUTFILE parm:

```
OUTFILE: PMTCTL CTL(OUTPUT) COND((*EQ F)) NBRTRUE(*EQ 1)
```

The CTL parameter specifies that the OUTPUT parm controls the prompting of the OUTFILE. The COND parameter specifies that the relationship (OUTPUT *EQ F) is tested. (Note that the to-value of the SPCVAL list is used.) The NBRTRUE specifies that if one (1) of the conditions is true (the *only* one, in this case), the OUTFILE parameter will be prompted.

A label can refer to a group of PMTCTL statements allowing you to condition a parameter by several controlling parameters. Statements in a group can be logically related by using the LGLREL parameter to specify *AND and *OR relationships.

DEPENDENCY DEFINITION STATEMENTS

The DEP statement can be used to define a required relationship between parameters. DEP uses a syntax similar to PMTCTL. A common example is a message-sending command. If MSG is specified, MSGID cannot be. This dependency can be enforced using the following statement:

```
DEP CTL(MSG) PARM(MSGID) NBRTRUE(*EQ 0) MSGID(USR1234)
```

The CTL parameter on this DEP statement indicates that the PARM relationships must be true only if the MSG parameter has been entered. The PARM parameter indicates that the MSGID parameter will be tested. NBRTRUE(*EQ 0) indicates that MSGID may not be specified. If the relationship is invalid, MSGID USR1234 is displayed.

USER-WRITTEN CHOICE PROGRAM

The use of a choice program is not for the novice programmer. It can be fairly complex depending on the level you want to support. Figure 14.5 contains a choice program written in RPG III. While a choice program can be written in CL, for performance reasons, it is typically written in another high-level language.

```
 E                      VAL       50 12
 E                      MSG     1 04 30
 E                      PMV     1 08 10
 ICTLPRM     DS
 I                                          01  10 CMD
 I                                          11  20 KWD
 I                                          21  21 OPTION
 ICHCTXT     DS                               2000
 I                                    B   01  020VALCNT
 I                                    B   01  020VC
 I                                        03 602 VAL
 I                                        01  30 TEXT
 IVALUES     DS
 I                                    B   01  020VALLEN
 I                                        03  12 VALUE
 C           *ENTRY     PLIST
 C                      PARM              CTLPRM
 C                      PARM              CHCTXT
 C           CMD        IFEQ 'SLTDAYS'
 C           KWD        ANDEQ'DAYS'
 C           OPTION     CASEQ'C'          CHOICE
 C           OPTION     CASEQ'P'          PERMIS
 C                      END
 C                      ENDIF
 C           ENDPGM     TAG
```

Figure 14.5: Sample choice program (part 1 of 2).

```
C                     MOVE *ON      *INLR
 /EJECT
CSR         CHOICE    BEGSR
C*  Create the "choice text"
C                     MOVELMSG,1    TEXT
CSR                   ENDSR
 /SPACE
CSR         PERMIS    BEGSR
C*   Build the permissible values list
C                     DO    8       VALCNT
C                     MOVE PMV,VC    VALUE
C                     Z-ADD10        VALLEN
C                     MOVE VALUES    VAL,VC
C                     END
CSR                   ENDSR
**
day of week, Monday, Tuesday...
**
*ALL
MONDAY
TUESDAY
WEDNESDAY
THURSDAY
FRIDAY
SATURDAY
SUNDAY
```

Figure 14.5: Sample choice program (part 2 of 2).

Choice programs can provide two levels of data:

- Choice Text: The information that will appear to the right of the parameter value when the command is prompted.

- Permissible Values: The list of allowable values that can be typed into the parameter. This list is displayed when the cursor is in the parameter value and the user presses F4.

Choice Program Parameters

The choice program itself must be designed to handle (or ignore) either or both of the preceding options. Two parameters are passed to the choice program:

- A controlling parameter.
- A valid values parameter. See Table 14.4.

Table 14.4: Choice Program Parameters.

Parameter	Type	Description
Controlling Parameter	Char(21)	Contains the command name, parameter name, and a control character.
Values	30 or <=2000	The choice text or a list of permissible values.

The controlling parameter is made up of three subfields:

- The command name.
- The command parameter keyword name.
- A controlling option.

These values are generated by the OS/400 command prompter.

The command and parameter name occupy positions 1 to 10 and 11 to 20, respectively, and contain the name of the command and the parameter that invoked the choice program (see Table 14.5). Position 21 contains either the letter "C" or "'P." This should be checked by the user-written choice program to determine the type of choice data being requested. The letter "C" indicates that 30 characters of choice text is requested and the letter "P" indicates that a list of permissible values is requested.

Table 14.5: Controlling Parameter Subfields.

Subfield Type	From / To Positions	Description
Char(10)	1 to 10	Command name: The name of the command that invoked the choice program.
Char (10)	11 to 20	Keyword parameter name: The name of the parameter requesting the choice text.
Char (1)	21 to 21	Controlling option: C = Choice text is requested. P = Permissible values is requested.

Valid Values Parameter Subfields

The valid values parameter must contain one of the following values, based on the controlling option:

1. If the controlling option is "C," the command prompter is requesting that your choice program return a 30-character string containing the choice text (Table 14.6).

Table 14.6: Valid Values Parameter Subfields.

Subfield Type	From / To Positions	Description
Char(30)	1 to 30	Choice text: The text to appear to the right of the command parameter value.

2. If the controlling option is "P," then a structure, or *repeating list* of permissible values, should be returned. Table 14.7 contains the structure for the permissible values repeating list.

Table 14.7: Permissible Values Repeating List Structure.

Subfield Type	From / To Positions	Description
Bin(2)	1 to 2	Number of permissible values being returned.
Char(*)	3 to *	Permissible value.

Individual Permissible value (pos. 3 through *):

Subfield Type	From / To Positions	Description
Bin(2)	1 to 2	Length of the permissible value.
Char(*)	3 to length	Permissible value being returned. The length of this value is specified in the 2-byte binary prefix.

LIST PARAMETERS

There are three types of list parameters that can be created.

- A *simple list*, containing multiple, like values. Created by specifying MAX(*n*>1).

- A *mixed list*, containing multiple, unlike values. Created by specifying ELEM statements for a parameter.

- A *complex list* or list of lists, containing two or more lists. Created when MAX(*n*>1) *and* ELEM statements are used.

Simple List Parameters

When you need to pass multiple similar values to a command-processing program, you can create several parameters. This, however, forces you into a maintenance cycle. Every time another value is required, another parameter has to be added. For example, a user-written command that accepts days of the week could be written as follows:

```
SLTDAYS  DAY1(MONDAY) DAY2(TUESDAY) DAY3(WEDNESDAY)
```

There is an alternative for this type of command where repetitive parameters are needed.

Using the list feature of command parameters, a similar command could be written as follows:

```
SLTDAYS  DAYS(MONDAY TUESDAY WEDNESDAY)
```

The complete command definition source is shown in Figure 14.6.

```
SLTDAYS:  CMD    PROMPT('Select Days')
          PARM   KWD(DAYS)  TYPE(*NAME) EXPR(*YES) RSTD(*YES)  +
                 SPCVAL((MONDAY) (TUESDAY) (WEDNESDAY) +
                 (THURSDAY) (FRIDAY) (SATURDAY) (SUNDAY)) MAX(7) +
                 PROMPT('Days to include')
```

Figure 14.6: Command definition source for SLTDAYS.

The MAX parameter of the PARM and ELEM statements can be used to create a simple list. A simple list requires that a value greater than 1 be specified for the MAX parameter. For example:

MAX(7) allows the command definition to accept up to 7 values for the parameter DAYS. The command-processing program also has to accept a parameter of this type. To do this, the parameter defined in the CPP should be a repeating list. Simple lists can be processed with CL, but RPG, COBOL, and C are more suitable languages. When a simple list is passed to the CPP, its structure is that of a repeating list. It contains a prefix of the count of the number of elements on the list. See Figure 14.7.

Number of items on list	Item 1	Item 2	Item 3	...	Item *n*

Figure 14.7: Simple or repeating list structure.

For example, the DAYS parameter (see Figure 14.6) is a structure with the format listed in Table 14.8.

The *declared length* of a simple list is calculated by multiplying the number specified for the MAX parameter by the length of the parameter and adding 2 for the 2-byte binary prefix containing the element count. For example, if MAX(7) is specified for a 10-byte parameter, the length of the parameter can be up to 72 positions.

$$\{ \ (7 * 10) + 2 = 72 \ \}$$

The parameter in the command-processing program should be designed to handle a value of at least the declared length for a simple list. It can be designed to

Table 14.8: Day's Parameter List Structure.

Positions	Type	Description
01 to 02	Bin(2)	Number of days specified
03 to 12	Char(10)	First day (if specified)
13 to 22	Char(10)	Second day (if specified)
23 to 32	Char(10)	Third day (if specified)
33 to 42	Char(10)	Fourth day (if specified)
43 to 52	Char(10)	Fifth day (if specified)
53 to 62	Char(10)	Sixth day (if specified)
63 to 72	Char(10)	Seventh day (if specified)

handle more than the number of elements (e.g., to avoid program maintenance in the future) but not fewer.

The *actual length* of a simple list is the length of the value actually passed to and processed by the CPP. The actual length is calculated by multiplying the value of the element count by the length of the parameter and then adding 2 for the 2-byte element count prefix. For example, if three days where specified on the DAYS parameter of the example SLTDAYS command, then the element count would be equal to 3. Multiplying that value by the length of the parameter produces 30. Then adding 2 produces a result of 32.

The CPP for the SLTDAYS command should be designed to handle 0 to 72 bytes. It should also not attempt to change the data beyond the actual length of the parameter being passed or unpredictable results can occur.

Figure 14.8 shows the RPG III code necessary to process a simple list created by the example SLTDAYS command. The program receives the parameters DAYS, which is defined as a data structure. The data structure is made up of two subfields:

- A 2-byte binary field for the element count named NUMDAY.
- An array named DAY that consists of 7 elements, each 10 characters in length.

The code shown in Figure 14.8 easily can be modified to handle other data types that may be used for a simple list by changing the attribute of the array elements. For example, to process numeric parameters, change the attribute of the array elements to packed decimal.

```
SeqNoE...................Array+RecElemLenPDAArray2LenPDA
     E                   DAY        10  7

SeqNoIDSName.NSEUDSInitialvalue+++++++++++PFromTo++DField+
     IDAYS        DS
     I                                      B   1   20NUMDAY
     I                                          3  72 DAY
```

Figure 14.8: RPG III code to process a simple list (part 1 of 2).

```
SeqNoCLOn01n02n03Factor1+++OpCodFactor2+++ResultLenDXHILOEQ
       C           *ENTRY    PLIST
       C                     PARM            DAYS
       C                     DO    NUMDAY    X
       C                     MOVE DAY,X      DAYWEK 10
       C                     EXSR RUNDAY
       C                     ENDDO
       C                     SETON                        LR
        /EJECT
       CSR         RUNDAY    BEGSR
       C
       C    Do some work.
       C
       CSR                   ENDSR
```

Figure 14.8: RPG III code to process a simple list (part 2 of 2).

Mixed Lists

A mixed list or element list is a parameter that is made up of one or more ELEM statements. These ELEM statements represent a type of "data structure" that is passed to the command-processing program. Typically, ELEM statements are used for a list of values that are related to a single entity or to a range. For example, an item number might consist of a warehouse number, a bin number, a slot, and a partial ID, while a report to be printed might require a FROM and TO date range.

The mixed list shown in Figure 14.9 contains four elements. The command-processing program for this command must define a data structure that can receive these elements. The data structure must be at least 9 bytes in length to accommodate the parameter.

```
MIXA:      CMD  PROMPT('Sample Mixed List')

   /*  Command processing program is XMPL0910  */

           PARM  KWD(ITEM) TYPE(ITEM) MIN(1) +
                 PROMPT('Item Number')

ITEM:      ELEM  TYPE(*CHAR) LEN(2) MIN(1) EXPR(*YES) RSTD(*YES) +
                 VALUES(NE SE NW SW MW MS NO SO ES WS) +
                 PROMPT('Warehouse') FULL(*YES)
           ELEM  TYPE(*DEC)  LEN(2 0) MIN(1) PROMPT('Bin number')
           ELEM  TYPE(*CHAR) LEN(1)   MIN(1) PROMPT('Slot')
           ELEM  TYPE(*DEC)  LEN(3 0) MIN(1) PROMPT('Part ID')
```

Figure 14.9: A four-element mixed list definition.

A mixed list, like a simple list, contains a 2-byte binary prefix containing the count of the members on the list. In the case of a mixed list, however, this number is always equal to the number of ELEM statements specified for the parameter. So, in the example shown in Figure 14.10, the field NUMOBJ would always equal 4.

```
SeqNoIDSName..NSEUDSInitialValue++++++++++PFromTo++DField+
    IITEM         DS
    I                                      B   1   20NUMOBJ
    I                                          3    4 WHSE
    I                                      P   5   60BIN
    I                                          7    7 SLOT
    I                                      P   8   90PART

SeqNoCLOn01n02n03Factor1+++OpCodFactor2+++ResultLenDXHILOEQ
    C             *ENTRY    PLIST
    C                       PARM            ITEM
```

Figure 14.10: Mixed list parameter declaration in a CPP.

There are many differences between simple and mixed lists. The primary differences are that a mixed list can accept a fixed number of elements, and each element can have unique characteristics. On the other hand, a simple list can accept a variable number of elements, each with identical characteristics.

Complex Lists

A complex list or *list of lists* occurs when a PARM statement contains a MAX value greater than 1, and that same PARM statement is also a mixed list of ELEM statements. For example, to define a parameter that accepts multiple qualified object names and an object type, one PARM, two ELEM, and two QUAL statements are needed. See Figure 14.11.

```
COMPLEX:     CMD   PROMPT('Sample COMPLEX List')

    /*  Command processing program is XMPL0912   */

             PARM  KWD(OBJ) TYPE(OBJ) MIN(1) MAX(128) +
                   PROMPT('Object(s) to use')

OBJ:         ELEM  TYPE(OBJNAME) MIN(1) PROMPT('Object name')
             ELEM  TYPE(*NAME) EXPR(*YES) DFT(*ALL) +
                   SPCVAL((*ALL) (*FILE) (*PGM) (*CMD)) +
                   PROMPT('Object type')

OBJNAME:     QUAL  TYPE(*GENERIC) EXPR(*YES)
             QUAL  TYPE(*NAME) EXPR(*YES) DFT(*LIBL) +
                   SPCVAL((*LIBL) (*CURLIB *CURLIB)) +
                   PROMPT('Library')
```

Figure 14.11: Sample complex list command source.

Because the elements of the mixed list can be variable, the command analyzer generates a special structure to handle complex lists. This structure contains offsets and values to the parameter values specified when the command is run. See Table 14.9.

The first two bytes of the list contain the number of items specified for the list. For example, if the parameter name contains four items, the 2-byte binary prefix would contain X'0004' (the binary equivalent of decimal 4.)

Table 14.9: Complex List Structure.

Positions	Description
01 to 02	Number of elements on the list
03 to 04	Offset to first element on the list
05 to 06	Offset to second element on the list
07 to 08	Offset to third element on the list
09 to 10	Offset to fourth element on the list
etc.	etc.

Immediately following the count is a list of offsets to the parameter values. These offsets are used to locate the parameter data within the rather large parameter passed to the CPP. For each value on the list, a 2-byte binary offset is inserted after the count value.

The list itself is passed in reverse order. This means the first item on the list is actually stored at the end of the data structure being passed. So the 2-byte binary offset values contain descending values. Figure 14.12 diagrams the complex list prefix structure.

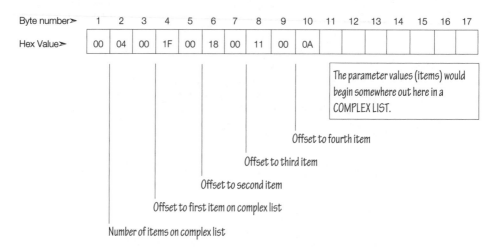

Figure 14.12: Complex list structure diagram.

Figure 14.13 contains example of RPG III code to handle a complex list. This code processes the list generated by the command source shown in Figure 14.13.

```
SeqNoIDSName.NSEUDSInitialvalue+++++++++++PFromTo++DField+
     ILIST      DS                                9999
     I                                      B   1   20COUNT

     IOBJECT    DS
     I                                      B   1   20NUMOBJ
     I                                          3  12 OBJ
     I                                         13  22 LIB
     I                                         23  32 TYPE

     IBIN2      DS
     I                                      B   1   200FFSET

SeqNoCLOn01n02n03Factor1+++OpCodFactor2+++ResultLenDXHILOEQ
     C          *ENTRY    PLIST
     C                    PARM           LIST
       /SPACE
     C                    DO   COUNT     X      50
     C          X         MULT 2         ELEM   50
     C                    ADD  1         ELEM
     C          2         SUBSTLIST:ELEM BIN2
     C          OFFSET    ADD  1         POS    50
     C          32        SUBSTLIST:POS  OBJECT
     C*
     C*     At this point, the data structure OBJECT contains the
     C*     object name, library and type for the object
     C*     specified for the X item on the list.
     C*
     C*     At this point, process the complex list item.
     C                    ENDDO
     C                    SETON                  LR
```

Figure 14.13: Sample RPG III code to process a complex list.

COMPILING USER-WRITTEN COMMANDS

Creating a command is similar to creating a high-level language program. There is a compiler for commands. It compiles command-definition statements into an OS/400 object with an object type of *CMD. A typical command compilation would be as follows:

```
CRTCMD  CMD(SLTDAYS)  PGM(WEEKDAYS)  MAXPOS(1)
```

The CRTCMD (Create Command) command compiles command-definition statements from a source-file member. Several parameters are described as follows.

- CMD—The CMD parameter identifies the name of the command object to be created, and the library where it is stored.

- PGM—The PGM parameter identifies the command-processing program (CPP) for the command.

- SRCFILE—The SRCFILE parameter identifies the source file that contains the member where the command definition statements are stored. This is an optional parameter that defaults to SRCFILE(*LIBL/QCMDSRC).

- SRCMBR—The SRCMBR parameter identifies the source member name where the command definition statements are stored. This is an optional parameter that defaults to SRCMBR(*CMD), indicating that the name specified on the CMD parameter be used as the member name.

- ALLOW—The ALLOW parameter indicates the environment(s) where the command can be run. This is an optional parameter that defaults to ALLOW(*ALL). Other options include: *IPGM for interactive programs; *BPGM for batch programs; *IMOD for interactive ILE programs; *BMOD for batch ILE programs; *IREXX for interactive REXX procedures; *BREXX for batch REXX procedures; *INTERACT for the interactive and external to a program; *BATCH for batch input streams; *EXEC to allow the command to be specified or run by QCMDEXC.

- MAXPOS—The MAXPOS parameter controls the maximum number of positional parameters that can be specified. Positional parameters are parameter values that are specified without using the parameter keywords. For example the following command contains two positional parameters.

```
CHGVAR  &DEC   %BIN(&OBJECTS 01 02)
```

The variable value &DEC is the first positional parameter. It is followed by `%BIN(&OBJECTS 01 02)` as the second positional parameter.

■ CURLIB and PRDLIB—The CURLIB (Current Library) and PRDLIB (Product Library) parameters allow the runtime current library and product library to be set. These libraries are changed for the duration of the command. When the command finishes, they revert back to their previous settings.

■ PMTOVRPGM—The PMTOVRPGM identifies the prompt override program name. This program is called by the command prompter after each parameter specified with KEYPARM(*YES) is completed. The prompt override program's job is to "pre-fill" the remaining parameter keyword values. Prompt override programs are used on several OS/400 commands, including CHGLIBL, CHGJOBD, CHGCMD, and CHGJOB.

REVIEW QUESTIONS

1. *Command definition objects are created by compiling a group of _____*

    _____ _____.

2. *The six command definition statements that can be used to create user-written CL commands are ____, ____, ____, ____, ____, and ____.*

3. *A _____ _____ _____ associated with a command is invoked by the command processor when the command is run.*

4. *The CMD statement is used to define the text that is used for the ____on the prompt display.*

5. *The PARM, QUAL, and ELEM statements are used to define each parameter of a user-written command. These command statements are referred to as*

    _____ _____ _____.

6. On the PARM, QUAL, and ELEM statements, the DFT parameter can be used to specify a _____ _____ for the parameter being defined.

7. The _____ parameter allows a list of values to be specified that can be used to translate the specified value to the value passed to the command processing program.

8. The MIN parameter is traditionally used to indicate that a parameter value is _____.

9. A value greater than 1 specified for the MAX parameter of the PARM and ELEM statements can be used to create a _____ ____.

10. When a simple list is passed to the CPP, it contains a 2-byte binary prefix of the _____ ____ _____ ____ ____ ____.

11. A mixed list or element list is a parameter that is made up of one or more _____ statements. A mixed list can accept a fixed number of elements, and each element can have _____ characteristics.

12. The CRTCMD (Create Command) command compiles command definition statements from a source file member. The PGM parameter identifies the _____ _____ _____ for the command. The _____ parameter indicates the environment(s) where the command can be run.

INDEX

%BIN conversion function, 47-48

*AND, 51-52
*BATCH, 13
*BCAT, 41-42
*BMOD, 13, 14, 25
*BPGM, 13, 25
*BREXX, 13
*CAT, 41-42
*EXEC, 13
*IMOD, 13, 14, 25
*INTERACT, 13
*IPGM, 25
*IREXX, 13
*NOT, 51-52
*OR, 51-52
*PROD, 14
*SERVICE, 14
*TCAT, 41-42

A

abbreviations used in commands, 1-2
Accounts Receivable sample program
  (ARJ801CL), 135-144
activation groups, ILE, 275
ad hoc queries, 258
Add Library List Entry (ADDLIBLE), 265
  overriding called programs using, 266
Add Message Description (ADDMSGD), 90,
  203-204
Add physical file member (ADDPFM), 2, 118
  batch processing, 142
addition, 46
advanced CL programming, 225-269
allocating message queues, 92
ampersand to indicate variables, 29-30

analyzer, command analyzer, 24
apostrophes or single quotes, xvii to delineate
  character literals, 2, 6, 11, 33-36
application program interface (API), 14, 18
  bindable APIs, 293-296
  CEE APIs (*See also* bindable APIs), 293-294
  ILE, bindable APIs in, 272
application support CL programs, 17-18
arithmetic expressions, 9, 10, 41, 46-47
  %BIN conversion function and, 47-48
AS/400 Database Programming, 255
asterisk and slash as comment delimiter, 4
Auto-Write function in Record Count application, 162-164

B

batch processing, 12-13, 18, 135-144
  Accounts Receivable sample program
    (ARJ801CL) for, 135-144
  Add physical file member (ADDPFM) in,
    142
  Clear Physical file member (CLRPFM) in,
    137
  commands ignoring overrides in, 141
  Copy File (CPYF) in, 136, 137, 143-144
  Delete Override (DLTOVR) in, 139
  error handling in, 122
  Format Data (FMTDTA) in, 136, 137-138,
    142
  labeled commands in, 3
  Member (MBR) parameters in, 137
  Override With Display File (OVRDSPF), 138
  Override with Database File (OVRDBF) in,
    138, 140-141
  Override With Diskette File (OVRDKTF) in,
    138

Note: Boldface numbers indicate illustrations.

Note: Boldface numbers indicate illustrations

Note: Boldface numbers indicate illustrations

Note: Boldface numbers indicate illustrations

Note: Boldface numbers indicate illustrations

Note: Boldface numbers indicate illustrations

Note: Boldface numbers indicate illustrations

Note: Boldface numbers indicate illustrations

Note: Boldface numbers indicate illustrations

Note: Boldface numbers indicate illustrations

Note: Boldface numbers indicate illustrations

The AS/400 & Microsoft® Office Integration Handbook

by Brian Singleton with Colleen Garton

This book takes a detailed look at how you can integrate applications in the Microsoft Office 97 product suite with data from your AS/400. Unravel secrets such as how to use your AS/400's output with your PC's data formatting tools or how to make attractive, professional reports with AS/400 data the easy way. Learn the secret of using visual query tools to point and click the creation of sophisticated information output and how to analyze and summarize the detailed (and often cumbersome) reports from your AS/400. Discover how you can combine the presentation capabilities of Microsoft Office with the database capabilities of the AS/400 to provide your company with the best of both worlds.

In the first sections of the book, Singleton introduces you to the essential knowledge you need to use Client Access as you integrate AS/400 data with the Microsoft Office applications. He covers installing and configuring Client Access, how to provide a seamless method of AS/400 integration with Microsoft Office using ODBC, the network drive functionality of Client Access, and the Client Access Data Transfer Function. He also covers TCP/IP's FTP file transfer function and how to use it to bring data from the AS/400 to your PC.

The remaining sections of the book cover the veritable Swiss Army knife functions of Microsoft Office. 320 pages. Level: Novice, Intermediate, and Advanced.

❏ BOOK C587 ....$79
ISBN 1-883884-49-7

TCP/IP Primer for the AS/400

The Essential Guide to AS/400 TCP/IP Concepts, Configuration, and Use

by Jim Hoopes, Robin Klima, and Martin Pluth

Imagine the rewards you'll reap as you connect your company's AS/400 to any other computer in the world! Wishful thinking? Not at all, since V3R1 when IBM started including TCP/IP free with OS/400. This book will show you how to simplify communications between AS/400s by throwing out SNADS and moving to TCP/IP, improve communications in your AS/400-to-PC environment, and lead your company into a whole new world of bargains and business on the Internet. *TCP/IP Primer for the AS/400* is the hands-on, how-to book you've been waiting for. It begins with the basics and proceeds through the various configuration options, utilities, and troubleshooting skills you need to connect your AS/400 to users within the office and around the world. 370 pages. Level: Novice.

❏ BOOK C561 ....$99
ISBN 1-883884-33-0

The AS/400 Owner's Manual for V4

by Mike Dawson

Midrange Computing's all-time bestselling manual is now V4R2-ready! Designed for AS/400 professionals at all levels, The *AS/400 Owner's Manual for V4* walks you through hundreds of AS/400 tasks from the perspective of how most shops actually work. Cutting through the dozens of parameters and options of AS/400 commands, *The AS/400 Owner's Manual for V4* takes you directly to the results you need. Offering much more than brief, to-the-point instructions, it also includes valuable descriptions that examine why AS/400 managers, administrators, operators, and programmers do certain things on the machine and how the AS/400 works internally. This edition is completely up-to-date for Version 4 of OS/400 and contains a new chapter about the Internet and TCP/IP. Wire-bound and concise, *The AS/400 Owner's Manual for V4* is the perfect workstation tool for anyone who does AS/400 operations, administration, or management. 464 pages. Level: Intermediate to Advanced.

❏ BOOK C5000 ....$59
ISBN 1-58347-001-8

AS/400 Primer

The Fundamental Concepts and Training for Programmers, Administrators, and System Operators

by Ernie Malaga

A must for every AS/400 shop, this comprehensive, 29-chapter book is perfect for novice and intermediate programmers as well as system administrators and operators. In a simple, straightforward style, Ernie Malaga not only explains core AS/400 concepts but also shows you—step by step—how to perform 30 essential AS/400 functions, including installation, troubleshooting, administration, operation, programming, and 25 other tasks!

You'll learn the essential technical concepts you need to get you up to speed on all areas of the AS/400. Increased understanding of the AS/400 will boost productivity and put all personnel in your organization on friendly terms with the computer. You'll find the *AS/400 Primer* will be a learning tool and a valuable reference for years to come. As one satisfied reader put it, "If you could only own one AS/400 book, this would be it." Don't power up without it! 435 pages. Level: Novice to Intermediate.

❏ BOOK C507 ....$99
ISBN 1-883884-25-X

 **ORDER FORM**

5 Easy Ways to Order!

BILL TO:

Name _____

Title _____

Company _____

Address _____

City _____ State _____ ZIP _____

YTQBZ

FAX
this order form to 760-931-9935, 24 hours a day, 365 days a year.

MAIL
your order to 5650 El Camino Real, Suite 225, Carlsbad, CA 92008.

EMAIL
your order to custsvc@ midrangecomputing.com.

PHONE
toll-free 1-800-477-5665 (Mon. - Fri. 6 a.m. to 5 p.m. PST).

ONLINE
ordering is available at www. mc-store.com.

SHIP TO (if different from above):

Name _____ Title _____

Company _____

Address _____

City/State/ZIP _____

ITEMS ORDERED:

Item No.	Description	Price	Quantity	Total Price

Subtotal

Add 7.75% sales tax (CA residents only), 6.25% sales tax (TX residents only), or 6% sales tax (NJ residents only). Residents of Canada add 7% GST.

Shipping/Handling—$6.25 per item (UPS ground, continental U.S. only)

Total

ADDITIONAL INFORMATION:

Daytime Phone (required to process order):

(___) _____ - _____

Fax (___) _____ - _____

Email _____

* Note: All prices are U.S. only. Please call for orders and prices outside the U.S. Prices Subject to change.

BILLING INFORMATION:

☐ Payment Enclosed (Make check payable to Midrange Computing.)

CREDIT CARD: ☐ VISA ☐ MasterCard ☐ AmEx ☐ Discover

Card # _____ Exp Date _____

BILL ME, P.O. # _____

Signature (required) _____

VISA **MasterCard** **AMERICAN EXPRESS Cards** **DISCOVER NOVUS**

Priority code: YTVAZ